Discipline Col:

Never have negative thoughts

Dream – visulize where you
want to go

Set new goals

Don't care what others think
of you.

System, Disipline, Action

Get book on succesfull person
list what he did to get there.

How *YOU* Can Make FIVE MILLION DOLLARS In Five Years

A STEP-BY-STEP WEALTH PROGRAM

by

Ross L. Anderson

While the author has made every effort to present factual and accurate information, he assumes no liability of any kind and does not represent himself to be a legal expert or professional accountant.

Published by Personal Financial Services, a division of Ross L. Anderson Inc. Newport Beach, California

Printed by Automation Printing, El Cajon, California.

Library of Congress Cataloging in Publication Data

Anderson, Ross L.
    How YOU Can Make Five Million Dollars In Five Years
    1-Finance—Success and Wealth. I. Title
81-51825

ISBN   0-96-6298-0-7

Table of Contents

Dedicated to the greatest principle in life which is to give and receive love, and to everyone who believes in that principle.

FOREWORD

Several years ago my brother, Ross Anderson, encouraged me to give up my job selling business machines and jump into the great unknown of self-employment and financial success.

At the time I had a family, regular working hours, an old car and a frugal life style. I was a little uneasy contemplating really becoming wealthy since I didn't know the first thing about it and I felt like it was beyond my reach.

Through many extended conversations with Ross he conveyed to me the same information that is contained in this book. Over a period of five years (which his program outlines) I have proven for myself that these methods really do work.

After implementing these basic ideas I have gone from having nothing to a very successful financial position. I own several beautiful homes, a new Mercedes, Jaguar and Rolls-Royce, a multi-million dollar business and many investment and income properties. My family and I travel worldwide several times a year and we now have everything we need or want.

Although you may not be able to visualize yourself being really wealthy, it can happen. It's no free gift. It takes a lot of sacrifice and hard work, but, if you will follow the outline in this book, a few years from now you can have all of the wealth you want. Best of all your time will be your own and you can have a true sense of freedom and independence.

I've done it and it works. All you have to do is *DO IT!*

Michael P. Anderson

ix

PREFACE

This book is much less than a scholarly tretise or disection of the inner workings and hidden secrets of some all-knowing investment group. It also isn't a dry textbook approach, or a head-in-the-clouds discourse on having a positive attitude. Essentially it's my personal account of my own financial progress and experience and is written as if you and I were sitting in a restaurant having lunch and discussing some elements of accumulating wealth. Some parts of this book may seem longwinded, repetitive or shallow. Although it may seem that way to you, in my own mind these lines of thinking are essential for "making it" and if it seems repetitive, perhaps I'm just trying to get you to believe that what I have learned is valid. I also present seminars and provide personal consulting services as a follow-up and expanded format for these ideas and methods. Additional workbooks and portfolios of project presentation are also available, either from bookstores or from our offices. All together, these ideas *WILL* lead a person to complete financial independence. This isn't blue-sky stuff. It really works. It's all worked for me and I've seen it work for many people I've helped. It's failed for the ones who won't follow the basic ideas and plans and it's worked for the ones who have followed through with the ideas and practices. It will only take you five years if you devote your time and energy to it.

If you think of yourself as an intellectual giant you just as well throw this book away. No one really likes arrogant people, and, regardless of where you think you're going or how you think you'll get there, this book isn't going to help you since you know everything already. For those who have

xi

a genuinely good self-image, welcome. For those who have low self-esteem, I welcome you with open arms. We can rebuild you! For those with lots of energy, we can channel that power into success, personally and financially. If you are tired and out of gas, we can revitalize you and charge you up.

Well, all of this really is a chat betweeen friends. Some of the ideas are personal but it's all happened to me and I don't mind sharing. Most success or investment writers prefer to come off as authorities who sit behind desks somewhere and dispense knowledge to all the little people who don't know the score. I'm one of the regular folks, and I've written about my highs and lows, a little philosophy, states of mind, and dialogues and procedures that will help you acquire wealth.

About half of this book is devoted to raising your confidence and self-image. It is critical that you come to realize that YOU, not someone else, can become very happy, first, and very wealthy, second. Try to absorb the ideas of self-worth as you read. Feel the flow of self-realization and self-value develop.   The other half of the book illustrates and discusses the mechanics and methods of getting rich. In these chapters, try to see how the thought processes lead to the closing of beneficial deals. Imagine, as you read, how these dialogues can change peoples minds, and get them on your side. These ideas are simply patterns that have worked for me and many others I've helped and observed.

So, just between us, let's start our chat.

Section One

The Psychology And Motivation

Discussions

CHAPTER ONE

Autobiography

This may be the least interesting and captivating part of this book but there are a couple of lessons to be learned from my experiences and I hope they'll benefit you. Someday we may meet and I'm certain you've had experiences from which I could learn. Ideally, we can all learn from each other and bypass our tendencies to make all of our own mistakes.

I'll summarize my early years in a few terse sentences. I was born in March, 1948 in Shelley, Idaho, and came from a poor family with a lot of love and a lot of problems. My Dad, Rex R. Anderson, taught me to work hard and to be organized, although he had trouble massing his talents into any great project. He's passed on now. I love him and always have. My Mother, Vera Clarke Anderson, taught the children in our family how to sacrifice, and we all still have great affection and love for her. My parents were, in a way, victims of circumstances. They were enveloped by

3

work and had jobs, while we were growing up, that paid so little that there couldn't even be dreams of affluence.

All of the children in our family, four boys, learned to work very early and had responsible jobs since we were very young. My brothers Rex C. Anderson, Christian Anderson and Michael P. Anderson all learned to work hard at early ages and learned to appreciate the barest of comforts. Rex and Mike have since gone on to great accomplishments in their personal lives and business enterprises. Chris has spent his past years developing and enjoying an appreciation of the arts and has little need for material possessions.

My early jobs started at about eight or nine when I delivered newspapers. I had a route in the country and delivered 13 papers, clearing 1¢ on each paper each day. At about age 12 I started shining shoes in a barber shop and scrubbing the floors on weekends. At the same time I worked a little in a cafe cleaning floors and peeling potatoes. At the time we lived in a 2 room apartment above a clothing store and paid $50 a month in rent. At age 14 I worked four hours a day and weekends in a dime store. I got $1 an hour and they paid me for about half the hours I worked, but I enjoyed the freedom they gave me in doing the work. They appreciated the great sacrifice I made of my time but limited their appreciation to a buck an hour.

At age 16 my family moved to Southern California which was the best thing that ever happened to me. Whatever else that environment teaches a person at least it offers some exposure to ideas and opportunitites. Within a few days of moving there I got a job as a boxboy in a grocery store. I worked hard for the company and always went the extra mile. After a year or so I received a great promotion to janitor at $3 an hour. I soon got the same job at another store and kept them both clean, working various hours from 3 A.M. one morning to 1 A.M. the next morning. That was more than enough to keep me busy but I had a few hours on weekends before and after church on Sundays, and I took a third job at a record store. All together I worked 16 hours each Saturday, 6 each Sunday and several hours each day. At this time I was in high school and later, when I went to Jr. College, I kept up the same work regimen. It's too bad that I didn't know more about relaxing and socializing, but I don't regret it now.

After a year of college I was a missionary for the L.D.S. Church in Michigan for two years. That experience taught me even greater tenacity and diligence. My efforts seemed to make some people happier for which I will always feel some satisfaction. After those two years, at age 21, I entered the world of business and bucks. On April 20, 1969 I awoke in my apartment in Anaheim, California at 7 A.M. I sat up in bed and said to myself: "I AM GOING TO BE RICH! I decided to paint houses since I knew that the jobs would be counted in hundreds of dollars. I borrowed paper and a typewriter to type contracts, borrowed a car to get to some houses and knocked on doors. Within eight weeks I made $10,000 for myself, which, at the time, was a lot of money. I had a few friends working for me, I knocked on doors every night and every Saturday and never had a single day when I didn't get work. I then travelled for about a year all around the globe and, for the first time, I understood clearly why there is such a great chasm between the first, second and third world countries. I couldn't believe it. I lost my fascination for travelling while in Africa, after 40 or so countries. There was so much starvation and disease and inconceivable ignorance. It was very depressing.

Before I began travelling I met a sweet girl, Alison Porter, in Rexburg, Idaho. While travelling I got butterflies for her. I came home but was drafted into the Army. After eight wonderful months I was discharged with an allergy.

In my spare time in the army I designed a complete jet airplane with detailed schematics and all. We still get those plans out when we want our friends to go home. They always leave immediately. I was proud of the plans and can't understand everyone's disinterest. After the army I went back into painting and got into sealing asphalt driveways. That business developed into an asphalt paving business which, for years, provided cash flow for my other projects.

While it took me 10 years to make my millions, I could have done it in half the time if I'd been able to learn from someone else. The asphalt business carried me while I learned how to make money. I developed an office supply business which was a profitable enterprise. I got into manufacturing men's cologne and women's skin products. These were marketed throughout the west in 110 stores and through mail-order. I began developing subdivisions in the western states and did that for two or three years.

During the next five years, from age 25 to age 30 I built two stereo businesses, had donut shops, an ice cream parlor and a sandwich shop. I built a Disco, when that craze started, for an investment of about $200,000 and its success led me to build another, the world's largest, holding 4,000 people, for two and one-half million dollars. I also built a small shopping center at this time, bought a gas station, a bedding factory, houses, duplexes, apartments, commercial buildings and I built houses and developed subdivisions. I also had a crew on the road who conducted warehouse stereo sales for me around the western states for a couple of years and I also had a lot of other, less notable projects going at the same time. During this time I had my financial ups and downs and I learned a lot. I also did well financially, and only had one business investment turn out badly for me. After building a 13,500 sq. ft. house which we lived in for 3 years, but never liked, we moved into another nice home I'd owned for a few years and discovered that life can actually be more enjoyable when lived in a simpler way. We still have all the comforts but less of the show and there's a lot less pressure for community and family recognition now. That's a drive and desire most of us have.

We still take lots of trips and enjoy lots of things but are very happy to be out of "show business." Curiously, we've learned that a Ford or a Cadillac can get us to the grocery store as fast as a Rolls ever did. A comfortable, but smaller, home has charm that a large palace just doesn't emit. You may have to do what I did and go through the stages of accumulation of a vast stockpile of material things. It may take that to get it out of your blood and I wouldn't want to deprive you of the satisfaction of seeing that you can do it yourself. All of that stuff never made me happy and it won't make you happy either but getting it is a challenge.

We now have five children with more on the way. The world doesn't need less children, it needs more children who have learned to care, to love and to be productive and improve and build society instead of debase and destroy it. We're trying to raise some average children who can, themselves, have enough courage and determination to live sensitive and productive lives.

Basically, I suppose the lessons I've learned in my life, which are outlined for practical applications in greater detail in successive chapters, could be summarized thusly:

1- Work habits developed in childhood and adolescence usually carry over to adulthood.

2- To appreciate every comfort.

3- Regardless of our beginnings, we can end up wherever we choose.

4- Optimism and love can overcome all things.

5- Things and people aren't always what they seem to be.

6- Open-mindedness. Not to be critical of others lifestyles, cultures, races or religions.

7- Tenacity for every good goal and project.

8- That happiness isn't tied to money but that money can provide some personal freedom.

9- Helping others can be a great satisfaction.

10- We can accomplish almost anything if we put our minds to it.

At this writing I'm 32 years of age and hope for many more happy years. There are many satisfactions and lessons behind us, but now, for my wife and I, our children have provided an insurpassable joy for us. We hope that the future years will continue to bloom with that same great happiness in our family.

Dany Coster 8/19/87
Hilton Head S.C. 43½ at
this time ? ? ?

CHAPTER TWO

Thesis

My thesis for making five million dollars in five years is simply this: money consumes so much attention and energy in a person's life, that ideally there would be a way to make the money necessary for an enjoyable life, and make it in a short period of time, quit making money, relax, and get on with living.

Money, and what people will do to get it, has to be the biggest joke ever put over on mankind as a whole. Think of all the people who have been killed, countries destroyed, families broken, hours worked, people cheated, lifetimes spent, schemes devised, crimes perpetrated, and so on and so on that have happened throughout history for one supreme reason: To get more money. Not only that, but the time-honored challenge is to find a way to do as little as possible and get as much money as you can get for it. As I think it through, it seems logical that we should each hope and work for as much money as we need to go through life and have and do what we want.

9

Considering that money has consumed so much of people's lives, let us put together a program that will make you a large amount within a few years. You can then spend your time, not in pursuit of more wealth, but in more productive and happy activities.

8/19/87

Hilton Head

Great Vac.

CHAPTER THREE

Develop Passion

Bob Davis

Take a look arond you at the people who have really achieved something or excelled in some field or endeavor, enterprise or talent and one of several things they usually have in common is that they have a great PASSION, an intensity, a single-mindedness for whatever they're excelling in. Choose your field, pick your goals, decide what you want and go after it like your life depends on it.

There was once a young man who wanted wisdom. He went to the wisest person he knew of, an old man wo lived nearby. He told the old man that more than anything he wanted wisdom. The old man took him down to the sea shore and they waded out into the surf. Suddenly the old fellow pushed the young man's head under the water, and, no matter how hard he tried, the old man wouldn't let him get a breath. After a few moments of this, the young man was released and allowed a breath of air. Bewildered, he asked the old man why he held him under the water. His response and his lesson was that when the young man

wanted wisdom as much as _____ ted a breath of air,
he would get it. In the same w_____ you decide on a goal
and pursue it with the greate_____ intensity, you will
either achieve it or die tryin_____ e the desire you'd
have for a breath of air if you w_____ held underwater.
That desire is a passion.

A real passion overcomes all _____ more important
than the weekends off, the expe_____ fun outings
with friends and the short da_____
greater than all and it doesn't giv_____
QUIT AND IT WILL NEVER F_____
there is no failure with passion. A_____
drive a consumate politician in e_____
friendship to manipulate and coerc_____
day, seven days a week *to get where he*_____
admire him for his tactics and m_____
certainly see how his limitless drive an_____
dreams of political power come true.

Look around you at the successful T.V. prea_____
religious zealots pursue their goals with an intensity that
would same Attila the Hun. You'll recall that Attila crossed
the Swiss Alps on elephants to achieve his military
objectives. These T.V. preachers get in millions of dollars
from many thousands of followers because of their
intensity. They inspire confidence because THEY KNOW
EXACTLY WHERE THEY ARE GOING. For them
EVERYTHING IS ABSOLUTE. Of course they disagree
on what the absolutes are, but that doesn't seem to make
any difference. Just watch them Sunday mornings. They
are *ELECTRIC*. All is simple, all is absolute, it is fail-safe
and it will never go wrong. People want to believe and they
want to follow someone who knows what he's doing. They'll
sell their possessions and send him the money. He can live
in splendor, become embroiled in scandal and even that is
overcome by his positive attitude. The scandal rolls off his
back like water off a duck. There is no failure. Are there

setbacks? Sure! Are there bad years? Yes! Are there insurmountable problems? Of course! Do they make any difference?!!! Will anything stop him? NO, NOTHING, *EVER!* He will not accept failure.

I read a book about young millionaires and all of them shared this same self-determination and intensity. All of them had experienced a lot of problems disappointments but they simply would not qu~~~ them went through bankruptcy or lo~~ money one or mo~~ ~~~

~~~ what ~~~ them and makes ~~~mon: They have the attitude that, regardless of what happens, NOTHING WILL STOP THEM. That's what makes them different and leads them to their inevitable success. There are no problems or difficulties greater than they are. They are simply bigger than anything and they will not accept failure. Does failure come? Sure, but they won't accept it. Will they learn from it? Yes! Will they mentally associate themselves with the failure and thereby lower their self-esteem? No! NEVER!!! In fact the failures are classified mentally as successes. Many lessons were learned. They were positive experiences.

I am not proposing that a person devote himself 100% to making money or anything else. I am simply stating that the way to get wherever you want to go is to pursue it 100%. That is why, later in this book, I propose a life-outline with different times to devote oneself to different avocations. That is, in fact, why I propose, in this book, to set aside five years for acquiring wealth, and then to forget the money. Of all life's endeavors, getting money is the least worthy of your time. But, at the same time, you need money to be free to pursue whatever else you want to do. So the only logical thing to do is to set aside a period of time to take care of this unpleasant task, devote yourself to it whole-heartedly for the designated period, get what you set out for and then forget it. When you get the millions you sought after, you can live off the interest without ever worrying about the principal money. Doesn't that make sense?

It's not just for money, either. Somehow if parents can instill in their children how to understand and use passion as a driving force they will work hard in school, work hard at a part-time job, work hard at home, play hard with their friends and relax with devotion in the time they've set aside for that. All things with intensity. And during the relaxing hours, or years, of a person's life, nothing else can ruin it because relaxing is the great pursuit at that time.

In chapter nine my outline for life timetable suggests different periods of intense dedication to various pursuits. Essentially a person could successfully enjoy a period of personal maturation and development ending at about age 18, spend a couple of years 100% dedicated to service to others (Peace Corp, missionary work, Vista ((domestic Peace Corp)), free hospital work full-time, etc.). Something to help others, pursued with the same intensity as outlined for the other pusuits, and with a *DATE OF TERMINATION*. Why a date of termination? Because you can stand on your head for an hour if you have to, but not for a lifetime. If you know that it is only going to last for a certain period it is easier to get through it and be completely devoted, knowing that after a certain period longer you won't have to do it anymore. That's the same logic used while pursuing money with 100% dedication. You MUST give up everything else but you can do it because you know it is only going to last a little longer and then you'll have all of the rewards from your labors while all the other "jokers" are still trying to raise the house payment. You must give up all else, BUT YOU CAN DO IT!!

When you are doing your two years of service you'll get tired of planting beans in some foreign field, exhausted with lifting old folks from bed to bed, and sick of cleaning bedpans, tired of trudging through snowbanks to share religion with others; in fact, sick of the whole idea at times, but *will you quit?* NO. NO. NEVER! You will do it and laugh, keep doing it and smile because *it isn't going to last forever.*

...ggies and so on, all in 2 or 3 months. During this time I did everything I was ordered to do, didn't talk back to anyone, followed the program, thinking all the time that boot camp would be over soon and if I went to Viet Nam or didn't, I would have made it through bootcamp, gritted my teeth, did what was asked and enjoyed it as much as possible, mainly because I knew that it wouldn't last too long. I'm grateful that I didn't have to go to Viet Nam, since I didn't want to hurt anyone and didn't want anyone to hurt me, either. That whole affair was a tragedy anyway and all of the lives lost there were in vain, unlike some previous wars where men fought and died for principles. Besides, the idea of rank and individual oppression in the military goes against my grain. I simply don't like people telling me what to do. The validity of the military is a subject in itself and I won't expand on it. It is vitally necessary to protect us, but the rank/status idea is so repressive of our most joyous personal feelings of freedom and achievement. The way I made it through my military tenure was by thinking of the terminal, short-termed, nature of that experience. That's how to get through the years of public service and the five years of 100% dedication to acquiring wealth. The idea is: "Yes, I can give up pleasure and leisure and the things everyone else is doing because I only have three years left to work."

If you don't have this capacity for passion in your heart, you'd better either develop it or resign yourself to a life of relative mediocrity. You aren't any different than anyone who has achieved the greatest in every field. Your intelligence has nothing to do with it. *IT'S ALL IN YOUR MIND.* We've all had problems and letdowns, but *YOU ARE GREATER THAN ANY PROBLEM. YOU ARE BIGGER THAN ANY DISAPPOINTMENT.* The idea and feeling is generative, cumulative; a building, moving, growing, exciting feeling inside.

Develop this *passion* in your mind and do whatever you do with intensity. Personally, in every job I ever had I went an extra mile or two. Even as a teenager I developed the idea of working intently at a job. At 14 years of age I had my own key to a large dime store. They paid me $1 an hour to work from 4 to 6 p.m. after school each night and after dinner I'd return to work for a couple of hours without pay, just to do the job well. I never got extra money for doing that but I was trusted and respected for being dependable and hard-working. I also raised my own self-esteem by seeing what I could accomplish. It didn't have much to do with the money either. The idea is to be super-active in your work period, super productive, positive and successful.

Since I was eight years old I've always had a job to occupy my time, I've got every job I've every applied for and I've never been fired, laid off or let go from a job. When I was 17 one employer had to cut down the staff and he tried to let me go but I wouldn't accept the lay-off, and told him so; in fact I told him I'd work for free if necessary but I couldn't accept a lay-off. *There can be no failure.* It is totally unacceptable and it can't even be considered. Anyway, in that situation I stayed at that job longer than any other employee, raised my salary by 3 times, had a couple of other jobs at the same time and all of the employers were happy. During those years I should have worked less hours and had more periods of play but I was looking for some recognition and I always got it in my job. If I had compartmentalized my time more I would have allowed play periods and played with the same intensity.

I was a missionary from 19 to 21 and worked early mornings till late nights, bypassed opportunitites to waste time, overcame fatigue and gave it all I had. I knew it was going to last two years, no more

candle from both ends and the middle, too. IT'S ONLY FOR TWO YEARS. IT'S ONLY FOR FIVE YEARS.

The five year financial plan to get five million dollars is a longer period because the money grows geometrically. The first year you may make $25 thousand, $100 thousand the second year, $400 thousand in the third year, 1.5 million dollars in the fourth, and 3 million in the fifth. Of course if you only went one more year you'd make $5 million more and $10 million the next year and $50 million the next and in only ten years you'd own the world. That is a natural, geometric, progression and everyone thinks that they'll go just one more year, but you won't because you only want $5 million and you're only going to spend five years getting it. Not one day longer. You can put up with a lot, knowing that it's all for a limited period of time. Your dedication and passion for what you are doing will make the days short and the five years will fly by.

18

Glen W. Turner (Koscot Interplanetary, Dare To Be Great etc.) is a real mover. Some people think he's a crook and some think he's the greatest thing since sliced bread. I don't know him and don't know how honest he is but, whatever else, HE HAS ENERGY. He will never stop. HE WILL NOT BE BEATEN. He's had tremendous legal problems but they will never stop him. He has a hare-lip too but he could be a quadraplegic and still have all the success in the world because:

1- He deserves it.

2- He wants it.

3- He's going to get it.

4- Nothing can stop him.

5-   Anyone who suggests that some problem is greater than he is has such a small mind that what they think makes no difference anyway.

A pessimist or a failure would be telling you now how Glen Turner finally got what's coming to him since he's lost a lot of money and has some legal problems. Personally I believe he is resting and digesting the positive lessons he's learned. He is a mover, has the energy to make things happen and will always, ultimately, come out on top of the heap.

When a person decides what he wants, sets aside a reasonable time period to get it, and then sets out to pursue it wholeheartedly HE WILL GET IT. It makes no difference if he's handicapped, less intelligent, from a negative background, different race, religion and so on.

A few years ago I used to go to a bank nearly every day to make deposits. Almost daily there was a young fellow in a wheel chair by the front door selling pencils. This fellow was almost totally paralyzed. He couldn't move either leg or one arm at all and could only with great difficulty move the other arm and hand. His head movements were uncontrollable and his eye movements were erratic. Now, many people sit in wheel chairs and sell pencils, and some who really are limited to that are making the most of their situation, but this fellow was different in a significant way. He had desire and spirit. In his eyes he had purpose and dignity. His great self was trapped in a body that was non-functional, but the immense courage he had radiated from him. I always bought a pencil from him and in his distressed and nearly unintelligible speech he would always ask, "Two?" He was giving me his pitch and selling me. I would usually buy two pencils and he would labor for several minutes to grasp another pencil to hand me. HE TRIED SO HARD. That was his greatness. Tears would come to my eyes as I watched him make his super-human effort to get another pencil for me. It was his great achievement. He would struggle to say the words "thank you." It was always a special experience to see this fellow working against all of the odds that were stacked against him. IF HE CAN DO THAT, WHAT CAN WE DO WITH ALL OR MOST OF OUR FACULTIES? Or any faculties at all. For that fellow, trapped in a body that he couldn't change, he was doing ALL HE COULD to change his circumstances and fulfill his innate and boundless destiny to be a dignified and successful person. Some people may not be able to see all of that in what I've described, but this fellow radiated tangible

...register your value on your appearances, but your value and ability are internal. It's not as much what's outside that counts as what's inside. *It's all in your head.* Your success is in your head and your failure is in your head. Later on in this book we'll explore the mechanics of making money. Don't tell yourself that you want to make money but just don't know how. You'll learn how. Right now we are talking about wanting it so bad your teeth ache.

At first impression, perhaps, some people think a 6'3" fellow who is 40 years old and wears a 3 piece suit is a stable guy and someone to listen to. For my money I would much rather deal with a 4' tall minority cripple WHO HAS ELECTRICITY IN HIS VOICE. He is the guy who is going somewhere. The tall, middle class conservative fellow can show me how to make 10 or 15% a year on my savings, but THE ELECTRIC CRIPPLE CAN MAKE ME RICH. Believe me! Believe me! It's true.

All the time I was putting my own wealth program together we lived rather modestly and I didn't go in for too much flash. Even a modest appearance isn't a limitation since the energy and excitement can overcome any negatives. I was also overwight and that didn't make any difference either. In retrospect, however, I would have felt healthier and stronger if I had lost some weight. I had always been a little heavy and thought that that was just how I was built.

A couple of years ago I decided, finally, to get rid of the excess pounds, gave myself three months to do it and pursued it with a passion. In 3 months I lost 75 pounds and 14½" off my waist. no big deal. It was all in my head, but I feel so much better that I wish I'd lost the weight years ago. But it still didn't slow down my financial progress. And it won't slow you down either. Nothing can. If you have no arms and feel less than aggressive and presentable, perhaps you would wear a diamond necklace to add a little flash. Get some nice clothes. If your internal self-image isn't up to par a few of these external decorations may lift your spirits for a while. I never had the clothes and diamonds. You may not need them either, but they might give you a little more confidence in yourself. If you can't afford real diamonds get some fake ones. Not to appear gaudy. Your clothes and jewelry shouldn't make you appear like a used car salesman in Hollywood. You should look confident and successful. If your diamond is fake, wear it with a disarming ease that shows that it could only be real. Get a gold watch with fake diamonds on the dial. Get some rich looking clothes even if you get them at a discount store. Get something with a little style. Later on you can get the real diamonds and $1,000 suits. If you feel like you need the jewels now and can't afford it, FAKE IT TILL YOU MAKE IT. Be comfortable with your appearance, with your diamonds and discussing large amounts of money. *Be confident and be excited.* Be comfortable and be successful. At the same time you radiate this excitement and energy, be completely at ease with your success. Act as if it is all taken for granted: It's just how things are. You are destined to be rich and successful, it is in your blood, things are going your way, you will be rich and nothing can prevent it from happening. Be disarming and at ease with your wealth, even if your wealth isn't in your pocket yet, it's in your head and you deserve it.

My idea of flashing yourself up a little if you have something you consider negative about your physical appearance is, for the most part, to improve your self-image. Some success promoters suggest you take all of your money and buy a Cadillac right at first and drive people around in it so they'll feel like you're a high roller. That may

that they put people off. You've probably seen a lot of them. They act too showy and too shallow. Get this in your mind:

1- You have success.

2- You have depth in your character.

3- You are at ease with your wealth.

4- You are *excited* and *stable*. This idea of yours is not a flash-in-the-pan. It is a well thought-out continuous idea that will not fail.

So be confident. Fix yourself up but don't go overboard. In this physical appearance idea for example, regardless of your skin color or build etc., you wouldn't want so many jewels that you look like a Christmas tree. One large diamond is nice and an expensive looking watch may be all you need. I have wealthy friends who think that a 3 piece suit looks more stable and business-like, more mature and respectable. I have never once concluded a business deal wearing a suit. Do it if you want to, but if you are more casual, relaxed with your success, well-dressed and one or two hints of wealth (jewels), you'll seem to have already made it. Later on you can add genuinely expensive stuff and it may impress some people who could further your wealth program, however that's an open question and all of the appearance stuff can be overcome by your correct attitude.

As my millions grew, by age 30 I had a new Cadillac, Rolls Royce, 13,500 sq. ft. home I designed myself, beautiful income properties that looked great and all of that may have inspired ocnfidence when people looked at them, and may have encouraged a few deals, but starting off you can have the whole show on your back. And act like it's fine that way, too. Everything to come across in a positive way. Always be confident and come across as KNOWING EXACTLY WHAT YOU ARE DOING. Not a cocky, know-it-all attitude, but a genuine projection of knowing exactly where you are going. I've known some really wonderful and deserving people who should have been able to do lots of deals but who always come across as not knowing what was going on. Too flexible in their confidence. Too doubting of their abilities to make something work out. But you are not like them, because FOR YOU, IT HAS TO WORK OUT. YOU ARE SIMPLY DESTINED TO BE WEALTHY AND THERE ISN'T ANYTHING YOU CAN DO ABOUT IT. IT MUST BE SO!!!

Years ago when I was knocking on doors for jobs to put new tar coatings on asphalt driveways, and even before when I knocked on doors to paint houses, I made up my mind that I would never end a day without having secured some work to do. I would not give up. Some evenings as late as 10 or 11 o'clock I was still knocking on doors, using a flashlight to show people how I could fix their driveways. I often apologized for being there so late, but told them I didn't want to pass them up since we'd be doing the work on their street the next day and I just wanted to see if they wanted us (me) to do their driveway while we were working there. Everyone seemed to understand simply because I acted like it was OK, and I never had a day when I failed to get at least one job. Even at that time I had some money and was buying lots of property and I had work to do, so how easy do you think it was still walking around late at night to try and find a $50 job to do? But I had to do it because I promised myself that I would never quit. And I never did.

In summary, then a postive and forthright attitude is the

of the woodwork. They are everywhere. There is no bad economy, there are no physical defects, there is no unfortunate turn of events. *There is no failure.....only success!* You must really believe that. I believe it because it is true.

Compartmentalize your time and devote yourself during the allotted period 100% to what you want from that time. Remember that success is in your head and if you can get your mind into a confident, happy and successful state, the rest will fall into place as you work at it.

I lived in London for a while and "sold books" there. That entire business was an experience in hype. I'll discuss it later, but an experience with a fellow I worked with briefly will illustrate the mental-success idea. For a few weeks I worked with a young guy named Ben. He had a great sense of humor and everyne enjoyed him but for some reason he "blanked" every night. He just couldn't place the encyclopedias. He went on like that for 2 or 3 weeks and one day something "clicked" for him and he placed (sold) two

25

sets. He was elated and excited. Every single night after that he placed at least one set but usually 2 or 3. He was on top of the world. Do you think all of the people he talked with changed all of a sudden? Of course not. The change was in his mind. He got his head into success, he accepted it and expected it and radiated the sure feeling to people he talked with. And he succeeded. Interestingly enough, he had a temporary set-back (one night without a placement) and he knew it was all over. Whatever turned on to get his head right turned off and blackened his mind. He became anxious and worried. He was *afraid* that he couldn't sell the books and he didn't. His sparkle was gone. But ALL OF HIS SUCCESS AND ALL OF HIS FAILURE WAS IN HIS MIND. After two or three blank weeks he quit the company. The lesson is obvious.

Don't let yourself get trapped in either two pits: 1. I can't succeed but it's not my fault, or, 2. When a degree of success comes many people start to coast.

Most people like to blame others for their misfortune. It eases the pain. Or they like an excuse for non-performance even if they have to suffer the consequences. An insurance salesman can have a day a week set aside for canvassing door-to-door for new clients. He knows, from experience, that he'll get 2 or 3 new clients if he spends the entire day at it. At the same time, though, he doesn't like to knock on doors. (Who does?) He knows that if he does go out he'll get the business since it's all a matter of numbers contacted and attitude. On his allotted day he wakes up and finds a terrible rain storm is in progress. Inside he feels good because he doesn't have to go out and knock on doors. It's not because he's lazy or doesn't like to canvass from door-to-door or anything like that. It's because of the rain and he can't go out in the rain. Even though he missed getting the new clients he is glad he didn't have to go out. This is a perfect example of having a good excuse for non-performance. Several others:

I couldn't get the loan because of tight money.

This is a seasonal business and this is the off-season.

Retail sales were down nationwide.

It wasn't a success because of high interest rates on our operating loans.

Etc. etc. Always an excuse except for the real excuse...ME. The real reason is because I didn't pull the thing together. I didn't make it successful.

your goal, and you never missed a day. The way to make it through the rain is in knowing that in only two more years you won't have to do this anymore.

The second point is in being satisfied when part of a goal is achieved. I started several friends in the house-painting business in a high-volume way, just as I had done. That was around 1969-1970. At that time it was easy enough to make $200 or $300 a day doing the work the way I did it. Fast and lots of it. Some days much more than that. I showed others how to do it but, when they got a few grand in their pockets, usually they would coast a little. It was hard for them to give up a Saturday to knock on doors to find houses to paint when they had some money in their pocket. After all, what difference would one Saturday make? Well, one Saturday might make a slow week, or a slow couple of days, but that seemed OK for them because they had been working so hard anyway, and it was only reasonable to take a day or two off. You can see their line of reasoning. They still had some money and it became a pattern that they would begin taking days off and, as you know, relaxing is much more fun than working and knocking on doors is the worst of all and if we just skip a couple of weeks and then hit it really hard we'll all be charged up. This happened so many times with so many people. But, the two weeks became a month or more and when another effort was made at the business the magic was gone and they hated what they had to do to start doing. Then they just couldn't get swinging again and they didn't pursue the business any longer.

The same thing happened many times in the asphalt business. People, I'd started patching and sealing driveways which is what I was doing, would see the money I was making and the property I was accumulating and they'd want it too. So, I'd outline a work schedule for them to follow to get exactly what I was getting or more. but, they wouldn't do it. Regardless of the financial rewards they wouldn't follow through. Here is a typical example of many conversations I've had with many people I started in this business:

X- "I'd give anything to have all of the property you've got."

A- What are you doing tonight?

X- "I'm going to the movies and shopping. What are you doing?"

A- I'm going to knock on doors to get more work.

X- How much did you make today?"

A- $600, how about you?

X- Nothing today, but I think next week will be good.

28

A- What are you going to do Saturday?

X- Well, I'm going to the beach. What are you going to do?

A- I'm knocking on doors to get more business.

X- But you're already scheduled up two weeks ahead. Why are trying to get more?

A- Because I am working. I deserve the best of everything and I'm going to get it. I can't depend on anyone else to take care of me and provide me with all the things I want, so I am

X- You know, you're right Ross, and I have to go to the beach this Saturday but next Saturday I'm going to do as you suggest.

Do you think it ever happened? No. They would not pay the price for success. There were a few exceptions to what I've described and today these people are all very wealthy. It's not that I taught them some great secret and shared my wisdom with them. I just told them how I was getting the things I had. Later in this book there is a chapter about the price we must pay for any accomplishment or achievement.

Most people will get a little money and coast for a while. They lose their intensity and passion and the dream begins to fade. The passion that can overcome our own selfish immediate desires is the motivation that will push us on to inevitable success.

If I have some legal problems I'd rather have an attorney represent me who will put his whole heart into my defense and never confine his interest in me to 9 to 5. Give me an attorney who will wake up at 2 a.m. and make notes on my defense. Give me an accountant who has genuine zeal for my interests.

If I have an IRS audit give me an IRS agent who is a 9 to 5 man, not someone who has a passion for his job. A passionate IRS agent will take his assignment seriously and will become so immersed in my audit that it will become "alive" for him. He will leave no stone unturned.

All of these things are what separate the exceptional person from the folks who will barely squeeze by during their lifetime or, at best, have a comfortable living, but bypass the real freedom a financially independent person can enjoy.

CHAPTER FIVE

Being Rich

Were a psychologist to read this chapter he might toss it aside as being erroneous and completely invalid. These ideas are based on my own observations and, through the years, they seem to hold water. That is, they seem to be valid.

If you eliminate the corporate folks and put together a group of a hundred millionaires and multi-millionaires, as sure as the sun goes down, they'll have a lot in common. Although there are exceptions, from my own experience I think you'll find the following basic characteristics are in common, and it should give you some insight into the desire you have that motivates you to acquire great wealth.

Most of these individuals will be from poor backgrounds. There is a great difference between how "haves" and "have-nots" are raised in general. A motivated person from a very poor background knows that the world has a lot more to offer than the hand he was dealt. He deserves a few aces up his sleeve, a few good hands and the opportunity to win and he knows he didn't get it when he was young. He knows what it's like to go to school with the soles worn through on his shoes and pants that are mended and years behind the current fad. He knows what it's like to be the odd duck in his class, social classification, because of the clothes he wore and so on. And, he didn't like it. (I didn't). He is determined to overcome his poor beginnings and have ALL of the things he couldn't have.

Most of this group will also share the NEED FOR RECOGNITION. Because of the material deprivation and concomitant social deprivations while young, this individual wants to be recognized. He needs others to see that he CAN and HAS acquired for himself the things that were never provided for him, and that are, in our society, proof of his validity and success. This person usually needs expensive clothes, luxury cars and a lavish home to provide him with *physical* possessions that can easily be recognized as proof of his *mental* or creative superiority. In the abstract they seem to provide that, but, by their nature, they provide no static feelings. The feeling must always be fed and expanded. Everyone must recognize me as a "success." That seems to be the feeling that motivates a person towards his goal.

Another similarity most of the people in this group will have in common will be *sexual anxiety.* In his book *THINK AND GROW RICH*, Napoleon Hill concludes that much energy for achievement and success is actually redirected energy from sexual frustration. That is, we have anxiety produced from sexual function or excessive stimulation which we are not able to fulfill or accommodate and it manifests its relief in the direction of exceptional energy in other endeavors. This pursuit could be a profession, the arts or, very commonly, in being a super-achiever. I know a lot of wealthy people and one of several common traits they share is that sex and sexual activity seem to be significantly more important to them than would seem to be the norm. There isn't a thing wrong with this. It makes life fun even though it produces a little anxiety at times since these types usually marry more reserved types who, by their very nature, aren't inclined to fulfill the rigorous sexual requirements. Someone else will have to tell you why these types attract each other. It is a ready-made partnership that provides automatic sexual energy that cannot be accommodated and can be successfully rechannelled to provide exceptional motivation for excellence in other areas.

My wife says she thinks these ~~~~~~ other ~

~~~~~ else, she ~~~~ preneurial type goes out on risky ventures or thin limbs every day and needs a more reserved and stable "mother" to come home to. Someone may know the answer, but I don't. In any case there is a lot of electricity generated that can super-charge and motivate a person to great accomplishment.

Another common trait seems to be *Physical proof of validity*. If you talk to me you can impress me with your intelligence and superior nature. In our western civilization, however, you don't need to talk to me to convey the message. You can convey it by what you drive, wear, and live in. If you are driving a new Rolls Royce I know that you must have done something right. Even if you just talked a friend into loaning it to you, you must be persuasive. If you stole it, you must have great confidence to drive such a conspicuous car around. If you're stupid enough to drive it around after you stole it, you must still be quite intelligent to have bypassed the double-tumbler locks. If someone just left the keys in it and you stole it, at least you have good taste in cars. And if it belongs to you, you either got the money as a gift, stole the money or earned it and bought the car. However you got the Rolls, driving around in such an excellent car seems to reflect on you, personally, in some way. Even if it shouldn't, I suppose it does. Diamonds are evidence of wealth and we can wear them all the time, even when we shower. When we see someone with a few carats of rock on their finger, our circuits register "that person should be recognized." So, if we acquire wealth and its trappings we have physical proof that we are valid and successful people.

Another similarity most of the millionaires in our group will have in common is their need of *flexibility for free souls.* Some people are just not cut out for the nine-to-five. They can be trapped in it for a while but it is just against their nature to have regulated hours. Left to their own instincts they are preditors and nomads who will roam, hunt night and day and provide more than their needs, but in an unstructured way. If these people can turn off their generators and cool their jets they can also relax completely and not feel guilty. Usually, these free people just can't be contained within the bounds of predictable and regular employment. They *need* to build, to grow and to have the financial flexibility to do as they please with their time. And they'll work hard to get there. There really can be no freer feeling than to have limitless opportunitites and movement.

We all have bounds to what we can do physically, but mentally we see wealth as the essential element in controlling our environment. We can travel, we can build, we can support philanthopic organizations, we can conquer disease through research, we *CAN* make a difference, but we must be *free* to do it.

Material wealth allows *creativity on a larger scale.* A child enjoys building with blocks and erector sets, and there can be an enlarged similar feeling when a person builds buildings. I've built a lot of houses and buildings and I felt great fulfillment when I could see my mental designs being materially realized. Out of all the types of building I've done, the most enjoyable was in designing and building homes. It is great fun, during construction, to move walls here and there and see mental images transformed into rooms and living quarters. You can do it, too. It's easy and it's fun. And you can make money doing it.

Some people find it fulfilling to build a bookcase or plant a garden. Building a block of apartment buildings is creative and fulfilling in the same way. But, to practice *this* art you need money to fund it. Some people want to become rich in order to fund the materializati~~~ their dreams. Th~~~

~~~g to

~~~ on here and there for

~~~o. He won't take you up on it because he can't. His time isn't his own. He has sold it to someone else for ten or twenty bucks an hour. All he has, in this world, is time and he has sold it to someone else for nearly nothing.

I once had a friend who worked in a corporate office of an insurance company for years and on the last day before his vacation he asked if he could leave ten minutes early. His boss told him he couldn't and this fellow was directed back to his work. He had sold himself out and had to do what his owner wanted. There isn't anything inherently wrong with being employed by someone else, but it is so restrictive and limiting. The real test of a person's satisfaction with working for someone is whether he has freedom and satisfaction in what he is doing, and is content with the compensation he is paid. Career criminals just can't get the hang of holding a daily job with regular hours. Neither can energetic spirits with an insatiable desire for freedom and wealth.

Our social training teaches us to want riches. It doesn't teach us how to get the wealth but society holds out this image of a rich and successful person who is everything we are supposed to want to be. And most of us go along with what we've been taught. There are other reasons for really wanting to get rich but, from my own acquaintances, these are characteristics shared by most people who succeed in their quest for money. You may share some or all of these traits. I think it's important for you to analyze why you want riches.

If you have a *non-material need* that seems like it will go away or be assuaged by *material success*, you should rethink your motivations. You should be happy in the first place and the wealth will allow you to expand freely in your own happiness.

CHAPTER SIX

If Ri~~ch~~

From the previous chapters we can see that striving for some material possession that will finally make us happy just can't happen. When we buy something, we feel elated. It lasts a while and then wears off. Then we have to buy something else. Usually we have to buy something larger or more expensive. From what I've heard and read about heroin, it's the same. It provides a "high," but, as immunity and insensitivity sets in, they need larger doses, more often and the effects last a shorter and shorter period of time.

In my own experience, every time I bought some land or diamonds or cars, or whatever, I felt a real "rush" of contentment, excitement and achievement. As I went on and on the thrill faded faster and faster. As a heroin addict wants more and larger doses, so does the internally unhappy person need more and larger deals to maintain the "high" of self-respect and public recognition, validation, euphoria and fulfillment. But, we all wake up in the morning and a new day requires a new "fix."

The only possible way around this mentally debilitating cycle is to have the necessary happiness and fulfillment in the first place.

So, what is there to be happy about?

There is a consuming and intrinsic joy available to each one of us just to be alive. We cover ourselves with blankets of self-doubt, low self-esteem, limited financial vision, worries and troubles and then wonder why we can't see the sun. When we go outside at night we look at the ground instead of seeing the vast display of the immensity of space. If we are religious people, we often look at our religious ideas as limitations instead of keys to unlock the universe and eternitites.

These, like all of my ideas on your success, are all in your mind.

A glass is half-empty or half-full. You either lost your money or learned a lesson. You are chained down by problems that seem insurmountable, or you realize that, regardless of current troubles, your happiness is intact. Your ideal happiness can never be taken away from you because it is based in non-material concepts. Your thinking may cloud these concepts but you can push the clouds aside. It is critical that a person finds his happiness in himself so that it can never be taken away.

In our western society we have much more opportunity for being happy. Many countries of the world, and I've travelled in dozens, have so great an economic, political or social oppression. Many countries have a rigid caste system which locks individuals in a social and economic class from which they can't escape. Ignorance is the great devil in most of these countries or societies. Because of a lack of education the populace can't see a way to improve their lot, can't envision class elevation, and in the most repressive

areas, don't even care. They accept their position as just being the way things are. Feeling that way, they aren't inclined to tune into the pure joy of living. Their hunger prevents them from contemplating the universe. If they only knew what was possible for them, they would go to a place in which it was possible or die trying to get there. In politically repressive areas, the populace is locked in chains and irons of control. In the communist countries, for example, the people are bound by economic controls (they generally can't own their own businesses), intellectually (all they know is what people tell them) and socially (their movements and meetings are controlled). When I was travelling in the communist countries I was constantly aware of the despair in everyone's actions and words. It all seemed so hopeless since th~~~
everyth~~~

~~~American
~~~ ~~~ ~~~ouring cities in the Soviet Union.

Senator Charles Mathias listed in the Congressional Record this sampling of questions that were put to Americans in Dushanbe, a city of the Tadzhik Republic in central Asia: Do you have laws in America? Can blacks marry? Can they marry whomever they wish? Are blacks given the day off on Christmas, too? Do you have bedbugs in America? Do they have only one eye? Can Indians talk? Do blacks speak English? Is it possible to send a letter to the USSR from the USA? Americans have artifical meat made of wood, don't they? Your sun rises in the west and sets in the east, doesn't it? Do any Americans immigrate to the USSR. The average American worker is too poor to buy his own tractor, isn't he? Is America near Israel? Is there a club for millionaires in the U.S.? Is it mandatory to join? Do you have statues of Lenin like we do? Do they permit capitalism in the U.S.A.? How many kernels are there on an ear of corn? Are all of you guides members of one family? Are young pioneers allowed to go to public school in the U.S.?" (U.S. News and World Report, June 25, 1979)

Can you imagine the repression that leads to such ignorance? In a society like that feeling joy in living is much more difficult because of their controlled existence. Even with the biases and bigotry in our western society we still have freedom of movement and expression. That, alone, is reason enough to be happy.

You may have some mental disabilities or you may be physically impaired. You may be unattractive, uneducated, unskilled and uncertain about yourself. But, *YOU ARE SPECIAL.* There never has been and never will be another you. YOU ARE GREAT. YOU ARE WORTHWHILE AND YOU CAN SUCCEED. Not just financially, but in many worthwhile pursuits in life. Your innate goodness and greatness should permeate your heart, mind and body with a happiness that can never fail you. This is the joy and *continuous* fulfillment that will carry you through ups and downs, good times and bad. It can transcend illness and disease. I believe it can even transcend death. It's the inner feeling that will be your friend when others fail you and your companion as you acquire wealth. It helps you see that *ALL* of the deals in the world can never make you a great person and a lack of any or *ALL* deals can't make you any less, either. Feeling this way, you are greater than any problem or any transaction. If a deal falls through, it makes no difference because, in the greatest possible sense, the deal has no importance at all. Thinking this way, you can never get backed into a corner, because there are no corners. You can't have any big problems because there aren't any big problems. It surpasses your own weaknesses and the weaknesses of others. Those weaknesses aren't permanent but your joy is. Feeling this great freedom you can pursue your wealth and real estate acquisitions without fear. There is no fear because nothing can go wrong that has any lasting significance. You are, at once, part of everything and greater than everything. This feeling can never lead you to feel better than anyone else. It can't make you arrogant or repressive because you realize that everyone has the same great position as you. And you are happy with that feeling.

A great cause of depression and anxiety is the inclination we have to focus our thoughts on ourselves. When we spend some time and effort helping others there is some inner satisfaction that deepens our happiness. It's even better if we help others anonymously, without recognition. If we do it for recognition, that, in itself, is our reward. If no one knows, the reward is inside us, and that's where our happiness lies. You may think I have my head in the clouds I don't. I've been "around the block" experienced the heights an worst problems in life a great authority but I ca what makes people ha

Another key point i ʌnger on past bad experiences or grudges. You car ge the experience, but you can learn from it and the negative feeling. It may be hard. It may seem ible, but *YOU CAN DO IT!!* If you hold a grudge, t person it will hurt will be you. The person who hu ended you is in a different world and the bad feeli only harm you. If you've had a bad experience, ever it is, you can overcome it. *ANYTHIN* elieve me. I've been taken advantage of and had m ngs hurt in the worst possible ways, but got through ook perseverance and patience but the joy of living ame it. You may have terribly depressing and excru g problems like this, also, and I know that YOU CAN ERCOME THEM. Does it hurt inside? Sure. Wh gets the very worst, do you think about killing y lf? Probably so. But, can you overcome it? YES! YES! And afterward you will be even better

41

positioned to have a successful life, because you have learned from your experience.

There are so many reasons for happiness. If you stop and consider the hopes and dreams of mankind since the beginning of time you'll see that most of these dreams have been realized in our society. People have always wanted warmth, food, health services, transportation, entertainment, communication, travel opportunitites, justice, free speech, indoor plumbing, food preservation, economic opportunitites, religious freedom, and on and on. While you may not have every one of these ideals, our society affords them all. We have everything that everyone in the history of the world has hoped and worked for. Shouldn't that produce some happiness in itself? We are living the wildest dreams in the history of the world. This is a time like no other time. While the news media assaults us daily with negative happenings around us, we often overlook the sheer joy of living in such a progressive and expansive age.

We can look around us and see people who have everything going for them and who achieve little or nothing. We can also see people who have nothing and make everything. These are people with joy, ambition and vision in their hearts. These people overcome all obstacles to achieve their goals, AND THEY SUCCEED. Their joy and happiness is tangible and real and can never be destroyed by the problems or misfortunes that come their way.

Helen Keller was deaf and dumb, blind and uneducated because of her afflictions. She had most of the cards stacked against her. She had the perfect excuses for non-performance and little achievement. How could she succeed? She couldn't hear, couldn't speak and couldn't see. How could she learn if she couldn't communicate? If she hadn't been afflicted with blindness she could have used her eyes to learn. If not deaf she could have heard to learn. BUT SHE HAD PURPOSE AND *SHE WOULD NOT*

ACCEPT FAILURES. She wouldn't, she couldn't, and *SHE DIDN'T!!* She learned to utter and refine gutteral sounds and form them into speech. At first crude and later intelligible. She became one of the great speakers of her time. She learned braille, learned to understand words spelled with fingertips in her palms, learned to "hear" by feeling throat vibrations and mouth movements of those speaking to her. She authored books, became a great humanitarian and friend of world leaders. She became the greatest. From a person who had NOTHING. Except the desire, the joy, the appreciation of a universe she couldn't see, songs she couldn't hear and the desire to help others. She wanted to help people who had all of their physical faculties but just couldn't grasp the great and consuming idea of joy that transcends problems, happiness that overcomes heartache and an indomitable spirit that will succeed. It's not economics. It's life. Money is part of life and you can have all you want. But greater goals and joys, that will never fail you, are within your reach. In fact, they are in your mind. Open your thinking. Be grateful. Realize what you have. And, feeling this way, how could you ever fail?

CHAPTER SEVEN

Status

Have you ever thought about what motivates class distinctions in most societies? I'm not a sociologist and my intellectual development hasn't matured fully but I reason that humans find security in being classified and assigned, either by themselves or others, to a certain class. Every class has its own demands, expectations and rewards.

In a book I read about status worldwide, the distinguishing characteristics of the classes in different countries were all outlined. As you know, in America the idea of success is to have a big home, an expensive car, a camper or motor home, a pool and tennis court, etc. etc. In some arctic countries the people couldn't care any less about homes and cars but they distinguish status by the number of reindeer a person has. A person will spend a lifetime accumulating a large herd of reindeer so as to be recognized as wealthy and successful.

In some near eastern countries the populace couldn't be less interested in reindeer or homes and cars, but *they* devote their lifetimes acquiring silver bracelets for their arms, and their status is designated by the number of silver bands they have. To them, the silver bracelets mean everything. In America, we don't want silver bracelets but we do want the things that our society has taught us to equate with wealth and success.

There are, however, certain human feelings and hopes and dreams that have always been and I think that more of these are realized or possible in the American society than at any other place or time. As mentioned in the previous chapter, mankind has always wanted to be healthy and have health services available. People have always hoped for a steady food supply, the means and freedom to travel and move about freely, the provision of diverse entertainment, education (as opposed to ignorance), a heated place to sleep, economic opportunity (that is a social structure in which it is possible to acquire something), religious freedom, free political expression and so on. For the most part, American society allows for the realization of most of the hopes and dreams mankind has always had.

Staus in America is very important. That may be why the U.S. has deveoped so rapidly into the world leader in more ways. People want to raise their social or financial position and it's very possible here, thus, rapid development and expansion.

Status is such a seemingly inherent part of the human mind that almost any means is utilized to form class distinctions. In a sanitorium in Switzerland all of the patients were tubercular and terminally ill and their status was designated by the severity of their illness and how near death they were. The more gravely ill were in the upper class and those very near death were the elite. Isn't it interesting that even in such a situation people will find status in the only way they can, through the only thing they have in common: their illnesses.

Well, in America, like good boys and girls, we have learned our lessons on what will make us successful and recognized.

We may not like it, in the abstract, but that's how we've been trained and that's how we think and that's the way it is. Those who don't go along with the program are classified as misfits and derelicts.

So, we all have this carrot hanging out in front of us. The carrot is an endless list of things we must acquire before we can be completely happy, fulfilled and have status recognition. There is always one more thing to get and then you'll be happy. In my own life the progression has gone something like this: (Keep in mind the way we feel; that everything would be so neat, so perfect, if only......) When I was young and coming from such a poor background, not just monetarily poor, but I could never develop a genuinely good self-image. So, I was poor in many ways, economically, socially, physically, characteristically and so on.

But, I always had a carrot in front of me. I always knew what I wanted next. My self-image never really improved and solidified until I was 19 years old and went out to do missionary work for two years. While as a teenager I had been able to work 2 or 3 jobs and do them very well, I was only paid what the job paid. In that way I was limited since there are only so many hours to work. When I was a missionary my ability seemed open-ended and I saw no limits to what could be accomplished. I arose earlier, went to bed later, was more intense and single-minded than others around me and I was very successful at my assignments. That was a great period for me to get my self-image raised up. It's a pity I didn't do it years earlier and I never would have settled for excelling in hourly-paying jobs.

This motivation for status and recognition can sometimes drive a person to particularly notable accomplishments. A few years ago I had dinner in Las Vegas with a 25 year old fellow who was very successful financially. Somehow, when he was 16 years old he got hmself jacked up and motivated. But what can a motivated 16 year old do? Not much, right? Wrong. He was 16 during the period when motor homes were really catching on and he went to the largest dealer in Denver and asked for a job selling. Of course he was turned down, but *wouldn't accept no for an answer.* He asked the owner to let him sell for one month and then, if he wasn't the top salesman, he wouldn't take any pay for his time. This excited young men worked the 3 summer months and made TWENTY THOUSAND DOLLARS in commissions. That was back when twenty grand was worth a lot. In fact, you can still buy a lot of groceries with $20,000. This fellow stayed in school, continued to sell part-time, got into real estate AT AGE 16, and by the time he was 20 was 100% independent. From there to age 25 when I met him he'd had a few ups and downs but had a general trend up, up, up in his projects.

Well, if I had had any idea that I could have gone out and tackled the world at that age I would have done it. But no one told me and it never came to me on my own. But, at age 19 I figured it out and it all fell together exactly as I knew it would.

After returning from that two year assignment my first "carrot" was to get a chunk of cash since I had never before had any amount of money. I've described in previous chapters how it happened, but in eight weeks I made ten grand. I had never had any amount of money before. Thus I got my first carrot.

I was on a great "high." I next wanted to travel so I took my money and a year off and travelled around the world to about forty countries. While I was travelling I got drafted and between coming home and going to the army I put together another reasonable sum.

Out of the army, I went directly back to my program. The next "status carrot" was to buy real estate and put together a few small deals which became larger and larger deals. All during this time I kept thinking that as soon as I got this one more deal I would somehow feel "full" inside. I saw as my crowning achievement the purchase of a beautiful 3 carat diamond for an engagement ring for my sweetheart. I really loved that beautiful stone and I had something most people can never get. I was elated, but alas, it didn't seem like I had everything I needed after all. From there, in the relentless struggle up the status-ladder, I wanted more than one business, so to the asphalt busines I added an office supply business, manufactured men's cologne in Los Angeles, manufactured women's skin products in Riverside, then more and more land projects and then I wanted to build a beautiful new home. I KNEW that, whatever else, when we had a wonderful house to live in I would feel like I finally was happy. And the house made us happy for a while.

Then, I added a retail business, then commerical properties, then new food service businesses, then entertainment businesses, then a shopping center, then apartment buildings, duplexes, houses, subdivisions, and on and on from here to yonder. I kept thinking, "just one more deal, then I'll be happy and then I'll rest." After having all those projects and properties it came to me that if I had the biggest house in the state it would surely lead to a permanent feeling of well-being, so I built a forty-odd room house that was so big and elaborate and well-furnished that it would boggle your mind. Then I needed a new Cadillac, than a Rolls-Royce, then I wanted a second Rolls-Royce.

At this time it suddenly came to me. I had been slowed down by some problems in a large project and it got me thinking: I don't feel as good now as I felt years ago when we didn't have anything. But, I had been doing everything our society teaches us to do to be successful, happy and in the upper crust.

To clear my thinking I got some professional help (from a psychiatrist....."gasp, how awful, and he seemed like such a nice boy" I suppose some people observed.). He told me what was so obvious but I had never realized. He said I could keep going and going until I owned the whole world but would never be happy until I was happy inside. On the other hand, he said, if I was happy inside, then all of the external stuff was meaningless. If a person feels inadequate inside they grasp for status. If they have their own status and internal image in focus, they don't care what projects to others. The one exception to this is if having a certain appearance will further our own self-interests. Then it is purely for show business and has nothing to do with feeling and status.

Of course, money can give you the free time and flexibility to do what you want but it will *NEVER* make you happy. It seems like it would, it does provide temporary elation and euphoria but IT DOESN'T LAST. That is why so many rich and famous people are so unhappy, even though they have a secure status position. The fame and reknown can never put something inside from the outside. It can't. But, that's the status/recognition carrot idea in our country. No one ever tells you that it's a big joke. Yes, the money is fine, the carrot is fine, but not to make you happy. The previous chapter dealt with real happiness. In this chapter I hope to convince you of the futility of the status climb.

First get your head together, then realize that you want the millions for flexibility and adventure and *then* go after the money.

If you think 16 or 20 years old is too young, then waste 10 or 20 years before you set aside your 5 years for wealth. If you really believe that a person must be 40 or so to start making it, then wait till you're 40. You could coast in an unrewarding job during the days and watch TV at night for twenty years. Of course your children will be grown up in 20 years and you won't be able to use the money for travel (exposure) and adventures for them. But wait, if you must. BUT........WHY NOT DO IT *NOW?* If you're 20 now or 40 or 50. It makes no difference. you will NEVER be younger than you are today. Set aside your time period and get going. If you do this and really work for five years you'll have the millions. If you don't do it, in five years you'll be sitting somewhere thinking of reasons for not being productive. The cards are NOT stacked against you.

In summary, my advice to you is to not get caught up in either the status idea or the false idea that you'll feel any happier having money. I finally got everything you can buy with money, nearly, and learned that lesson. On the other hand, wealth can provide you with endless personal freedom, for time and interests. Clear your mind first. Get your happiness together and then go after your Five Million dollars. YOU CAN DO IT!!

CHAPTER EIGHT

What It's Like When You Finally Get Rich

Just for a moment, as you sit there relaxing in your chair, envision what it would be like to be on a small south sea island with everything just the way you want it. Companionship, food for the picking, balmy weather, no demands on your time, no competition. Just relaxation, health and contentment.

So, we sit, we dream, we visualize, sometimes we even try to inject realism into our dreams to be sure that it really would be that good, and we long for that best of all possible situations. However, the realization of our dreams doesn't ever seem to be as good as we think it will be. So it is with the acqusition of great wealth. Although it does a lot of positive things for you, it isn't a panacea for all ills. In a previous chapter we explored the basis for real happiness and if you aren't happy inside, there aren't any external possessions that can make you happy.

If you *are* happy inside to begin with, then the material wealth you accumulate can take care of many periferal problems. If you always remain cognizant of your internal happiness and why you're getting rich, then you won't be so disappointed when you get it. If you are from a poverty ridden background you know that the greatest challenge in such an environment is to get the car started every morning. Being rich means that the car always starts.

Do you dread answering the phone, knowing it will be some bill collector or creditor? Riches may not make all your phone calls trouble-free but you won't have that sinking feeling when the telephone rings. Being wealthy will bring some good news in the mail instead of overdue bills every day.

Perhaps the greatest of all the blessings of wealth is freedom. Freedom with our time and our movements is the wonderful sensation available to us. To really be free. While some friends of mine were travelling in the Soviet Union they were driving a car through the Ukraine. They took a wrong turn at a crossroads which was a slight variance from their pre-declared itinerary, and, less than half-a-mile down the wrong road they were stopped and told that they had departed from their authorized itinerary. They were being followed all the way. I was also followed all of the time I was there, although I took a few short-cuts and lost my "friends." It is all so repressive.

As I was going through a great mountain range, a hundred miles from nowhere in every direction, we had many unexplained stops, as are common on Russian trains. In fact, they often dismantled the wall and ceiling panels to search for contraband or whatever. In my compartment was an elderly fellow who, I determined, was going to see his grandchildren. He showed me several pictures of young children and conveyed that he was going to see them.

During one of the many stops they checked everyone's papers again and on one of his papers a number was illegible or smudged. Without any discussion at all the Russian officers just took the old fellow and threw him off the train, out in a snowbank, crying, and the train pulled away and left him in the most desolate mountains possible. Well, I'm sure that was the end of that guy. And, no one seemed to care much. There was little I could do with soldiers pointing machine guns at me. This isn't a fairy-tale. It's how these people live. Whenever you see travel logs of Russia they always show the beautiful subway in Moscow with its tile walls and artwork. Yes, the subway is beautiful but what about the people? They are repressed, generally depressed, drab and unhappy. That is political repression.

Freedom is supreme to me.

In Africa I saw many thousands starving to death. Everyone seems to accept the death all around them. It's part of their society. These people are pressed economically. Most of them earn a dollar or two a week upon which they support themselves and their families. These people are so dejected, so repressed and with no apparent way out. What a pitiful lack of freedom.

Here, in the first world countries, we have political, social, philosophical and economic freedom. We have more of everything than anyone has ever had before. But we, too, are bound. We are enclosed by our mental hang-ups and lack of flexibility caused by the necessity of making a living. If we are bound in that way, then being rich can free us.

The greatest "high" in having lots of money (millions, always think in millions) is that you are finally free. As Martin Luther King Jr. said, "FREE AT LAST, FREE AT LAST, THANK GOD ALMIGHTY, I'M FREE AT LAST!!!"

When you finally rise above your living expenses, when you get much more than you need to live the rest of your life, more than you need for your philanthropies, your giving, your family (everyone seems to want to give money to their family), when you have more than you can spend for all of these, you can throw your arms skyward and exclaim, *"I'M FREE AT LAST."*

If you were to keep your properties after you gain wealth, you'll still have a few strings tying you down and a few worries. Of course, having your money in the properties will insulate you from inflation but still require a little of your attention even if you employ someone to take care of it for you. But, even if you keep some properties, you will still be free.

Whatever else the money does or doesn't do, you don't have to worry about living expenses. Never again will you think about money to spend. And the basic stuff is all taken for granted. If you have the bucks you can take trips anywhere, whenever you want to. And you don't have to limit your expenses while you travel. Not that you will spend twenty grand on a vacation just because you have the money. Maybe you will and maybe you won't. The important thing is that you'll do exactly what you want to do without considering the expense. Personally, I enjoy hamburgers once in a while. I don't want steak all of the time. I also like bean sprouts for salad and they must be the cheapest food you can buy.

A middle-class couple on their yearly trip to Europe may spend five grand on their trip. When you take your European trips, it may be every month or every five years and you may spend $3,000 or $30,000. The point is that you'll do whatever you feel like doing. You may feel like driving a used Chevy (some do) or a $250,000 Rolls-Royce Camargue. It won't make any difference. You'll drive what you please and go where you please and not go where you don't want to go. The chains are broken and you are finally free to do as you please.

However, the kids still have dirty diapers, the dog still gets sick in the living room, you still argue with your wife, (not about money, but you'll think of something) and life goes on. You can't let the money detach you from your family and lose them. For example, if you have an argument about something and you think...."I don't have to stay for this. I'm going to South America to unwind," and if you do go it won't work out in your best interests. You can only do that trick a few times and you'll lose your family. Go to South America to unwind, but work your problems out before you go, and take your wife with you. Don't envision money as your ticket away from unhappiness. It simply isn't. The unhappiness is in your head and the money is in your pocket.

A great joy in life, a great fulfillment, even for self-indulgent sorts for the most part, is in being able to help less fortunate people.

H. Ross Perot, a Texas multi-billionaire, since becoming very wealthy, has continued to live in the same modest house he had before, drives the same 15 year old car and lives his life as if he had never become rich. But, he has used much of his money to fund some dramatic one-man projects. Help to refugees, political prisoners, hunger abatement and so on. Well, there are plenty of good causes in the world and there will be a great satsifaction come to you when you give your support and time to them. You'll have every blessing life can offer, so why not share it? There is an even greater satisfaction in doing it anonymously. If you do it for the show, you may get a little public recognition (which will be your reward), but a greater reward is to do it anonymously and have your happiness in your heart. It's the same old idea I've already repeated over and over. The lasting joy must be inside and can never come from external stuff, in this case recognition. The recognition will be a temporary high but it will not last. The lasting stuff is inside, so give of your time and money.

Also, after you acquire substantial financial reserves, you'll have an endless stream of people come to you to sell you something, get you to invest in some venture, or just want a handout. This may not bother you but it will seem like everyone wants your money. Some people feel threatened by this and become obsessed with the idea that they are going to lose their riches or that everyone is trying to get their money. Some become recluses and misers and hoarders because of this feeling. Be open, be free and don't let other people lock you in your den of gold.

In summary, when you get your wealth you'll feel elated at times (because of the freedom), depressed at times because you're still living in the real world), happy for where you can go and what you can do, and unhappy because sometimes when you get there it isn't much fun.

But, overall, the great blessing is *FREEDOM*. For the past couple of years I've stayed home a lot and played with my children and I've never been so happy. We take plenty of trips and try to spend our time enjoying each other, getting to know our children better, teaching them and being close to them. If I were an avid gardener or hunter or fisherman or skier I would pursue those avocations now. I got into health food and exercise and have really enjoyed that a lot. Before long some other hobby or interest will catch my attention and we'll spend some time at that.

Apply that feeling to yourself. Project yourself into the future, when you have your riches, and see that you can do whatever comes along, whatever interests you, go wherever you want to go, and, do whatever you want to do. Just DO IT.

CHAPTER NINE

Life Outline

There are certain times in a person's life when they are more liable to do certain things than at other times.

Muhammad Ali was the greatest fighter, he had several comebacks, but eventually he became too old to be the champ. Even after that there wan't anything wrong with him, it's just that he couldn't do that thing as easily.

Look at a five year old child. Children that age have ENERGY. I wish I had that much physical energy, but I don't. For me, that period is past. In the same general way there are certain periods in a person's life when the ideas I'll set forth here can be more easily implemented, and at other times the ideas will be difficult.

Colonel Harlan Sanders, the fried chicken king, didn't start his restaurants and franchises until he was 66 years old. At that age he got himself jacked up, on the road and promoting and he was very successful. But, how many 66 year old men do you know of who could begin at that age? There isn't any reason why they can't but most people that age feel like that period of their life is a time to slow down and relax. There are other periods in a person's life that, ideally, would be devoted to raising a family and so on.

Let's examine a list of ideal accomplishments that a well-balanced and successful life would include. You, personally, may want to add to or delete items from this list.

A happy childhood.

Adolescence with social development and acquiring the ability and desire to work.

A period of free public service.

A time to acquire financial resources.

Marriage and raising a family successfully.

Travel and adventure.

Philanthropic endeavors.

Obviously, some periods in your life are better than others for these various goals. My argument is that the ideal time to acquire your wealth is between the ages of 21 and 26. Before that five-year period a person could have a year of travelling around the world and two years of public service and after 26, marriage and family. I suggest waiting until age 26 to get married for several reasons. By then your emotional development is complete, and later marriages are generally more successful, and because many marriages can't survive what you'll need to do to become very wealthy in only a few years. It will require your attention and time and full dedication and it leaves little of you to share in a marriage. You can't give your days and nights to becoming wealthy and still have sufficient attention for a mate.

I am an intense and passionate person. If I'm doing something, I do it. If I'm not doing it, I don't do it. At the same time, I'm not completely inflexible. It's just that there seems to be so much more pleasure in something if it's pursued with full attention. If we go to a restaurant we expect good service and food and a quiet atmosphere. If we go to a movie we dislike talking and interruptions. The movie seems to be more enjoyable if it is the sole activity and object of our thoughts. At the movies, let's watch the movies. When we are talking, let's talk. When we are making money, we are making money, and when we have children, we owe them our attention. A wife can't share her husband with something that requires all of this energy, 20 hours a day. We'll discuss that in greater detail later on.

If a person has his wealth he can marry and retire at 26 and get on with living. As the years pass, many happy endeavors will occupy his time. If you segment your life, it will give you security and direction.

YOUTH: Age 0 to 12 should be a time of play and social development. Children can learn to, and want to, do chores around the house and it gives them self-esteem to see that they can accomplish tasks and that they are admired and respected. At about 12 a young person should start an income-producing experience to learn the correlation between his own efforts and rewards. This could be an hour after school each night and 2 or 3 hours on Saturday. From this experience, and from learning to provide for his own needs, he'll develop life-long habits for work.

By *AGE 14 OR 15* he should be making his own way as far as most expenses and major purchases are concerned as well as having his own time to cultivate and enjoy friends and pursue sports or whatever else interests him. Girls, at this age, shouldn't limit their activities and skills to domestic pursuits. Although they might well end up being a wife and mother, they ought to get some exposure to other skills and talents.

At *16 OR 17* he should have some savings from his own work, plenty of experience in dealing with people from several years of working with them, and a clear understanding of how he can take care of himself. This person is a grateful child. His parents haven't spoiled him or deprived him. They've pushed him out of the nest and helped him up when he fell. They did it several times and he learned to stand on his own. He has a healthy interest in various ideas and pursuits. He knows how to work with people and how to work with friends and he has 2 or 3 grand in the bank.

AT AGE 18, on leaving high school, this person should get some exposure to see what the world is like. If he travels and experiences different cultures before college or financial pursuits it will change his perspective of the world and what he could and should accomplish with his life. If he goes right into college he still has his head in the American cloud, without realizing what life in the rest of the world is like. He should take a grand or two, go to South America, travel and work, then to Europe, work and travel and then on to other parts of the world. He can travel some, work a little, spend a little and then on and on to new experiences. You may think that eighteen years old is too young to take off around the world, but if this young person has been working for years and cultivating his own support and independence, he will be ready for the trip. He'll still stub his toes a few times, but the experience and exposure of travelling has virtually no substitute.

If he does this for a year he'll meet hundreds of interesting people and get exposure that will change his life. He'll come home with his eyes open and ready to get on with his life.

I believe that *EVERYONE* should, ideally, devote a couple of years of their lives, full-time, in service to others.

Unpaid. Even if we have little proclivity to altruism, we are the recipients of so much cumulative service that it's only reasonable to contribute freely of ourselves. If a person does this while he is young it will always be in his mind that he has really given of himself and accomplished something. This service should be unpaid, full-time and 100%. In other words, not a 3 hour a day commitment with fun in the afternoon and pleasure in the evenings. I'm talking about 20 hours a day, 7 days a week immersion in a project. It may be the Peace Corp, Vista (the domestic Peace Corp), missionary work, nursing work at an understaffed hospital, perhaps in exchange for room and board, or offering yourself as full-time, or more, help in a nursing home. Or, rebuilding flood-damaged poverty areas, or teaching children in a backward location with no schools, or working 90 hours a week in a refugee camp in Asia, or on and on.

GIVE OF YOURSELF. Give your time, all of it and all of your energy. Give your love, your feeling, your interest. your *passion.* Knock yourself dead doing it and at the end of a 2 year period you will have a feeling of joy and accomplishment inside that you won't be able to contain and it will always be a tremendous satisfaction. It will stay with you during your whole life and no one will ever be able to take it away from you. And, when you are finished with the two years you'll only be 21 and have a year of travel behind you, with all of its exposure and experiences, and a 2 year gift to mankind that few people make. But *YOU* did it and now you are ready for another segment of your life.

If I have to paint a bedroom I can either spend 30 minutes several times throughout the day to get it done, or I can work for 4 hours straight and get it out of the way. My philosophy and practice has always been to get the unpleasant task finished and get on with something else. That way the painting doesn't take the whole day and it leaves free time *later* with the work already done. I feel the

63

same way about getting rich. Get it over with and take the money and run.

If you want to do it in a year you'll have to rob banks unless you hit a hot stock or hot crap table. There is no need to take ten years. It simply doesn't take that long. Five years isn't too long a time, generally you won't make a billion dollars in five years but you can make a few million. It will require all of your time, energy, passion and ability.

Remember, as we have previously visualized, the intensity that you had for your year of travel and 2 years of service? Remember how, during your two years, as you worked 80 hours a week in a rest home, you grew so tired of bathing incontinent people, lifting angry old people, and felt like you would die in your tracks if one more person threw up on you? But remember how you kicked yourself in the rear-end and went on with it, with even more dedication and energy, DETERMINED NOT TO GIVE UP?

Well, during your five year period you'll get twice as tired, with more pressure and anxiety, but stirring up all of your energy and passion you will continue and pursue your goal with an all-consuming zeal, because *you will not be beaten, you will not fail.* It will only last for five years and *you can make it.*

But, this five years requires *ALL* of your interest and time. It is so much more difficult to acquire your great wealth if you have a wife and family, for several reasons. Your wife will feel jealous of the time you *MUST* spend in your business. You won't have much time for her. It isn't fair to your children not to be with them and raise them. At the same time your wife will feel less and less important to you as your investments gain more and more sigificance. You can't serve two masters. A family is so much more important than money but we also want the money, so what is the logical thing to do?

Obviously, make the money first, in a short period of time, and then get married. If you do it that way your wife will never compete with your projects for your time, she'll feel more important because you'll be spending your time with her and you'll both be secure in your finances instead of having the fiscal instability most new marriages have.

You'll both be more experienced and mature and that will encourage a successful marriage. It makes sense to wait for marriage and make the money first. If you are making your millions and don't want to lose a fine potential spouse, hire her as a secretary, keeping it all business, and she'll have a great understanding of how you've made your money. It might be difficult to keep it all business, though, and in any case, you won't have much time for socializing and division of efforts. Overall, it makes sense to wait for marriage and make the money first.

So, from *21 TO 26*, you'll gain financial success and I suggest marriage and starting a family when you're 26. You'll have all of your money and all of your time for your family. And you can spend the rest of your life taking care of them. You'll also have all the time in the world to pursue common interests with your mate, and for developing and enjoying your own interests. A goal of mine, for my free time, is to build an orphanage farm for unadoptable children, kids with defects that cause them to be bypassed by most adopting couples. Everyone wants the easy way: young, white, healthy children. What about the challenge, the accomplishment? There is my soap box again. We need to put ourselves out and do the exceptional and *accomplish something*. Why not?

If you follow this type of plan you'll have many years to do as you will with your time. If you are older now, it may be a little more difficult. It you have a family it may seem harder to take some risks that are necessary for your financial success, than if you didn't have to consider your dependents. BUT YOU CAN DO IT, REGARDLESS OF YOUR AGE. No matter how old or young you are you can make millions of dollars if you put your mind to it and

STAY WITH IT with all of your energy. There are thousands of examples of older people who have begun a new vocation or pursuit and have been eminently successful. AND YOU ARE AS GOOD AS ANY OF THEM.

CHAPTER TEN

Will You Pay The Price?

Let me save you some time and trouble. If you're not going to pay the price to get rich, you might just as well not start. If you want to get to Los Angeles from New York City there are several ways to get there but there aren't any short cuts. The shortest way is to fly in a straight line. But you still must fly. You must get to the airport, buy a ticket, get on the plane and so on. There are certain things you must do to reach your destination.

Any great concert pianist has put in many hours of practice, usually several hours a day, to acquire the great skill he has. If he doesn't practice he doesn't have the skill.

There is a price to pay for any achievement and, although I would like to be a skilled pianist, I'm not willing to "pay the price," or, in other words, do what is necessary to be a pianist. I also won't pay the price to be a great artist, a successful stamp collector or a theoretical mathematician. I want to have those talents and skills but I don't want to badly enough to do what is necessary to get them.

The price to pay for being a successful parent is to give up some personal pleasure and preference for the benefit of your children. As a parent, sometimes, I would rather relax and read the paper, but my children want to play. For myself, I would rather read the paper. To be a good parent I will play with my children. I will give up some immediate pleasure for a long-term goal. It is the same with any worthwhile endeavor. You must give up immediate pleasure for a long-term goal.

If you don't want to do that you'll never excel in anything worthwhile, let alone follow the program for wealth I'll outline for you. It is going to require a lot and, if you pay the price, you'll get it.

It's really important to give up the free time, much entertainment, much socializing and frivolous activities to be able to commit yourself 100% to your financial success. You may know of people who have less devotion than this and have still made millions of dollars, but I'll bet they didn't make it in only a few years. To make it in such a short time you must eat it, breath it, sleep it, bathe in it, and live it. It will be you.

Of course, there are many things that you would rather do, but, *for five years* you can force yourself to do this. You can give up the pleasure of the easy life for your long term goals.

What does that mean in the day-to-day practical sense? When you're starting out making your initial nest egg of five or ten grand it means working nights and endless hours to make your sales. It means working more hours when you'd rather just rest for once. Making one more sale each day. Going on and on even when you have thousands in your pocket. When friends invite you somewhere and it conflicts with your work, which will you choose? For your financial success you will choose the work EVERY TIME. Over and over you will give up your pleasure for your success. BUT ONLY FOR FIVE YEARS. If you thought about doing it for a life-time it would make you sick. YOU WANT THE PLEASURE, and you'll get it in five years, and have it 24 hours a day while the folks who are playing now will be having their 2 or 3 hours of diversion each day. They will still be struggling financially and you will be completely free.

Discipline yourself. Control yourself. *YOU CAN DO IT!!!*

Gain this self-control, achieve your wealth and on that final day of your program you will have a tremendous satisfaction inside because you will have given up five years of pleasure, but you'll have a lifetime of pleasure ahead of you.

Think it over.

CHAPTER ELEVEN

Partnerships

There are always perfectly good and logical reasons why a partnership is the right thing to do. There is always a matching of talents or abilities, strengths and weaknesses, each person adding to the business or transaction just the talent that is needed. In theory, it will all work out perfectly and the logic is so sound, and you will anticipate the problems and how to solve them, but with very rare exceptions PARTNERSHIPS NEVER WORK OUT.

Of course, even if you know that, your partnership seems like it will be an exception. It always does. I believe in a positive attitude and optimism, but, as far as partnerships are concerned, you just as well forget the idea of it working out successfully. There are, of course, exceptions but they are so rare. If your partnership doesn't work out, you may somehow salvage the business or enterprise, one partner buying out the other, selling out completely, or struggling through unhappy years as partners, but it will almost surely end in bitter feelings and no friendship. One

71

exception to this is to have a partner who is so silent in the business or transaction that you can't even hear him breathe, let alone have any control or input.

I have a friend who lived in the midwest several years ago and had a thriving pizza business there. He had a good friend and they decided to pool their talents and go into the business together to add more locations. Naturally, it seemed like they were matching talents and the synergism of their skills would produce a great and successful business enterprise. When they went to sign the legal partnership papers their attorney told them that they could go ahead with the deal if they wanted to, but as sure as the sun shines, when all was said and done, they would end up enemies.

Of course, they knew each other better than that and there wasn't any way it could end up in an unhappy way, so they didn't take his advice. Within 3 or 4 years they were no longer friends or business partners.

Years ago I started a food service business with a good friend. We had several locations and a thriving business. We had been great friends for many years and, at first, the partnership seemed to be working but it just couldn't last. Let's say it wasn't his fault or my fault. Let's just say that partnerships almost never work out. Tempers wear thin, divisions of responsibility become more vague, even if they're spelled out in a contract, and feelings change. The initial excitement wears off and the day to day grind sets in and some aspects of the partnership that were clouded by euphoria before the partnership began now have clearly emerged and become big problems.

I have a couple of friends who bought an apartment house together and drew up a very detailed contract to outline their individual responsibilities. The building turned out to be a good investment and they made money but they ruined their friendship.

Even though they had a very specific contract they each began to feel like the other wasn't pulling his own weight. At first, they'd talk about it and try to settle the differences of opinion but the problems became lingering bad feelings that wouldn't go away. In the end they sold out their friendship for fifty grand.

In real estate transactions, there is often a real case for taking in a partner, particularly one with money, if they are completely silent in the deal. There can't be two chiefs. If they'll put up the money and let you work hard and give them an excellent return, that's great. If they want to coach you and prod you into working hard it isn't advisable. You'll give them several times the return they'd get at a bank and you need the money, so, IF THEY'LL JUST KEEP QUIET, it could work out. They usually don't and it usually doesn't.

Millions of people have money in the bank at 5 to 8% interest, and they'd love to let you use it to get them a higher return, but before you jump into any partnerships with them, think about it.

74

CHAPTER TWELVE

Whom Do You Trust?

Well, you can't trust everyone, as we all know, but you *can trust:* your family, your wife, your banker, your attorney, your accountant, your religious leaders, your key employees and your friends, right? Ha-Ha. The joke's on you. You can't trust any of these people.

If you are a religious person you can trust God. Most of the time you can trust and depend on yourself, but you should NEVER TRUST ANYONE ELSE. If you'd rather, I can write an entire essay about how wonderful it is that there really are some people you can depend on, who will NEVER let you down. I felt that way for many years, but one-by-one I found out that everything was not as it seemed. There were lots of people who trusted me too much, also, so I'm not any different than anyone else. I never intentionally misled anyone, but I was very optimistic and persuasive and a few people should have examined my proposals more closely. I never once knowingly took advantage of anyone, but a few times my optimism overcame some reality and the people involved just depended on me. Only in one deal did this trust ever work out to anyone's disadvantage. Still, I learned that, whether intentional or unintentional, you should not take anything at face value.

There were, however, many people I personally trusted, who intentionally and knowingly deceived me, stole from me, damaged my most special relationship (which we've put back together, but the heartache was almost terminal). And from all of that I learned that EVEN THE MOST TRUSTED AND RESPECTED PEOPLE *WILL LET YOU DOWN*.

All of this is very important to you. Don't be an infant. I had travelled around a lot, put together lots of deals, lots of exposure, lots of experience and NOTHING could surprise me. But, someone was lying to me, someone was stealing from me, all was not as it seemed in my marriage, my community leaders were renegades when they were out of town and really wonderful guys within the city limits. Some of my church leaders were more immoral and vile than the people I least respected. My employees, who were very well rewarded for their work with me, were stealing on the side. I could go on and on, but the point is that these were respected and trusted people and they all turned out to be so different than they seemed. I should have been more careful in my marriage, more careful in my business and more wide awake when it came to people.

I'm not recounting this to belittle anyone, but to help you see that you really must look deeper at things. All of these business and personal problems worked out just fine, but I must have used exceptional energy working against the odds. You can save yourself some problems and hurt feelings if you don't place much dependence, respect and trust in anyone. Then if they let you down, it won't cause any damage.

People are just people and they ALL have problems and weaknesses, but if they let you down it will hurt you to whatever degree you trusted them. Don't trust them and it can't hurt you. Don't depend on them. Don't think any too highly of anyone because when the truth is known, that degree of respect and trust will turn into a commensurate degree of hurt. And, the one thing that is tough for a positive, successful, ambitious and aggressive person like you to overcome is hurt feelings. Too much respect and trust equals too many hurt feelings and the ambition will drain out of you so fast it will scare you.

Be cautious, be doubting, don't believe them, see through them. Is the community leader an embezzler? Don't be surprised if he is. Is your religious leader a liar, an adulterer, and the least of all? Maybe so. Is your business partner skimming the business? (He couldn't be because you've known him for 20 years and you've been through so much together--right?) He's probably skimming. But how could he do that to you? I don't know, but maybe he is.

Do you get my point? When this trust is betrayed it is absolutely devastating. So, my advice is not to trust them in the first place. Will you pass by someone who is genuinely worthy of your admiration, respect and trust? Yes, you probably will. Will you pass up a lot of trouble and hurt feelings and disappointment? YES! YES! YES! You can get where you need to go without depending on these people. The one exception to that is with your mate and, if you're smart, you'll include your wife in all your plans, hopes, dreams, and projects and NEVER let anything become more important than your marriage. Make your plans and projects live for her, too. She'll help you through. Listen to her. Help her see that what you are doing is for her. Talk out your problems until you both understand each other. But, even after this, don't blindly trust that all is well with her and that you can coast in your marriage. Unknown to you, she may be unhappy inside and have to look elsewhere in an effort to understand herself. Be sensitive. Be smart.

You may wonder how this affects your finanical success. It's difficult to separate being a full-time husband from a full-time investor. In order to get your millions in five years you can't easily share your attention which is needed by your investments. If you are married, be careful. Don't sacrifice a good marriage for a few million dollars.

Interestingly enough, most people see themselves as exceptions to most rules. Perhaps by now you may believe that most people will compromise your friendship, but, at the same time, sincerely feel like you can trust *YOUR* friends. If you must, do and find out for yourself. If you want to avoid a sad end, don't do it. It will hurt you and ruin a friendship, too.

After a financial problem I had, caused by my own stupidity, I advised a good friend of mine that the greatest lesson I learned from that experience was not to trust people or believe what they said. Yes, he said, he had learned that lesson too, and always the hard way. Then he went on to tell me about a large transaction he was putting together with a local businessman. It was a multi-million dollar deal and right off I could see that he had his head in the clouds as far as dealing with this other party was concerned. I cautioned him about it and advised him not to trust the guy, and to either skip the deal or put it together in another way. "Well, he said, I can see that in a normal circumstance you would be right and normally I'd approach it that way. HOWEVER, this case is different." My last advice to him was that he would regret it later if he depended on the other principal to do what he said he would do. As the deal developed, the other fellow not only figuratively put his arm around him, but literally put his arm around his shoulder and told him a tale that would make your eyes water if you saw it on TV. The drama and dialogue were great.

This guy said to him, "I trust you to do what you said you'd do in the deal, and you should trust me to do what I've said

I'd do. Some of the things we've talked about aren't on paper, we can put them down sometime if you want to (ha-ha) but as long as we understand each other it will come out alright." And, he said, he felt just like my friend was his son. The guy's attorney minimized the significance of the unwritten agreements and the constant requests from my friend for more and more key information critical to the success of the project. It all flowed so well that my friend was never reluctant to give them the plans, documents, leases, leads, specifications and etc. and all the while Mr. X would reassure him and "blow in his ear" to keep his confidence. Not only that but most of the people involved went to the same church as my friend, and I could go on and on.

Take one guess how it all turned out. I'll wait a minute, take a guess. RIGHT!!! Correct on the first guess.

From the very first day the whole deal was a set-up and a scam. The people involved knew from the start that they would gradually get all of the information they wanted, have unclear legal documents signed and ultimately end up with the whole project for themselves. And they did. My friend didn't hurt them at all because they never trusted him for a minute. He was hurt because he really believed.

What they told him never materialized, and, as a result, he lost millions of dollars. I hope he's finally learned the lesson.

By cautioning you to have this doubt in your relationships with others, I hope you don't become obsessed with the idea that everyone is trying to take advantage of you. If you feel that way it will breed such pessimism and cynicism that there won't be any way that you can then function in a positive and confident way.

Just open your eyes and see things for what they really are, not what they seem to be.

Diogenese, the Greek scholar and philosopher, has been carrying his lamp around for over 3,000 years, looking for an honest man, and he hasn't found one yet.

CHAPTER THIRTEEN

Give Gifts But Not Loans

As you put your fortune together, you'll feel lucky, blessed and fortunate. Friends or acquaintances will come to you for participation in deals of all kinds. They will have the idea, they'll do all the work, and they'll make it a success, and all you have to do is put up the money. I've done this so many times it would make your head spin. The logic seems sound: You only have so much time but you do have some extra money. They have lots of time but no money. If you'll just do this one deal they will be forever grateful. Don't do it.

They won't be grateful, and, in fact, they'll end up resenting you. After all, it was their idea and they did the work, and *all you did was put up the money.*

I had a long-time friend who was working for $3 an hour in a food service business. I made the agreement with him that I would build and finance some similar shops, pay for all equipment and GIVE him half of the business. We would pay him a good salary and have yearly dividends from the business to split. He had *no* financial exposure and never obligated himself for 1 cent to get the business going. I took all the risk.

He DID organize the locations, hire the staff, work long hours, manage the business 100% (as agreed), paid off the capital costs, etc. All of which was as we had agreed. The businesses were *very* successful and made plenty of money. He was grateful for the opportunity since he would never have been able to do it himself, there was lots of money to pay back all of the money I fronted for the set-up. I was grateful since I got my money back and had 4 more businesses and didn't have to manage them.

Perfect, right? Wrong.

Let me explain the progression of thought in a deal like this. It's all very natural and believable and the psychology makes sense.

At the beginning there is euphoria in starting a new enterprise. There are obstacles but they are all overcome by the positive attitude. The locations are beautiful, the equipment is new, there aren't enough hours in the day to spend in the business. It is all so exciting. And the money starts to roll in and the good feeling increases. Then, after a period of time, it appears that this is a stable, continuous business and the monotony starts to arise. The only way to surmount the monotony is to get more deals or more locations.

So, we added another location, then another, then another. Then, because it is a successful business and it's making money, my investment is repaid and I've got back all I've put into it, so I'm even, BUT HE'S STILL STUCK RUNNING THE BUSINESS. He has to stay, he agreed to stay, but he's still putting in the hours and I'm home sleeping.

But, the business is making lots of money. How could he resent the fact that I'm not there working too? I kept my part of the agreement and he gets a good salary for managing besides splitting the profit.

As he spends longer and longer thinking about it, it becomes clear to him that he got into a bad deal. He has made the business what it is, it's really his business, but I own half of it and don't have to do anything.

Of course I put up the money, but I got the money back and he knows he could have gotten the money anywhere. So, he's locked into a bad deal. He is overlooking the fact that there are lots of people with ideas and lots of people to spend time in a business, but, there are few people with the money.

The money partner in a business should get 75 to 90% of the business since *HE* is the key person. Everybody has time, but everyone doesn't have money. But, he couldn't see it that way. I never suggested that we re-adjust the split, but he wasn't happy with even a 50-50 split.

Naturally, if someone feels that way it won't be long till the wind is out of their sails and they become unproductive and depressed. They also become resentful. First they appreciate the help, then they expect it, then they demand it, then they resent it. If you won't take my word for it, try it yourself and you'll see.

You could find a very wonderful and deserving person who was down on their luck and needed a little boost, and give him a check for $500 every week just to help him out. He would be so grateful for your generosity and help. After a few months of your checks, he would begin to count on them and expect them. After a few more months, if the checks were late, he would be upset and a little irritated. He might even start to call you and ask you why the check was late. Then he would tell you that he was counting on you and would appreciate it if you could make the checks a little more often. After a while longer, if you quit sending the checks, he would probably have very ill feelings toward you. In the abstract, grateful, but in the here-and-now, resentful.

And it's not because of a defect in the person. Was my business partner a good friend? Yes. Nice guy? 100%. Hard worker? I'll say he was. But it was a BAD DEAL.

So, when you begin making money, if you really want to do someone a favor, give them some money outright. Don't lend it, don't invest it in their enterprises, don't discuss repayment. it's a straight gift. If you can't afford a straight gift, keep the money. No loans, no deals, no partnerships, no expectations.

And, you'll probably keep your friend.

Section Two

DISCUSSIONS ON ACTUALLY MAKING MILLIONS

CHAPTER FOURTEEN

The Mechanics of Acquiring Wealth

You can get rich selling or doing almost anything. You can work for a dollar an hour and if you can work 5000 hours a week you'll make $260,000 a year. Unfortunately, you can't work 5,000 hours a week. Some people seem to believe that just because they work hard and put in lots of hours that they are on the road to success. You can have three jobs and kill yourself off working but if they are low-paying jobs you simply can't ever make much money.

The first question you should ask yourself is not "What do I know how to do?" The first question should be "how much money do I want to make?"

If you want to make a hundred grand become a doctor. If you want to make a million a year, don't consider becoming a doctor. They don't make that much, except through investing. People who pursue a career in law or medicine solely to make money are misled.

There are hundreds of easier ways to make more money than they'll ever see, than to spend years in classrooms and practice, and receive the small return they get.

If you want to heal people, become a doctor. If you want to see justice done, become a lawyer and so on through the professions. That is the only valid reason for any of those career pursuits. But, never, ever, for the money. You can make more money while you sleep than a professional person will ever make in his or her practice.

In the first place, when considering wealth, you should realize that it's highly unlikly that you'll ever get really rich from your own efforts or from the efforts of a few employees. There are several ways to accumulate material wealth, but the fastest and surest is through real estate, because LEFT ON ITS OWN, IT WILL BE WORTH MORE TOMORROW THAN IT IS TODAY, and the great goal in front of you is to buy it today and LET THE PROPERTY MAKE MONEY FOR YOU. You can invent the hula-hoop and make millions. You can patent silicon chips or light bulbs and make a killing. You can discover viral treatments that were heretofore unknown and retire from that one idea.

However, most people don't have that one great new idea, even though there are thousands and millions of ideas untouched. That leaves other options open for making money.

IF YOU CAN MAKE A LITTLE MONEY YOU CAN TURN IT INTO A FORTUNE.

You can have a few hot dog stands and make a hundred grand a year or so, or make that much selling tires or furniture or whatever. Many people would see the hundred grand as a very comfortable living and spend it as they made it. I see the money as a way to acquire real wealth and be free for a lifetime.

As discussed previously, isolate an endeavor that has the potential *to make more money than you require to live.* Never settle for less than two or three hundred dollars a day. I've never met anyone who wasn't worth that much although most people don't make anywhere near that much. On second thought, I've known a few people who weren't worth a dime, but there were very few. After you get this income source, and we'll discuss later many ways to start, then live modestly and save a few thousand dollars, five or ten, and you're on your way. AFTER YOU MAKE THE FIRST TEN THOUSAND DOLLARS YOU ARE OFF THE GROUND AND NOTHING CAN STOP YOU. It's harder to make your ten thousand nest egg than it is to make millions out of it.

If you are a family man now, with the responsibilities of caring for others, in some ways you are more limited. You can't bet all of your money on one roll of the dice. If you are alone you can lose and pick yourself up and get on with it. A family needs some security and continuity. But, even with a family, you should never sell yourself short. You ARE worth a few hundred a day. If you live in a community with virtually no opportunity, then you must move. Your only alternative is to waste your life away with no possible chance for real freedom. So, move if you must. Do you think that you can't move because you don't have the money? If you really want to, you can. Beg or borrow the money, sell your possessions, but move and expose yourself to a waiting opportunity. That opportunity you select will allow you to save a few grand, and that amount, say $5,000 will become $10,000 and 20, 40, 80, 160, 320, 640, etc. IT WILL, but first you need the five thousand.

When I started it was by painting houses, as I've related and then asphalt repairs and paving. Then office supplies (office supplies sales sounds trivial, the average office bought only $20 worth of supplies a month, but with 1,000 accounts that's $20,000 a month at 50% profit or better. How do you get the thousand accounts? Hoof-it and get 5 new acounts a day as well as taking care of the existing accounts. (You'll need one full-time employee for telephone orders and shipping but you'll still end up with your yearly hundred grand for yourself). Open a small store or shop and promote it to death. I don't care what product or service you have.

If you have put yourself in a city or area with enough potential customers you'll get your hundred thousand. We'll discuss in a following chapter an idea for selling cookware, although I'm not saying that cookware is something *you* might do, but it's a good example.

You can buy a dozen big sets of cookware for $600 to $800 and make three or four thousand dollars off them. If you don't have the six or eight hundred, buy two or three sets, get lots of promotional literature or type some yourself and get it printed at a quick printer, and sell the two or three sets.

Yes, it's a modest start BUT IT *IS* A START. Even if you only have one set, be smooth, be professional and they'll know that you have at least a few thousand more sets in your warehouse. After a while you'll feel like you have a warehouse full of the stuff, too, because you'll be so confident and assuming of your closing the sale and ultimate success.

Give yourself the basic opportunity to make a small amount and you'll be on your way to millions. Always think in millions. A hundred grand isn't a lot of money, but it is 1/10th of a million. As soon as you get to your first million, the others just keep piling up.

After you have selected pots and pans, or any other means to make your first few thousand there are then several ways to make it grow geometrically.

You can gamble with it in Las Vegas. If you bet red or black on roulette, you'll have close to a 50-50 chance (less the two green slots), and if you called ten in a row your $5,000 would become, if the house would keep raising your table limit: $10,000, 20, 40, 80, 160, 320, 640, 1,280, 2,500, and on your tenth spin you'd win $5,120,000.00. It takes about fifteen minutes for ten spins and that would be an easy way to get your five million. If only you could get the ten spins.

Before I gave up gambling a couple of years ago I had ELEVEN spins go *AGAINST* ME. In order to stay even on a loss, the next bet has to be twice as much as the one before. So, if you lose $1,000 the next bet has to be $2,000 to get back the thousand you lost and to win this one. If you lose again the next bet has to be $4,000 to come out.

I won't say what I lost, but doubling eleven times finally got my attention and my money. I quit and the 12th spin came out in my favor, but I didn't have a bet down. FORGET GAMBLING IN LAS VEGAS, OR ANYWHERE ELSE, AS A WAY TO YOUR WEALTH.

Also, forget illegal means to wealth. Drugs and rackets and scams and so on are so far beneath you that you shouldn't even think about them. Make it honestly and sleep nights. Life is too short to make money illegally.

In the file of legitimate opportunities there are several ways people make large sums of money, but the easiest, lowest risk, and most stable and certain is in real estate. Remember that we are talking about millions of dollars. You can run a business and make a great living, but it's tough to make anywhere near millions of dollars in a business in only a few years. You may be able to do it in a large business, but how can you develop a large business and have a CASH RETURN of five million dollars in only five years?

So, my recommendation is to make your money in real estate. Not as a broker or agent, they're on every corner, but as a buyer and developer.

I have a friend who worked in a loan office for a mortgage company. He saw dozens of deals come and go and he regularly got his pay but with no growth or progress, even though he was in a perfect spot to find and take advantage of real estate opportunities. Over lunch one day I asked him

91

why he didn't stick his neck out a little, buy some properties and get on the road to wealth. So, he did. He jacked himself up, kicked himself in the rear end and bought and improved or developed several properties in the first year and made about $300,000. He just had to take a chance and get himself going. He benefitted from a lot of my experience and made more his first year than I did in my first year. I made all the mistakes myself and no one gave me the time of day. I told him more during lunch than I learned in a year. That's why, following this program, you'll start out with the benefit of my experience. *YOU JUST HAVE TO DO IT!* I keep stressing that because most people, even when confronted with the simplicity of buying, improving and selling real estate, still seem to feel like it's something other people can do, but they can't.

The basic reason that real estate is the best field to immerse yourself in is because you make money on it in many ways:

1- You'll buy properties for much less than they are worth.

2- You'll sell properties for their value, or more.

3- You'll make improvements that will dramatically affect their value.

4- You'll make 10 to 20% a year in inflation, NOT ON YOUR INVESTED MONEY BUT ON THE FULL VALUE OF THE PROPERTY.

Inflation doesn't know how much, if anything you have invested. All inflation does is go on and on, with your property worth more tomorrow than it is today.

So, in summarizing, when exposing yourself to ideas to allow you to make money, first of all get into something to provide cash flow for living and some besides, then take that money and get into real estate. In following chapters we'll talk about the mechanics of putting the deals together. Not theoretical stuff either, but deals I've done and ideas that really do work.

THEY WILL FOR YOU,. TOO!

CHAPTER FIFTEEN

Leverage

Depending on where you put the fulcrum, a long lever with a lot of LEVERAGE can lift a big load.

The great advantage of real estate for investing and making large amounts of money is it's potential for *VERY HIGH LEVERAGE.*

If you can buy a duplex for $50,000 with $2,000 down (I've bought plenty with this down payment), or buy diamonds outright, or buy futures contracts or put the money in a savings account, you'll have very different gains. Let's look at the comparative gains in the aforementioned potential investments.

First the bank deposit. If you save your money in any savings account you'll earn from 5¼% to around 8% interest. To be generous let's say 8%.

If you were to invest the $2,000 in diamonds, depending on where you bought them, the return would be something like this: Diamonds, because of their unusual source (85% from one company ((DeBeers))), and unusual distribution controls are not easily purchased from anyone near the real source. Consequently, a number of people are always making a profit on your purchases. Even if you buy from a broker and resell to him they'll normally pay you less, when you want to resell, than they can buy the stones from their source. So, when you resell you won't even get wholesale price. Diamonds have had their ups and downs, but assume they'd even appreciate 20% a year. With the tremendous spread between wholesale and retail and the difficulty of selling high enough to make a profit, the 20% will never cover the differential. If you're lucky you may end up even. I've bought and sold plenty of diamonds and the only case in which they have provided good returns is in the long haul.

If you pay $2,000 for a diamond, in a couple of years you'd be able to get your two grand back and, as the years pass, your investment will increase in value. Over the years you'd probably come out ahead of bank interest.

Futures are contracts you can buy agreeing to buy or sell nearly any commodity or metal (pork bellies to silver ingots) at a time in the future for a price which is determined now.

You can usually buy on margin (deposit of 10% or 20%) with a broker and secure the contract as if you had paid the entire amount. In other words, if silver was trading today for $20 an ounce and you bought a futures contract to purchase and take delivery of 850 ounces of silver in six months at $23 an ounce. You are betting that, within six months, the price of silver will be $23 an ounce or more. Then you could resell at a profit.

In 1979 and 1980 the silver market had some very volatile price fluctuations. It went from $14 an ounce, up to nearly $50 an ounce, and, almost overnight, back down to about $10 an ounce. You can make a fortune in any futures market fluctuation, depending on whether you've agreed to buy or sell. If silver is now $20 an ounce and you agree to buy 850 ounces at $23 an ounce in six months and you had to pay a 10% margin, your total obligation to buy would be 850 x $23 or $19,550. If you paid a 10% deposit you'd pay $1,955 to your broker to secure your promise to buy the silver.

You *buy* the contract from someone willing to *sell* the 850 ounces in six months at $23 an ounce. *That* person is betting that the price will be lower than $23 in six months, and you'll have to pay him more than the market price. *You* are betting that the price will be higher than $23 in six months, and you'll be able to buy the silver under market value.

Let's figure it both ways. Let's say that in six months the price is still $20 an ounce. You have to pay him $23 an ounce, so you've come out 850 X 3 = a loss to you of $2,550. Usually you won't actually take delivery of the silver. The trading is done mostly on *contracts* to deliver, rather than *actual* delivery. Instead of actually forcing you to pay the $19,500 for the 850 ounces, the contract seller would probably take the $3 per ounce price differential from you, which would total 850 X $3 or $2,550 and cancel the contract. He probably never had the silver to deliver in the first place, so all along what he was really doing was simply betting: if, in six months, the price was above $23, he'd lose. If it was below, he'd win.

If, on the other hand, in six months the price was $26 an ounce, the contract seller would owe you $2,550. You would probably not actually pay him the $19,550 and demand delivery of the 850 ounces, but collect the difference between the market price and the lower contract price. You could force him to deliver the silver and he could force you to take it. A couple of years ago a group of futures traders demanded delivery on some massive potatoes futures contracts on potatoes that never existed. They didn't want the price differential, they wanted physical delivery. So, the contract seller had to buy up potatoes on the open market to fulfill the contract.

In any case you can make or lose money two ways: Buying on margin, just paying a deposit on your agreement to fulfill a contract. And on the actual fulfillment of the contract.

The futures market is a whole game in itself. You have to place your bets and wait and see.

The Hunt brothers lost nearly one *billion* dollars in one day when silver prices fell and their brokers demanded that they meet the margin call. The brokers wanted more money to secure the difference between the high-price agreement and the falling market price. They could have made it just as fast.

But, you can use the *leverage* and make much more than just the rise in market price. The key element in any leverage is to USE THE SMALLEST AMOUNT OF MONEY TO SECURE THE LARGEST POSSIBLE DEAL. If you can, you'll also do it WITH THE LEAST POSSIBLE LIABILITY AND EXPOSURE TO LOSS. That's why, in your contracts on properties or whatever, you leave yourself as many ways out and as much flexibility as the other person will agree to. It only makes sense but many people don't do it.

Overall, unless you *immerse* yourself in the futures or commodity markets, you have a lot of exposure. Lots of people have bad experiences in these markets, while some real experts make a killing.

Even an unskilled person CAN, however, do well in real estate with much less chance of failure. So, I recommend real estate.

Let's see what you can do with the same $2,000 as the down payment on a $50,000 duplex using LEVERAGE.

There are at least six ways to make money on the real estate:

1- Buy under value.

2- Leverage.

3- Cash flow.

4- Equity

5- Tax savings.

6- Appreciation.

1- If you buy at full value and sell later at full appreciated value, you'll make money just from inflation. But, you should generally buy under value. It's like buying a car. You should never pay full price for a car BECAUSE THERE ARE PLENTY OF CARS OUT THERE FOR SALE AT MUCH LESS THAN FULL PRICE. So why pay full price on real estate? Sometimes you may even pay a premium price for a piece that, for some special reason or use, will make you much more than the regular returns. But, usually, try to stay under value. By doing that you've already made money because there is always someone out there who will pay full price. You just have to find them.

2- If you put your $2,000 in a savings account you have no leverage. They'll pay you 8% interest on just the $2,000. In a real estate deal you'll make a profit, not on your $2,000 investment, but on the full value of the property. LEVERAGE is the reason why you should never own real estate free and clear until you have your wealth program completed. Why pay $50,000 for the duplex when you can make as much profit on it with only a $2,000 down payment? Use the leverage.

3- When you buy the duplex, if at all possible, and normally the only way to buy, should result in a positive cash flow. That means you'll have more money coming in in rents each month or year, than you are paying out each month or year. There are a few yearly expenses to divide by twelve months that are also included. Your rents will be your total income from a property. So, you know what that amount is, if you have full occupancy and the vacancy factor doesn't go down. In figuring your occupancy factor be a little cautious and figure a vacancy here and there. I'm the last one to recommend that you be conservative in your optimism and motivation, but you should realistically consider some vacancies and all potential expenses. These include: the mortgage payment, property taxes, insurance on the property, any management fees, maintenance and repairs and miscellaneous (i.e. L.I.D.'s ((local improvement districts)) assessments for street, sewer, sidewalks, etc., not included in the property mortgage or taxes, etc.) Add all of those together and the total, per month, should be less than you take in in rents. The positive difference is your CASH FLOW. That's money in your pocket. Money you can spend.

If the payout is higher than the rents, you either have to get the price of the property reduced, pay more of a down payment, get the terms rewritten for a longer payout, or have lower payment arranged with a balloon payment in 1, 2 or 5 years. If you can't do any of these, you'll have to pay out of your own pocket to cover the loss each month. This loss is called the NEGATIVE CASH FLOW. If you have a continuing source of funds you might want to do deals with a monthly loss, since, in the long run, you'll make a bundle on the property. My own feeling has always been: why buy properties with a negative cash flow when there are plenty of properties, that with a little work and negotiation, will break even or show a positive return?

The $2,000 in a savings account will never pay you a cash flow every month, unless the bank pays you monthly interest of $13.50, before taxes on interest. A good real estate deal using the same $2,000 will pay you some cash every month. Maybe $100 a month, more or less. For $13.50

100

interest you can get a bag of groceries. For $100 a month cash flow, you can subsidize the monthly loss on another good income property that has a negative cash flow.

So, the cash flow in real estate can leverage itself into even more deals. Since the mortgage payments are static and won't change but the rents you charge will rise, before long your rents will cover the loss on the subsidized property, freeing up the $100 to be used on another property. It can, and does, grow geometrically. In fact its natural growth, using leverage, *is* geometric. The only reason people interrupt the natural pattern is that they become lazy, disinterested, or tired of keeping track of properties.

4- *Equity build-up.* Another advantage of real estate is that your renters are making your mortgage payments and declining the principal (paying down the original amount borrowed) as well as the other advantages already outlined. On the $50,000 duplex, depending on the interest charged and length of payback, perhaps $1,000 will be paid on the principal during the first year. That amount increases each year. In the early years most of each payment goes for interest. But, a thousand dollars is a thousand dollars and that, in itself, is a 50% return on your $2,000 down payment investment.

5- *Tax Savings.* It is really important that you get a good accountant as soon as possible. Many C.P.A.'s or regular accountants overcharge and dispense poor advice. Many are real professionals and aren't too expensive. Your tax structuring is an important part of your wealth program.

People who are energetic and buy and sell property and keep the economy rolling are rewarded by the government: they pay little or no taxes.

In this example, let's assume you paid full value for the duplex. Every building lasts only a certain length of time and the I.R.S. assumes that part of the life of the building is used up each year. This declining value, on the building, is called DEPRECIATION. When you buy a property, part of the price is attached to the land, usually 20%, and part to the building, usually 80%.

Commercial and housing units are usually accorded a 40 year life. When you buy your duplex it may be 15 years old with 25 years left of its allowed life. As a practical matter, buildings last longer than the time allowed them in depreciation. Your $50,000 duplex, times 80% of value in the building itself, divided by 25 years left in its life, equals $1600 a year in depreciation. You can take that right off the top of your taxable income. If you're in a 35% tax bracket you'll save $560 off of your tax bill.

6- *Appreciation.* This is the whole ball game in one word. Inflation makes your properties appreciate all day, every day. While you sleep, when you're travelling, all the time. It's true that there are periods of market adjustments when inflation is less than other times but, as far as anyone can tell, inflation is here to stay.

One problem you'll have in some of your deals is that you'll deal with middle aged or older people who are still living in the 1940's. Some of them remember the great depression in the 1930's and retain the "save and buy" mentality of the 1940's and 1950's. They don't realize that there is no way to "save and buy" today.

In the 40's and 50's the usual course of events was for a young fellow to get a steady job, save $20 a week out of his pay check, and in a few years he would have a few thousand dollars to pay down on a house. If he had a good job he could then save for a few years and get another property as an investment. There was very little inflation. The house he wanted today for $15,000 would cost about $15,000 next year and he knew if he just saved up $4,000 he could buy it. It was just a matter of how many years it took him to save the down payment. It was important for his peace of mind to make a sizeable down payment. That's just the way things were done. Many of these people still think along those lines today.

Today, with 15 or 20% inflation, or more, if you want to buy a house for even $50,000, that house will appreciate $7,500 or more each year (typically). So a person would have to save his 20% or $50,000 or $10,000 plus 20% of the inflation, $7,500, compounded every year.

If he saves for five years the property will be worth:

Beginning value $50,000.

First year- $57,000.

Second year- $66,125.

Third year- $76,044.

Fourth year- $87,450.

Fifth year- $100,567.

So, if he takes five years to save his down payment, he'll need $25,000 down, if he holds to the 25% down payment. So he has to save $5,000 a year, over $400 a month. Meanwhile, the house will cost him more than twice as much, and instead of making $400 a month mortgage payments, they'll be over $800. Hopefully, his wages will have doubled, but the point is that he could have had the same house for $400 a month, even after his wages increased.

So, he'll have the same house, pay twice as much for it, twice the down payment and twice the mortgage payment, simply because *he waited to buy it*. You can work hard and save up your nest-egg, by burning the candle at both ends, but in a nice stable conservative job it will never happen, until it's too late! But you simply cannot save a little each month and ever come out ahead of the game. The property values are going up faster than you can save.

That's the way things are, so to *take advantage* of inflation, *YOU OBVIOUSLY HAVE TO OWN THE PROPERTY*. The same force that was previously working against you is now working for you. The more you can get it on your side, that is the more property you own, the better. While you can work and earn a certain amount of money, as you accumulate properties *THEY* will make you money.

A $100,000 property in any good location will appreciate 20% a year, or $20,000. With your tax savings and cash flow and depreciation *this one property* should make you a hundred dollars a day, more or less. That's over $4 an hour, 24 hours day, and it will increase every year. When you get a million dollars in property, it will pay you $1,000 a day and climbing. If you buy your properties right and sell them right it's even more. Where else but in real estate can you do so much with so little?

So, let's examine inflation and appreciation on your $50,000 duplex. Top be conservative let's figure it will appreciate 15% a year. If have chosen a good location and completed some inexpensive but cosmetically dramatic improvements, or if you have abided by your copper-clad rule not to pay full value, it will be a higher rate of inflation. Iron-clad would mean that you *never* pay full value, but sometimes you will. Remember that you've only invested $2,000 and appreciation alone has returned you $7,500 on your $50,000 duplex in the first year.

So let's add up the total comparison.

Savings account: $2,000

160   8% interest
_____

$2,160   total

Because of inflation, at 20%, your $2,000 is worth $400 less than when you deposited it and you are $240 in the hole.

Let's compare the duplex deal with the above:

1-	Buy under value	0
2-	Leverage	0
3-	Cash flow	1,200
4-	Equity	1,000
5-	Tax savings	560
6-	Appreciation at $50,000 value	10,000

total return $11,760.00

In this case your $2,000 investment has given you a return of 645% on your money.

Now lets compare the duplex deal if you bought it for your usual 20% under value.

1-	Buy under value	$10,000

2-	Leverage	0
3-	Cash flow	1,200
4-	Equity	1,000
5-	Tax savings	560
6-	Appreciation at $60,000 value	12,000
total return		$24,760.00

In this, more typical, case, your $2,000 has returned 1,250%.

Do you realize that this is 1,250% as compared to 8% bank interest. You may think those figures are high, or very optimistic. Hundreds and thousands of deals are done just like this every day. If you can swing this same deal for $1,000 down, your return will be 2,500%. You may even get it with no down payment at all. If you don't believe that deals with this potential exist, then don't look for them, and leave them for people who do believe. It's all in your mind anyway.

Remember, also, that your property appreciation is not on your net worth, but on the total values of the property.

When you are four years into your five year $5 million wealth program, you may have a NET WORTH of $3 million and total assets of $8 million in investments. These investments, at 15% inflation, besides all the other advantages and returns, will provide an annual return (increase in value) to you of $1,200,00.00 a year, PLUS CASH FLOW, DEPRECIATION AND TAX ADVANTAGES, ETC. The appreciation alone is $23,076.23 a week or $3,296.70 a day. Plus a grand a day in cash flow and no taxes to pay and on and on. No matter how you figure inflation, you can use it to your advantage.

As you assess the comparative advantages of savings accounts vs. real estate, these are the distilled observations:

Savings accounts are secure, as there is virtually no risk. You don't have to manage your money so there isn't any work to do.

Real estate has some inherent risks, and that's why the rewards are higher. You do have to do some management and leg work in real estate, so there is some of your time involved.

As far as the futures, commodities, diamonds and other potential investments: they are all viable investments, but, in my opinion, involve more risk and require more skill and expertise. I don't think any of them are as forgiving as real estate. If you make a mistake buying a piece of property, just wait and the value will catch up to you through inflation. No one has the corner on real estate since it is everywhere and is an uncontrolled market. And, with real estate, there are often people in trouble or in a hurry who will sell you their property for far less than it's worth. You just have to do what's necessary to find them.

Keep this in mind: If you worked hard for five years and ended up with only one large property, it would support you for the rest of your life, would eventually be paid for, and you could raise the rents to keep up with inflation on just one piece.

Isn't it incredible that most people never get that one piece?

CHAPTER SIXTEEN

There Is Always A Pitch

As I was shaving this morning, I noticed that my self-heating shaving cream failed to get hot. The can was obviously nearly empty and it said on the label that the last couple of shaves would be cold to indicate that it was time to buy a new can.

I envisioned that for six months or a year the research and development people in their company tried to get *ALL* of the shaves hot, but, for some reason, couldn't get the chemical reaction to last till the can was empty. On the surface that would be a defect, and the research people would see it that way. But, deferring to principles of marketing, the chemists and engineers could send the product with that defect over to the advertising department, and those boys would make everything alright and seem just fine with the product. The only way to do that with their shaving cream was to *make the defect a positive selling point.*

Negative view: We can't make the last few shaves hot.

Positive view: This product is so advanced that it even signals you, in the last few shaves, that it's time to buy a new can.

FANTASTIC!!!

There not only is a sales pitch for every product or transaction WITH positive selling points, there is a pitch for a product or transaction with obvious defects, and often the defect is the selling point.

There are many examples in my own experience to relate.

Years ago, when I was painting houses, part of the pitch was that my paint had "mildew inhibitor" in it. The chemical eliminated the growth of mildew which shortened the life of the paint. For interior surfaces, our paint had a "vinyl bonding agent" to increase surface strength for scrubability.

These facts didn't present themselves as the entire pitch, but as part of a smooth and confident delivery with a beginning, a middle and a close. If I knocked on doors to paint houses, my opening was: "Hi, I'm Ross Anderson. We're doing some house painting up here and we're finishing up a couple of jobs next week, so I stopped to see if you have any painting you need to have done while we're here. That's the first pitch. (Reply: I don't know, let me ask my wife.) Their next question might be: "How much do you charge?" Or else the wife might just come back to the door to see what I want. Then I'd repeat the first pitch in a little different way and add a little. "We always fill up our schedule with other jobs and you'd probably save 30 or 40% off our usual charges." (Pitch). Then, "I can look at what you wanted painted and tell you exactly what it would cost you."

Then, typically, they'd say, "Why don't you look at these three rooms and see what it would cost?"

THEN YOU'RE IN. Once they ask you in or ask about the products, or ask for an estimate YOU'VE GOT 'EM. Then you see what they need to have painted (or....) all the while figuring on paper to make it look like you're getting the price as close as you can.

Always come out to an odd figure. obviously you have it right down to the nitty-gritty if it's figured to an odd figure.

Then *offer them choices*. If we (pontifical we, it's really just you at this point, most likely) do this work next Wednesday and Thursday (always sound as if you're busy and have plenty to do. You may not have anything to do, but you can call them back, after you have the job and move the work up.).... if we do it next Wednesday or Thursday we'll paint these four rooms and the beams in the hall for $516. If you want to we can use a cheaper paint but it wouldn't last as long and, in my own experience (vast), you'll be a lot happier if you go with a better product. If you plan on living here a long time you might want to spend another $40 for a vinyl bonding agent that makes the paint surface stronger and makes the paint last, maybe eight years instead of five years. It all depends on how long you plan to be here. Anyway, how does $516 sound if we do it next week? Price and time....it sounds like you've got the work, and you're just scheduling now.

Answers could be: "The price is too high." Response: "Well, we could use less expensive paint." Naturally they would decline to use a cheaper product. You might offer to wait thirty days for half of the payment, or some other arrangement to close the deal. If they respond positively then you'd offer the extra vinyl for $40 more. $40 isn't much for a primo product and the stuff is only going to cost you a buck or two. The natural response is yes, but even if the response is no they are still confirming the job: "No, I don't want the extra vinyl when you do the job."

Then you offer: "Let me fill out a contract and we'll be here next Wednesday about 9 A.M. Be assuming and positive and natural and *FLOW*. The only possible conclusion to your visit is to make a sale. You know it, and by your attitude, they know it.

Then you fill out the contract. Near the end it specifies a 3% extra charge for payment upon completion or else they can save the 3% and pay half now and half on completion, or a 10% deposit or whatever. Then you sign and they sign, get a check and you're on your way. I always make it a point to take long enough but never too long. I act as if I can wrap *any* deal up quickly enough to do it right but not waste any time. The unspoken idea being: Let's take as long as it takes but you and I both have other things to do. The same way when you're executing the work. Get it done and get out. The paint job will actually take only a few hours but by scheduling Wednesday and Thursday it sounds more extensive.

Anyway three rooms will require 10 or 12 gallons at $3 or $4 a gallon, since you'll buy from the manufacturer or on a close-out, but never retail or normal wholesale from a paint dealer, and you're in the job $50. You'll get $556 less your costs and you have about $500 for a few hours of work, and you'll do another job the same day. Most painters may charge less and skip the second job and go home and drink beer. BUT NOT YOU. You may charge a bit extra for the paint, because of its high quality, but your price is very fair. You'll do the second job because you don't want to drink beer; you want the money.

All of this sounds as if this paint is made of solid gold. I once watched them make the paint we used. They have a big vat of water to which they add a bucket of pigment, a handful of vinyl and some seaweed derivitive to make it thicken up. The seaweed stuff must have cost them nearly nothing and it made it so thick that it HAD to be high quality. These guys were charging me $2 a gallon for the stuff, which was a bucket of water with some pigment and "jello" in it. An ounce or two of another chemical tossed into the vat was the mildew inhibitor. All pitch. All show and no go. Or just a little go. What I'm conveying by this discourse on paint manufacturing, is not the simplicity of making paint, but rather that the selling is all in the pitch, not really in the product or service.

I'm not suggesting that you paint houses. I'm showing you the development of the pitch and presentation. There is always a pitch.

When we had an office supply business we either had cheap carbon paper or expensive carbon paper. The pitch on the cheap stuff was that it wasn't quite as clear and didn't last as long, but was so much cheaper than the expensive stuff, and would save them a considerable amount over the period of a year. The pitch on the expensive stuff was that, even though it cost more, the copies were so much clearer and presented so much more professional an image, and the stuff lasted so much longer that the cost was neglibible over the period of a year. Sell them whichever one you have the most of, or whichever one you'll make the most money on, and they'll know they got the best deal. It's all in the pitch.

A few years ago we had stereo stores and sold all brands of audio equipment. That business was 95% pitch and 5% product. 95% show and 5% go. As I look back on how we sold the stuff, and it's the same if you go buy something today, it really wasn't dishonest, and the things we told people weren't lies, but the pitch certainly served our ends. I'm relating these dialogues to show you that it isn't necessarily the product you have, or your position, it's what you can convince yourself, and others, your position is, and how you present the pitch. The selling is not always in the product it's in your head. If you get your mind into what you're doing and REALLY BELIEVE IT, and act like you believe it, they'll believe it too. BECAUSE THEY WANT TO BELIEVE. *EVERYONE* WANTS TO BELIEVE.

If we had lots of expensive amplifiers we wanted to sell, we'd tell them: "This is more expensive, but if you spend a little more now you'll never have to buy another stereo." If we had lots of cheaper amplifiers to sell, we'd tell them: "This one doesn't have quite as much power, but it's a good buy and will last you several years. By then the products will be changed so much that you'll want another stereo anyway."

If we wanted to sell them lots of power, we'd say: "This has 150 watts (75 watts a channel, but who's counting channels?) and the extra power will virtually eliminate all distortion from your system. You'll forget the cost difference and the sound will be so much better."

If we wanted to sell them a lower powered amp, we'd say: "This unit has 40 watts, with all of the basic functions, and these speakers are very efficient and usually require only about 4 or 5 watts a channel, so you have plenty of extra power. You can spend the extra $300 for a bigger amp, we have lots of them, but why buy it if you don't need it? Besides, if you buy this amp I'll give you a pair of these speakers for $380, which is half-price. How does that sound?" They can only respond that it sounds like a good deal. Then, we'd give them a price build-up—amp, turntable and speakers, only $730, and "let me show you what the payments will be if you finance it." You have the assumption of sale, close, low pressure, quick, exact and you already have them looking at payment figures. The pitch continues: "If you want to fill out a credit application they'll have it approved by 1 o'clock and you'll be all set. We'll put the products back for you, to make sure that no one sells them." It's all assumed, so natural.

They almost have to go along. Once I felt a surge of this mental magic come to me, during one of our big stereo sales, and I sold eight big stereo systems in 25 minutes, just to see how short a demo, and how quickly I could close. I hustled them up and had a girl take the applications and I *ran* back out and grabbed the next warm body. *I WAS COOKING.* Everybody bought. We can assume that I didn't run into just the right people. It wasn't the people, it was me. And it's not *your* product, it's *you.* I didn't really have to even ask anyone if they wanted to buy. We knew from the first word that they would buy. They knew it, I knew it, and all we had was to show them something, very quickly, so they could see what they were buying. That experience was exceptional, but from it I learned that even in two or three minutes I could get someone to buy a stereo system, IF I REALLY THOUGHT I COULD.

If someone wonders why the amp is so heavy, it's because it has massive heat sinks on the transformers. If they wonder why it's so light, it's because it's completely solid-state and they have eliminated the bulky parts other amps use.

If they wonder why it has so many controls, it's so you can personalize the sound to your exact tastes. If they wonder why there are so few knobs, it's because the manufacturer simplified the controls and eliminated the functions they discovered most people never use. If we wanted to sell them undamaged speakers it was because they shouldn't buy damaged electronic products since you can never tell when they'll quit working and how badly they're damaged. If we wanted to sell damaged speakers it was because they are barely damaged at all, they are $100 less and the sound is exactly the same. All pitch.

In asphalt, the sealer has asbestos fibers in it to make it last, sandwiches are made with rolls which are baked twice each day, windows are washed with chemicals that leave a protective, transparent film, chairs have special lumbar support springs, paint has mildew inhibitors and on and on and on. The PITCH is the reasons to buy.

In a real estate deal, the negative way to look at a demolished wall is that it looks like the building will fall down. The positive pitch is that you estimate it will cost

$3,000 to repair the wall, but to get on with selling the property you lowered the price $10,000. You will gladly (pitch--you really won't) make the $3,000 repair but the selling price will be $10,000 higher, or if they want to go to the trouble to make the repair "maybe they could even do the work themselves for $1,000 in materials," you'll knock off the $10,000.

The negative problem turns out to be a selling point on the property. In fact, the very first thing you could do, is to take them around back and show them the wall. They're going to see it anyway. Then give them the pitch. "The best thing about this property, aside from the full-occupancy and cash flow (it may actually be a negative flow, but who's counting) is that you can save about $10,000 off the selling price if you want to do a few repairs yourself. Let me show you."

You're not ashamed of the falling wall and they *may* be able to pay themselves $9,000 to fix it. *FANTASTIC!!* Then go on with the other good aspects of the property. The one criteria for using and openly bringing negative items to a · buyer's attention is if they will eventually discover it themselves. Always minimize the negative aspects. Be disarming. In many deals I've done, problems were raised which could have turned into big obstacles, but by bringing them out, discussing them briefly, and getting past them as if they don't merit any more time, they are tossed aside as small concerns. There is a lot of pitch in all of this, but you have to believe the pitch, too.

Give me anything and I'll sell it. AND YOU CAN, TOO!! i.e. "It's true, this manure smells awful, but there isn't any better fertilizer and the odor doesn't last long," or, "These fertilizer pellets are nearly as potent as natural manure, but they eliminate the odor, and for the little extra the pellets cost you, they are worth it because they eliminate the terrible odor."

You can be on either side and make it seem like it's correct.

In a real estate deal, as you encourage the seller to accept your offer, part of the pitch might be to show him how he is far ahead taking less money on the down payment and carrying a larger second mortgage. If you feel and act like they'll come out better, you have to believe it yourself, then it will seem normal and natural to them. Later we'll discuss all the reasons it's better for them but the idea is that you can even sell a low down payment and a long-term mortgage to them as a "plus."

Or, whatever else you need to put the deal together.

If you see it as a plus and act as if it's a plus, *they'll probably see it the same way.* It's in your projection, your attitude, your demeanor, your casual acceptance of the surety of the deal, as if there's no question about it being in their best interests, and, usually, the people will believe you BECAUSE THEY WANT TO BELIEVE. And you can see why both sides will come out ahead.

Any side of any deal. In a duplex: "The heating system works perfectly and you won't have to spend a cent on it." Or, "we allowed $5,000 off the selling price to repair the heating system, but it shouldn't cost more than $2,000 to fix it. Let me show you what's wrong with it, it doesn't amount to much." Your honesty and forthright manner will disarm the wary buyer and he'll feel like you're being completely straight with him. Then on to more positive aspects of the building. IT WORKS. And, you can do it.

I have used this attitude for years in all kinds of businesses and all kinds of deals, and it has never failed me. The basic idea is to see *everything*, even a defect, as a selling point.

Recently I paid a fellow $2,500 for a pipe system that runs through my fireplace and heats water. I still don't regret buying it but if I'd stopped to consider the initial outlay, and how long it would take to get my investment back, I ma

117

have looked at it in a different way. But, the fellow's pitch was great and *HE REALLY BELIEVED IT.* Everything he told me was true, I'm sure, and the system works just fine. I would never pay $2,500 for some pipes but I would gladly pay that much to someone who is excited and has a confident and believable pitch. Besides that, the guy deserves it. It was his own idea and he works hard at promoting it, and HE'S EXCITED.

Think it through and cultivate in your demeanor and personal presentation the ability to see everything in the best light. Just use your head.

One day I was sitting in a bank, closing a loan, with the usual optimism, confidence and positive attitude toward whatever deal we had going, and a fellow sat down at an adjoining desk to talk with another bank officer. A few days earlier this fellow had called me about renting one of my buildings to put a flower shop in. He hadn't committed to the lease but I had given him some encouragement on the certain success of his building in that location. If I had a flower shop there I'd have people eating flowers. And, so would you. It really was a great idea and the location was perfect.

Anyway, as I sat near him at the bank, he didn't notice me but I could hear all he was saying. He explained that he wanted to borrow some money to start a flower shop and also needed some money to buy a motor home. He said he wanted to get both loans but, if he could only get one loan, he really wanted the motor home. I couldn't believe it and my bank officer and I nearly laughed out loud. What a pitch. In applying for a business loan, he tells them that he wants a motor home more than the business. He should have had a few pages with projections, suppliers, costs, mark-ups, cash-flow analysis (show biz stuff) that should all have been part of his positive presentation and conversation. He should also have assumed that he was good for the loan and acted like it. Instead, he was talking about his motor home.

118

Bank officers, like everyone else, want to be convinced. They want to believe. They want to see dedication and intelligent decisions. In this case, the intelligent decision certainly wasn't to buy a motor home. The motor home will depreciate and no one uses them much anyway. The same money in an income property will make you a pile of money.

I've done million dollar deals with the same attitude as buying a lawn mower and you will, too. You deserve the loan, you expect the sale, you know they'll buy and you always have a pitch. In later chapters on the mechanics of real estate deals we'll go into successful pitches.

If you think the word "presentation" has a more positive connotation than "pitch," then use it, instead.

This idea, in summary, is that *THERE IS ALWAYS A REASON TO BUY*. There's an advantage to whatever you're offering and a logical reason why everyone should accept it.

I am grateful that my can of shaving cream let me know this morning that it's time to buy another can. I'd better go do it.

120

CHAPTER SEVENTEEN

Establishing And Building Credit

If you don't already have some established credit, don't despair. If you have bad credit, we can rebuild it.

Reaching a position in which you have borrowing power from here to yonder is just a matter of progessively larger loans, making repayments and getting more and more of a track record.

For the most part, bankers are not very clever or ambitious. It's true that they have their hands on the purse strings, but if they were very smart they wouldn't be working for the small salaries they receive. They have job security and that's about it.

But, it's their game and you have to play it by their rules. It's ironic that the least creative and clever people can control the funding for the most creative. Bank officers are like building inspectors. They aren't well paid and they aren't the smartest guys down the road lately, but they do have some control over some of your activities and you have to make them feel important. If you get into an argument with a building inspector, usually, you'll come out the loser, one way or another.

Be friendly with inspectors or bank officers, compliment them, make them feel important but don't let them take advantage of you. If you're getting a loan from a bank and the officer is being arrogant and making you feel as if you're begging, ask the bank manager to have another officer handle the loan or else go to another bank. You are their customer and you deserve some respect and consideration. Often, these people with so little real accomplishment and influence, enjoy raising themselves above you. YOU are the customer and you are doing them a favor by doing business with them.

In any case these are usually the types you're dealing with and it can work out to their advantage, and yours, to have a mutually friendly and respectful relationship. A lot of it is in your attitude and you should come across as knowing what you are doing and using the banks help in getting there.

There are several sources for obtaining money and we'll discuss how to build your credit with each of them.

FINANCE COMPANIES. These guys have a license to steal. Of course they take high risks, much higher risks than a bank will take and they need the extra interest to absorb their consequently higher defaults. Limit your indebtedness to finance companies. Use them to build your credit, if you need to, and fund an extra high profit deal if necessary, but not as a normal part of your financial program.

If you don't have any credit now, or if you have bad credit, these procedures will establish good credit for you.

Go to a finance company to borrow a small amount of money. If you don't have credit you might as well skip the banks for now. Talk with the manager of the finance company and tell him *EXACTLY* what you are doing. You don't need the $100 loan (start as low as you have to), but you want to establish a repayment record to establish your credit. If he won't loan you $1,000, or $100, ask for $50 and agree to put the $50 in a security fund that they'll hold for you to insure the payments. Then pay it off in a few monthly payments. Don't pay it in two months or less because you won't show regular payments unless you've made a few.

When that first loan is repaid, wait a couple of weeks and then borrow $500. Leave it in a security fund with the finance company, if you have to. Next time, get $800 or $1,500 and *use* the money this time. Keep your payments regular and make them a few days early each month. The people will continue to loan you larger and larger amounts. You'll have a dollar loss on the first loans since the interest is so high. But you're getting credit. After two or three of these and a couple of other small loans you will, at least, have some credit references.

Charge a cheap chair at a furniture store. Don't get anything expensive, in fact you should wait for any frills till later on, but get a cheap chair on credit, get a lawn mower on credit, or get some other inexpensive item on credit, and then make regular payment to pay if off. Something to show a consistent pattern of payments. Then, when you first go to a bank officer for a loan, HE'LL HAVE SOMEONE TO CALL who can tell him that you always make your payments early. Remember that the bank officer wants to make the loan to you, he wants to have confidence in you, and he would like to have a couple of references who will tell him that you're good for the loan and help him believe.

After a few small loans with finance companies, say up to $2,500, you'll approach a banker, tell him exactly what you are doing and get a $500 or $1,000 loan *UNSECURED*. It is important that they trust you on an unsecured basis. He may ask for the pink slip on your car or a UCC1 form on

123

your furniture, but you really need the *UNSECURED STATUS*.

If you must, offer to deposit the money in a savings account in the bank. They can't lose. There *IS* a way to put the loan together. Tell the officer that you want to establish a payment record with them. Tell him your plans. Ask his advice (it will make him feel important, but think three or four times before you let his advice discourage you) and let him know about how your plans are falling into place.

Get the $1,000 loan, then a $3,000 loan and *use* the three grand instead of leaving it in the bank. Have a checking account at that bank and, as your credit develops, open a checking account at another bank and start to build your credit there. Within a year or two you'll have several banks with your record of payments, and each of them will be ready to loan you thousands of dollars when you need it. While one bank might not loan you $50,000 for the down payment on a large property, five banks might each loan you $10,000 which they have long ago learned that you can, and will, repay. Even while you are building your credit this way you'll be buying real estate for nothing down and, if necessary, using the finance company or bank as references.

In turn, as you get larger and larger loans, the real estate holdings will give some support to your financial stability and success in the banker's eyes. He will see that you are buying property and that things are falling together, just as you told him they would.

SAVINGS AND LOANS (S & L's) These institutions usually provide mortgage money, often their own money as opposed to a bank selling your mortgage on the secondary loan market. You can get second or third mortgages through S & L's quite easily, once you're established. That is their primary business and they normally are more flexible and understanding than a bank. But they don't have so varied a group of people apply for loans either. A bank officer talks of odd ducks of every sort. Most people dealing at an S & L are doing real estate deals and have a little more sophistication. You can develop your relationship with an S & L the same way as a bank. Start small. Take a second or third mortgage, even if you don't need it. Give them plenty of equity on a small loan amount and MAKE ALL OF YOUR PAYMENTS ON TIME OR A FEW DAYS EARLY.

Do this a few times, for larger and larger amounts, and when the time comes that you need a $100,000 second mortgage, the S & L will be familiar with you and your repayment record. This is such a simple procedure and it works, but most people won't go to the trouble to borrow small amounts of money that they don't need just to establish credit.

Another source of funds is a *loan broker.* This is an individual or a company that acts as a liason between a lender and a borrower. They find funds available for loans and search for borrowers and match them up. They usually charge a few percent of the total loan from one or both sides, plus the interest on the loan and, typically, the cost of the money is higher than through conventional sources. However, sometimes it's worthwhile if it's the only way to make a deal fly. You have to decide if the figures add up for any particular deal.

Another reason, besides high interest and costs, that I personally don't like dealing with loan brokers is that they are usually quite unresponsive. If you have cultivated a good relationship you can *call* the bank and arrange a loan in a couple of minutes. Even if you have an established relationship with a loan broker, he may take days or weeks to put you in touch with a lender. They usually have to beat the bushes and find the money, or else convey the information on the proposed transaction to third parties for their approval.

It's so much easier when you talk with someone, at a bank, for example, who can either tell you yes or no for sure.

I once called one of my bankers and asked him if I could get $130,000 to do some building. "Sure," he said. I asked him to deposit it in my account and I'd sign a loan agreement the next time I came in the bank. He made the deposit and I wrote checks on the funds and the next time I was near that bank (one of the several developed sources), I stopped and signed a note.

No questions asked, no red tape. Only a pleasant five minute conversation on the telephone. THAT is a cultivated relationship, and yours will turn out the same way if you take care of them. It starts small and grows and grows. I got the 130 grand that time without even signing a note, simply because he knew I would do what I said. He knew from past experience. if I hadn't developed the past performance I wouldn't have had him as a source. *Develop* your sources. Loan brokers are alright if you need them, but they're too unresponsive for my blood. I don't even care if a lender is going to tell me no, if he'll tell me outright. I usually have trouble waiting for "the answer." They are always going to have "the answer" next Thursday or sometime like that. Sometimes banks tell you the same thing. It drives me nuts. Tell me yes or tell me no, but please *tell me*.

Another source for money is through *private parties*. These parties can be found through newpaper ads and through the grapevine you'll be on as you get established. You can advertise for funds yourself, and often you'll see ads for money to lend. On real estate deals these people often want splits, part of the action, for their loan participation. Many of these sources are viable lenders. Sometimes the money is at good rates, although, typically, it is higher than a bank and they want a greater debt-equity spread.

Some, or many, of these private-fund sources, as a matter of course, loan a small amount of money on a property with substantial equity and insist on terms so difficult to fulfill that the borrower is backed into a corner before he even starts.

The borrower then defaults and the lender forecloses and gets the property for much less than value. Some private sources do business this way every day, and they are usually very inflexible. They won't let you pay late, and, in fact, want you to default so that they can foreclose on the property and get it for themselves.

If you have a good cultivated relationship with a bank and the time comes to pay a loan, if you pay the interest, or a little principal, or nothing at all, usually they'll "flip" the loan. In other words they rewrite it as a new loan. That's the same as paying the previous loan off and getting a new one. Often, entrepreneurs will have loans at several banks and use funds from one loan at one bank to pay a loan at another bank. Then another bank will loan money to repay the first loan and the second bank will loan to repay the third bank and so on.

The amounts usually increase, in this circular loan procedure, and this arrangement must not be interrupted (i.e. a bank refusing a loan) or your house of cards will fall down. This is, at least, a poor business practice, if not illegal in some way. My banker told me about a fellow in town who had done this for years and spent the "float." All of the local bankers knew about it, but the guy always paid his loans off and thus had perfect credit. He was borrowing in the hundreds of thousands of dollars and had to keep the loans going to avoid having to ultimately pay it all back. That guy either has to come up with some cash eventually, or stay healthy. If he got sick for a few months he'd be a goner.

Occasionally, I would recommend that you get a loan at one bank to repay a loan at another bank if you need to. If you have lots of projects going it is much less conspicuous and less obvious what you are doing. It's much better to just flip the loan and keep the deal clean and simple.

In summary:

Start your credit today. Borrow larger and larger amounts.

Cultivate a good relationship with your banker or lender.

Repay your loans on time or early.

If your bank becomes unresponsive, change banks. Move your accounts.

Be careful with splits and partnerships unless it's worth the risk and the only way to organize a deal.

The most desirable source for borrowing any money will require little or no security or collateral, no credit checks, no long applications or waiting for loan committees. After you have cultivated your financing sources, they will usually treat you this way.

It is also quite easy to put deals together using funds *from the sellers*. You can even come out money ahead and with a flexible enough contract to allow for most possible contingencies and unforseen complications. We'll discuss those arrangements later, but the sellers themselves are definite financing sources.

TODAY is a good day to start your credit. If you can't do anything else, at least *TODAY* go see a finance company and borrow $50 or $500 with a payback as previously outlined.

Your $50 loan will be your first step up your mountain of millions.

CHAPTER EIGHTEEN

The Necessity of Cash Flow

You probably can't start off making *large* real estate deals to get yourself accumulating wealth. You'll be able to do deals that have an even, or positive, cash flow, some with a small negative flow, but your early deals probably won't pay your living expenses to start off.

As you know, you have to eat, have a place to sleep, a car to drive and money to live on. You can live modestly, like I did at first, but you still need some money to get by.

You might be able to do some deals at first that will give you a cash flow, but usually you need a little income.

So, one of the first objectives is to get going in something that will take care of you while you are acquiring wealth. There is a lot of difference in having a job that pays you a grand or two a month for a short time while you're getting somewhere and having the same job as a career. To get somewhere, it's fine. To keep it is the pits. One is positive and one is negative. But, you do have to make some money, so what should you do?

For you to start your investment portfolio you'll feel a lot better if, for example, you have five grand in your pocket. A couple of thousand of that will be the down payment on a property. A grand or so will be to improve it, and a grand will carry a potential negative flow for two or three months while you improve it and fill it with renters.

So, let's say you need five grand before you really take off and you'll feel more secure if you're not dead broke. The five grand is easy BUT NOT IF YOU ARE IN A POSITION WHERE IT COMES HARD. For example, you need five thousand dollars but you must make it in addition to making a living. If you are in a job that only pays enough for a living you will never get the five grand. If you're selling pencils for 10¢ each and clearing 8¢ on each pencil, you are making 80% profit, BUT HOW MANY PENCILS CAN YOU SELL? If you sell 1,000 a day you'll only make $80.

Select your field, and make sure, somewhere and somehow, it *can* give you a chunk of money.

For example: (I did this myself years ago, so I know it works.) Most people don't like to paint their homes, and in a previous chapter on pitches, I outlined part of the sales presentation I used while painting houses. Many people want painting but never get around to calling a painter, and when I came around and offered to do some painting while we were working in the area, they were very interested.

You could do the same type of thing if you haven't made your "nest egg" yet. There are lots of goods and services to be sold, and the money is to be made, not necessarily by having a totally unique product but in the promotion of that product or service.

Be confident, positive and sure of yourself, as well as casual in your certain manner. In this business, for example, don't be arrogant, but let them know that you are doing lots of work, you keep very busy and if they have you do the job, fine, and if they don't, fine.

You really *are* doing them a favor and if they have you do the painting (or whatever) while you are working nearby it will cost them less. In the last chapter I outlined some of the responses and phrases I used in this type of presentation.

Anyway, in this scenario, you have isolated something most people don't enjoy doing for themselves. You can be careful and learn how to paint. I didn't know how. And, most important, you can make hundreds of dollars a day. I don't know how many hundreds, but you *can* make hundreds. Most painters probably make $100 a day, but you can bet your boots that they're not out knocking on doors to get the work. They also aren't going anywhere, and they'll never be rich. But YOU will be and it doesn't matter if you need to spend 6 hours a day door-to-door, you'll do it *because the work will come.* It has to. You won't let it not happen. It's not just painting. It's asphalt sealing, window washing, and sales of very high profit stuff like cookware and so on. But, don't be the salesperson who makes $30 to $50 a set for sales of cookware. Find a source (easy) and buy the stuff from an importer or direct yourself and make $300 or $400 a set. Make your appointments in the morning and afternoon and keep 5 appointments each night. 5, 6:30, 8, 9:30 and 11 p.m. Give them a five ply sauce pan, regularly $26 just to hear your short presentation. Guarantee them that it will only take 30 to 45 minutes since you have another appointment afterward. By the way you can get the sauce pan for a dollar, if you look around a little.

Keep five appointments each night and with a positive attitude you'll sell two or three of them at, perhaps, $400 a set, and make $200 or $300 profit each. You can buy the best five ply cookware, for example, for $60 to $80 a set and they sell for $400 to $500. That's brand name stuff. Go for an off-brand that sounds legitimate and buy it for $30 a set and sell it for $180, plus only $21 for a sixty dollar knife set (costs you $3) and, somehow, you'll get a couple of hundred profit from each sale.

Some people won't have two hundred to spend, but many will and if you come across the right way they'll get the cookware instead of new tires for their car. You expect it from them and they'll do it. If you go with an off brand make sure it has lots of pieces, lots of layers and a good brand name. No one wants "Industrial Cookware," but any woman would want "Kitchen Chef" brand. Anyway, you get the point. When you are through talking with them they'll think that "Kitchen Chef" is the finest brand ever manufactured and the reason they haven't heard of it is because it's only sold in the most expensive stores.

As your brochure will show them, with a price build-up piece-by-piece, the set retails for $660 and it's all right there on paper. Any importer will give you a letter with any suggested retail stated clearly, just to cover yourself.

And, the best surprise, saved for last, is that the set only costs them $180. As a financing plan (you're not in the financing business, but, with this plan, you can't lose) if they want to, they can pay $100 down (which pays for the cookware and $70 profit) and the balance of $80, plus carrying charges of $20 in two payments of $50 each, one payment in 30 days and the other in 60 days.

You'll have a few people move on you but you've already made your profit. A few will be late with the payment but you'll have systems set up to mail them statements and returnable envelopes to remind them. If you carry the $80 you've made $20 interest besides. Most of these people will be around for at least 60 days so you should be covered. If you hit them with buying the knife set, too, and the thirty-two piece ovenware set (retail $90, costs $6) you may get them into a $250 or $300 deal with $100 down and the rest on the cuff.

All of which you'll be into for $40. Of course you'll have monthly "threat" letters to slow payers, but that won't upset you because it's just part of the business.

Just between you and me, I don't know anything about the cookware business, except where to buy the product cheap, and all of the foregoing reasoning just popped into my mind, but don't you see how you can get an idea, develop a pitch and then go out and work it to death?

Name any product or service and you can make up the pitch and a resonable reason why a buyer can't live without it. You can do this, easily, IF YOU THINK YOU CAN. And, as always, you have to really believe it yourself. I'm just a run-of-the-mill guy, like you, and if I can come up with this stuff, I KNOW you can. Just isolate your product or service and make it work.

Have the right attitude, put in the time and really believe your pitch. Start a small business if you want to to provide your cash flow. I've had lots of 'em. But make sure it's in a place with potential, with a market. You might be the greatest thing on two wheels but how many bicycles can you sell in Podunk, Michigan? Don't laugh, there really is a Podunk, Michigan. I've been there, but there aren't many people there and you can't sell many bicylces. Give yourself some exposure. Have a side-street location, if you need to, but advertise like crazy.

Do your own ads and the people will feel your excitement as they hear your voice on the radio or see you on TV or read your personal notes in your ads in the newspaper. And, they'll respond. This gives you cash flow. Expand, get a better location and the public will see you're growing and share in your excitement. Hype. Hype. Hype. Go. Go. Go. Sell. Sell. Sell.

Find new suppliers and buy cheaper and cheaper, sell more, advertise more, buy more and expand! Can you *feel* the excitement?

You can find any product for your business. Food. Vacuums. Stereos, furniture, waterbeds, gifts, jewelry, anything! Advertise and get 'em excited. Paint the walls and invite the public to see your beautifully redecorated store. Tear out a wall and invite them to see your expanded facility.

Always a reason, always a pitch, more and more, always better deals (was there ever a really good deal?), more reasons to buy. Anyway, you get the idea of promotion.

This kind of high-profit, expanding enterprise can provide you with your necessary cash flow. Choose retail, door-to-door, any product and any service. Pick yours out and go after it. Do it in a place with some potential. Some small cities, 50,000 population, have less competition in a certain product than a large area has, so this idea doesn't automatically disqualify any area. Some areas, like Southern California, have a great economy, plenty of money and lots of potential buyers, but also lots of competition. Give yourself a large enough market.

Anyway, do something like I've explained or one of your own ideas and get your cash flow to live on and give you a little bundle to start on. It will help you a lot during this period to live modestly, too. I had several hundred thousand in net worth and still lived in a $110 a month apartment and drove a $350 car. If I'd been smart I'd have bought a house to live in, but I didn't and the rent all went down the drain. But it was very modest living and I used the money for investments. I could easily have spent the money on other things but getting somewhere was more important and I knew the apartment wouldn't last forever.

I didn't hate the place, either. I liked it because I knew I could afford better but chose not to spend the money.

But, as I say, I should have invested in a house with some of my cash flow, and not spent ALL of it on investment properties.

But the cash flow was there and it floated all the deals. You can do that, too. The important thing for you to realize is that you *MUST* do something to generate more than your living expenses. You can often get a property with little or no money down, but you really should have a few thousand dollars to carry any negative cash flow, for improvements or for unforseen expenses. As outlined, there are plenty of ways to make this money.

CHAPTER NINETEEN

How To Start New Businesses

You'll never really get rich in a small business. You'll make a good living and maybe another hundred grand a year if you're lucky, but you'll never make *millions* IN THE BUSINESS. However, a business provides cash flow for your investments, as outlined in the previous chapter, and the CASH FLOW, not the personal income, is the best reason to consider getting into a business. You should also know that to make a business successful, it takes a lot of time and dedication and that might draw your interest away from activities that would make you much more money.

If you start a business for the investment money it can provide and if you'll be dedicated enough to spend all the time necessary to make the business go and also to organize your investment projects, you'll kill two birds with one stone.

Without going into any great detail I'll outline how I got into, developed, and made money in several types of businesses. These may give you some additional ideas or encouragement.

I've never had a failure in a business enterprise and you don't have to either. I've had lots of problems because of bad judgement and incurable optimism, but never a failure, because I WOULDN'T ACCEPT FAILURE. There are certain signs that indicate that a business isn't going well and if those indicators are heeded and appropriate action is taken, the business can recover.

I've already explained, in a previous chapter, how I started in the house painting business, and the pitch I used, and how I started the asphalt business. The painting business can always remain a one or two or three man operation. The natural maturation of the asphalt business is that, as time goes on, a person has opportunitities to do more and more work and instead of renting, they start buying equipment. First a roller, then a truck, then a paving machine. Then, they add more employees and then more equipment and so on. Often the growth consumes all of the profit. If a person developed a business like that, perhaps the smartest thing to do would be to level off when a level was reached at which there would be funds for investing but no expectation to keep the business as a *life-long* business.

You can start off with very meager means. When I first began to seal driveways, I had an old pink Studebaker car and I'd put about 15 five gallon buckets of tar in the back seat and trunk and toss my brooms in and take off. It got the material to the job, and the jobs turned out fine, but it certainly didn't seem too professional. I had heard about buying hot asphalt to fill in holes and, on one job, I called the asphalt company and had them deliver a ton (the least you can buy) and dump it in the middle of the driveway. I only needed about 100 pounds of the stuff and didn't know what to do with the rest so I shoveled it into the back seat area of my Studebaker car. That raised the front-end about three feet higher and I somehow made it over to another job that needed some filling too. I told the fellow at the second job that I didn't always use the Studebaker for paving jobs. I told him we had a four-door Chevy we used on the big jobs. He though that was funny and I acted as though everyone hauled a ton of asphalt in their car. And the job turned out just fine. After that I got a truck and then the expansion just happened. But, you can see how it's possible to start out with nearly nothing.

If a person lives modestly and takes the money from the company and invest it wisely, in a couple of years, the investments will be growing so quickly that there is no longer a need for the business enterprise that provided the start.

When I started an office supply business, as previously described, I first found a wholesale supplier of products and then proceeded to knock on hundreds of doors, office calls, to line up customers. You can find wholesalers for nearly anything in a large metropolitan phonebook. I lined up customers each day and, although each office's monthly account was small, together they were an excellent source of capital.

Shortly after I started that business, I decided to manufacture and distribute Men's Cologne and Women's Skin products. I got the big national phone books, yellow pages, and got all the names and addresses of companies that could provide the necessary elements of the planned products. I had all of the national companies that deal in essential oils develop various fragrances for me. There were about 50 final products developed, and I picked the one that seemed most marketable. Through the changing and modifications in the formulas we ended up with a great men's Cologne product. I had various glass companies send sample bottles, label companies design labels, cap companies send their samples and so on. To make it a very distinctive product that would be able to penetrate that very select market, I designed a velvet bag for each bottle. Each bag had a satin ribbon around it with the label reproduced on the satin. I made calls to various box companies for the display box and got samples and prices from as far as Hong Kong and Japan. I selected a plastic box made for us in Los Angeles. I ended up with separate suppliers on every aspect of the product.

My wife sewed the first several thousand velvet bags and I labelled the bottles. I got a heat printing machine and had a metal die made to reproduce the label on the velvet ribbon and I did the printing of the satin myself. I went to L.A. and got the first shipment of plastic boxes and packaged several thousand bottles myself. The cologne had been mixed and bottled at a contract plant in L.A. and I picked up the filled bottles personally.

Work like this is a key element in the success of any venture. The willingness to work unlimited hours and do the labor yourself. After a while it will pay you to get employees, but on a limited budget you can get into some more intricate products and make them successful. I located the cardboard boxes for shipping and had the completed product.

Then the chore at hand was to market the finished product. I took a trip around the West and talked with the buyers of all the major chains. Toiletries is an iron-clad business, and it is very difficult to enter the market and get shelf space. I ended up, after several months of work and great persistence, with my products in 110 stores around the West. I then developed a line of women's skin products and had them produced at another contract manufacturer in Southern California. These products were primarily designed to be marketed through mail order. I had national advertising in major magazines for those products. It was all arranged by contacting the offices listed in the magazines.

This type of entrance into this sort of business requires you to, first, have an idea for a product that is different or with some other compelling reason for the public to buy it. If it's more beautiful, cheaper, tastes better, smells better, lasts longer etc. Some advantage, then take the products apart, element by element and find the cheapest and best source for each part of the finished product. As you secure each element, buy it with your cash flow, from whatever grass roots enterprise or job you have developed or found.

Start to develop your market as you are producing your products. Approach buyers with prototypes, if you think it's necessary, before you get into production, and get their ideas and criticisms. Then modify your product to meet their needs. If you are persistent, creative, and if you refuse to stop until you succeed, you can make nearly any product a success. When you talk with buyers feel out their interest and find out what it takes to get solid orders. Then produce, promote and ship.

I personally sent follow-up letters to each point of sale for my products and called the stores regularly for re-orders. They knew that I was interested because I acted like it.

If you pursue manufacturing a product, make sure you have a viable idea and then pursue it with all of your time and energy.

Another source of income, depending on the local market and financing conditions, is to build and sell homes. We subdivided lots of property and built many homes and buildings, and they have always worked out very well. As outlined in following chapters, if you find a hungry general contractor to do your construction you'll have a great profit potential simply in reduction of costs. I developed fourteen recreational subdivisions and one residential subdivision. I've been involved in other residential subdivisions, also, and normally you'll have to put in water, sewer and roads

141

when you subdivide. My own experience, and that of several friends who have done this, is to use the ground as collateral for a loan to make the improvements. The property owner will usually take a second mortgage for his position, since the added liability is offset with the added equity in an improved property. That leaves the property with a clean first position and it's excellent collateral on a development loan.

Have all bids signed and detailed before you close any loan or purchase transaction. In OPTIONS we discuss how to tie up a property while you're rounding up the financing and an option on bare ground will let you get *all* of the development details tied up before you commit yourself to the deal.

Engineering costs and survey fees must also be included. Subdivisions are really quite simple. Sometimes it's necessary to get a zoning change, and they are sometimes quite complicated. Leave yourself a long option period if you plan on trying for a re-zoning since it sometimes takes many months. After development, the selling of a few lots will provide funds for beginning the construction of one or more spec homes. Be modest in your spending, add lots of convenience touches that make the home interesting, but not radical or too great a departure from a conventional plan. You can make homes interesting if you put a little thought into them. This may seem so elementary and obvious to you but many homes sit vacant because of a lack of planning and imagination before construction. It's not just a matter of cost, either.There are so many decorative and interesting things to incorporate into a home plan, and they can make a substantial difference in the salability of the home, if you'll just stop and think.

When your homes sell, you'll make your money on the lot and on the house, itself. Even in slow economic times a careful homebuilder, willing to do some legwork to find mortgage funds and so on, can do very well.

Next, let's consider a retail business. As outlined before you need to select a product, put yourself in a sufficiently supportive area and build, promote and advertise. Nearly any product or service can seem exciting if it's advertised correctly. Don't pay too much attention to ad salesmen as you're putting your promotions together. They really just want your money. Some of my businesses have done well with short ads every day. Others have done much better with little advertising at all except for special sales, and then a complete saturation of TV, newspaper and radio. Overall, radio has been my best buy. Ads are cheaper and you can convey a lot of energy and excitement. You can do the ads yourself and sound as if your finger is in a light socket. They'll listen. I've usually done my own radio ads, recorded at the radio stations's studio, because the regular announcers are too drab or so well known that no one notices their voices.

Promoting and advertising your product is one of the most important elements in any retail business you may organize. If you use your imagination you can come up with hundreds of ideas that will attract customers to you. A few years ago, when we were doing lots of stereo sales, I bought about three dozen old surplus Army search lights, the big kind with five foot-wide beams. I made some calls and sold a few of them and made enough to pay for the twenty-five or so lights I had left. We would usually run ten or fifteen of them at a time and the traffic was fantastic. During our sales we'd run till midnight or 3 A.M. some nights and have all the lights sweeping around the sky and the people would come out of the woodwork. One night, between midnight and 3 A.M. we sold over $20,000 worth of stereos. It was all promotion. Bang. Bang. Bang. You can do stuff like that in a retail business, too.

In retail , getting the cheapest source for products is a main objective. By beating the bushes, making calls, going to product shows, and keeping your ears open you'll be able

143

to save a tremendous amount on each item purchased. Once again, this all sounds so simple, but it's always amazed me that so many retailers will buy their products, often at twice the price, through the worst sources possible. Make some calls, make some trips and get the good deals. Borrow bank money, secured by inventory, buy in quantity and promote the stuff to death.

There are so many other fields to develop businesses in. Look around you, define needs and develop a product or service to take care of that need. Don't be afraid to spend money but don't spend a dime more than you need to for maximum return. After a certain point your money is wasted.

All you really have to do to enter any business is to break it down into its component parts and take care of each of them, one at a time.

Often a person has an original idea but the prospects of putting a business together around the idea seem to overwhelm him. Even the most complex business is simply a group of simpler tasks and talents. The reason I would discuss something so obvious is because 99+% of the population is at a complete loss as to how to go about starting a business.

By their nature, some enterprises and businesses are long term and will only provide substantial money when they have matured over a period of years. They may be very stable businesses, but require too long a period to provide a large spendable cash flow, and, for this reason, you should skip them. If you are considering an idea for a new venture, think it through and make sure that the business can be aggressively promoted, is cheap enough to get into, and can provide a reasonably quick return. By your assiduous investing practices you'll by-pass the stable but long term boys in a year or two and be off like a rocket.

CHAPTER TWENTY

Financial Statements

Regardless of the size of a loan, purchase or transaction, some representation of your financial condition will probably be required. If you have applied for a car loan, they ask about income and assets and so on. If you are self-employed and looking for a loan to start a business or expand or for the down payment on real estate or for whatever purpose, someone will certainly ask for a profit and loss statement and a complete financial statement. When you are buying property quite often an attractive financial statement will make the seller feel more confident in carrying a contract with you. I once had an employee who was trying out his wings in real estate and was putting together a deal for a $300,000 property.

He had a financial statement prepared which showed his net worth at about $20,000. I went over his statement with him and we ended up at nearly $80,000 as his net worth, and everything completely justifiable.

145

It's a crime and you can do time in a big "hotel" if you knowingly provide false information to obtain credit but there are so many ways to improve the appearance of your financial condition without being deceptive. Have a good reason why everything is listed as it is, just in case someone asks. In all of the deals, loans, purchases, contracts, partnerships and deals I ever participated, NEVER ONCE did anyone question my financial statement or ask for an audited statement.

I, personally, prepared every statement I ever had and after a few years I had an accountant retype the information on his forms, with his firm name at the top and his disclaimer at the bottom. The disclaimer declared that the statement was unaudited and no representation was made so far as its accuracy was concerned. Nevertheless, it *was* on their forms and it *seemed* more legitimate than if I'd typed it myself, although the entire statement was a direct copy of the figures that I had provided the accountant.

As you start to acquire real estate and/or businesses you'll have more opportunitites to be optimistic on your statements. As your list of properties increases you'll grow geometrically, but everything will be very logical and confirmable.

Just for example, let's look at the statement of my employee which originally showed $20,000 in net and after our rewrite showed $80,000. This fellow owned his own home and owed $25,000 on it and valued it at $30,000 since he'd only had it a year.

I showed him that the interior decorating he'd done, wallcoverings, upgraded carpets, completely rebuilt and upgraded bathroom and extensive outside improvements including fence, lawn, garden, sprinklers, outside lighting and on and on, raised this value substantially.

While some houses like that were selling for only $30,000 he obviously had thousands of extra dollars in improvements. Some of this may be a little optimistic, but who's counting? It was obvious that his improved value was at least $40,000.

If he calls around a little he'll find an appraiser who appreciates lots of improvements in a property and will give him a written appraisal for the $40,000 figure. So, that increased his net worth $10,000 by the stroke of a pen.

He also had an old foreign car that he paid $1,400 for and valued at $3,000. If he had called around a little he would have found someone who saw that as a rare car with a significant value, perhaps $15,000. Paying that person a $20 fee for his appraisal, he could get a written letter of value estimation pointing out the excellent restoration value of that car and the ways in which it was more apt to be restored than some other cars of the same model and year (show biz). The person gets $20 for the letter, and my friend gets substantiation for the car's value on his financial statement. Thus, he adds $12,000 to his net worth. My friend (employee) had quite a collection of used furniture (antiques), and he valued it all at $500 when it was obviously worth ten times that much. I knew a few dealers around town who would agree that some of his pieces were really quite scarce and *if the right buyer* were to come along, he could get a very good price out of the antiques.

And on and on through all of his possessions. He ended up with a good financial statement, even though he didn't change the list of assets. He also had a good reason why everything was valued the way it was. Just in case someone asked him. In many years, no one ever asked me once.

If you, personally, don't own a home, car or antique furniture, you own something of some value. If you're broke, but own the dozen sets of cookware we discussed, you'll have letters from the distributor or importer showing them with a retail value of $600 per set. $600 times 12 sets = $7,2000 in inventory. It's not what they cost, but their value that counts. Don't ever let anyone tell you to list assets at their puchase price. Always list their full value, unless you

147

intentionally list some under value (after you get going), just to be able to show that you have a tendency to be conservative in your figures. I can sell you a car for $10 but that has *nothing* to do with its value. Its value is what you can sell it for if you wait for the right buyer.

You can sell anything for a high price and we usually list our assets at a high market price. As soon as you acquire your first income property you'll really be on your way. Those properties are fantastic for improving a financial statement. All in a very logical, honest and straight forward way. Just for example, read through this actual account of a deal I put together, visualize how you will do this, too, and "feel" how it all came together and fell into place. In a later chapter we'll explore this example further, so far as how to find deals like this etc., but for now let's look at the income-multiple idea in action.

I was offered this commercial building for $95,000 which was a fair price. The owner lived far away, hadn't seen the property for a long time, and was *VERY ANXIOUS* to sell. I suggested she fly over to look at the terrible condition of the property (it always sounds worse on the phone), but, because I was anxious for her to come and see it, she didn't come. I told her that it really needed a lot of work, we already had lots of property and didn't need any more, but that I'd put together an offer. I don't know how much work it actually needed but you can do a lot of cosmetic stuff for $1,000.

She ended up at $75,000 with $15,000 down. I offered her $65,000 with $5,000 down in cash and the other $10,000 of the down payment to go for improvements, which should be fine for her since the money would end up in the property she was holding for security. I didn't say when I would spend the ten grand on improvements but could have committed to do it within 21 months, which doesn't sound too long. I may have needed the 21 months to do the rebuilding for individual tenants I'd be getting in, to meet their personal needs. (That's the pitch.)

I had two acquaintances who had cosmetic work done on their income properties, and major work done on their residences with *ALL* work billed to the rentals. I wouldn't do this, but they did it, had the big deduction on the income property, their personal residences improved and they had very little exposure. If the bills were ever questioned it might appear that they had paid a high price for the rental repairs, but you know how you can never see all the electrical, plumbing and repair work after the walls are finished. So, in any case, they would have been covered even if they had committed themselves to complete the improvements by a certain date. I didn't commit myself to a date. In any case I paid the $5,000 down. It was borrowed for a year by which time the building would be sold, and ended up paying $65,000 with $5,000 down and not one cent of my money invested. The building had a tenant using part of the building and paying $600 a month which was $25 per month more than the first mortgage, taxes and insurance.

I convinced her that the great advantage of selling to me was that, come rain or shine, she would get her check the first of every month. I invited her to contact other people I'd bought poperty from to see if they didn't get their checks on time. Because I invited her to contact them, she didn't. I obviously wouldn't have suggested it if the payments were late, would I? I never had anyone ever call anyone else, because I always invited them to. If they had called they would have found that the payments were on time anyway, because I was always careful to be on time or early.

So, she accepted the deal. Se got her $15,000 down ($5,000 cash and $10,000 in eventual improvements), and I got a $95,000 building for $65,000. With no investment.

Now, here's the magic. The tenant was paying the mortgage. I painted a wall or two in the unused part of the building and placed ads to rent it. I rented one part for $200 a month, and another area to my own retail business for $400 a month. No one came along who wanted that space for $400 so I took it myself.

That gave me an income of $1,200 a month. To figure the actual value of a property, ALWAYS VALUE INCOME PROPERTIES AT 100 TIMES THEIR MAXIMUM MONTHLY RENTAL. If you're renting it for $600 now but have a letter (!) from a realtor (!!) showing that it could actually rent for $900 then it's value is 100 times $900 or $90,000. 100 x maximum monthly rent. So, on this property I valued it at 100 times the $1,200 monthly rent or $120,000. I only paid $65,000 for it and invested nothing, owed $60,000 on it and it was worth $120,000. In that one deal I raised my net worth $60,000. Actually $55,000 since I still owed the $5,000 down on a loan. I'd never have to repay the loan, anyway, since I would sell the property before the year was up, or else flip the loan and pay a few hundred interest.

Now, on with the magic. Property usually appreciates at least 15% to 20% a year and a year after I bought this property, even though I had leases signed which locked me in at $1,200 a month, the property was still worth 15% more than the 100 times the rent. So, a year later the property was worth:

$120,000	rent multiples at beginning
18,000	appreciation in one year
$138,000	total value at end of first year

The mortgage had paid down $3,000 so I owed $57,000 on a $138 building. Instead of repaying the loan on the down payment or even paying the interest I included the $5,000 note in another real estate deal by borrowing the down

150

payment for the other property and getting an additional $5,000 to repay the first loan.

Then it shows the first loan paid in full (good credit) and another larger loan. The second year the property appreciated another 15%, this time of the $138,000 appreciated value, or about $21,000 so was now worth $159,000. The mortgage had paid down another $3,000 to $54,000 so I had an equity of $105,000 not counting the $5,000 down payment loan repayment, since it was lost in other real estate deals by now. All of this $105,000 with an investment of ZERO DOLLARS.

Add to this, many other loans, many deals, purchases and sales and you can see where the millions start to show up on your statement. This example we've used is only *one small property.* You buy it low, low down, borrow the down if you can, rent or lease it after improving it a little, ending up with a tremendous equity.

And, you are able to show EXACTLY how you arrived at the value. Would you ever sell the property at that high of a price? Maybe and maybe not, but *EVERYTHING* over $65,000 is pure profit.

What if, for example, you only sold it for $120,000. This would be a tremendous reduction in its real value and the low price would move the property fast. You'd take only $20,000 down, which for you will be the down payment on a $250,000 property. The $250,000 property will actually be worth $350,000, but you'll get it cheap from someone with hot feet. After the $20,000 down payment to you, you'll have a hundred grand coming on a contract, only owing $60,000 less the pay-down, on the first.

So, you'll have a $40,000 second mortgage which you can either carry for 20 years and get a $400 check every month or else advertise it for sale at a 20% discount. Whoever buys the second mortgage will thus get the 12 or 14% interest on the contract PLUS your 20% discount which is a 34% return on their money which is an exceptional return for a regular saver.

If you sell the note at discount, which is easy, you'll get $32,000 cash besides their $20,000 down payment. You've already used the twenty grand as a down on a $250,000 deal, or else you used your twenty grand and borrowed twenty grand from the bank. If you have twenty of your own in it, the least the bank can do is match your money with another twenty grand, right?

After all, you repaid them the $5,000 loan and all the others too so there's no question about whether you're good for the twenty. So you got $40,000 and used it to get a $400,000 property, actually worth $550,000 but you paid them less than value, and now you sold your note at a discount and have another $32,000 to invest. This money will get you another property. Are you keeping up with this? The thirty-two will get you a $350,000 property, or else you'll make a deal with the bank.

Since you got, for example, the $20,000 loan to match your own $20,000 for the other deal, you'll pay them $10,000 on that note if they'll give you another loan to make the down payment on another property. So, you owe them $10,000 on the first deal and you'll be in it $20,000 yourself (because you are such a conservative type and like to be moderate in all of your equity positions and dealings. Cough. Cough.) That leaves you $22,000 on the note payment and you'd like to get $38,000 to go with it. That will total $60,000 when put with $22,000 left after you give the bank the $10,000 from the $32,000 realized when you sold the $40,000 note at discount.

Now, you only need, as you'll recall, $40,000 down on this $400,000 property but want to provide for cash flow, improvements etc. so you'll end up with:

The $20,000 plus the banks matching $20,000 down on a $400,000 property.

A $40,000 second for your equity.

You'll discount and sell the second for $32,000.

Pay $10,000 back on the first loan (excellent credit, pays early).

Get $38,000 to go with your remaining $22,000 from the discounted second mortgage sale. That's close to the first deal: the bank matching your down payment, and $38,000 is about a match for $22,000, right? Act like it is and it will fly.

Use $40,000 of the resulting total of $60,000 as the down on another $400,000 property and have $20,000 cash for any improvements or temporary negative cash flow.

Now, let's transfer THIS information to your financial statement. Remember that this is only one deal, but let's see how this shows up:

Under assets:

Cash	$20,000
Properties	$550,000
	$500,000

You only paid 400 grand each for them but one was worth 550 and one was worth 500 (100 x maximum rents).
You'll show under liabilities only one bank note for $38,000 and you paid 40 grand down on each piece.

Consequently you paid $40,000 down on $400,000 leaving a balance of $360,000 on each piece or $720,000 for both but they are worth, together, $1,050,000.

From this ONE extended deal you now have a net equity of $320,000 plus $20,000 in the bank or $340,000, ALL FROM THE PROFIT ON ONE SMALL DEAL, and, remember, that although the original building we discussed was worth $159,000 with appreciation we practically gave it away at $120,000. That's $39,000 under value and even though we did that, look at what we've done with the profit you made from the sale. Not only that, the bank loves you since you repaid them the $5,000 loan on the first property, $10,000 of the $20,000 loan on the second property, and a year early at that. You only owe the bank $48,000 and you're already in the million dollar area, so $48,000 isn't much, is it?

How will you pay the 38 grand in a year? Pay half of it and flip the other half and the interest. How will you even pay half, $19,000? Include it in a loan for another deal, or, within a year, you will have improved the property a little and sold it high, or perhaps you won't have even spent a nickle on it, but will have found a buyer willing to pay its real value ($550,000.). Plus your 15% appreciation, naturally, or a total of $632,500.

That last figure isn't even selling it high; it's just what it's worth. Selling it high would be getting 700 or 800 grand from it because it's right where someone wants to build his castle.

But you're selling it for $632,500 and you bought it for $400,000, you've paid $20,000 off the mortgage and owe $340,000 with an EQUITY of $292,500. Selling for $632,000, of course you'll want $100,00 down, much less than the 29% many people ask. But, in return for the small down of $100,000 you will need to get one or two percent more in interest than would otherwise be normal. The pitch is that the one or two percent won't make too great a difference to your buyer since you both know that he's going to sell it in a couple of years and make a couple of hundred thousand on it, so what difference does the extra interest make? It actually makes a lot of difference, but who's counting?

Anyway, on this one property you have an equity of $250,000 and he's paying you $100,000 down. So take $25,000 for half, or $50,000 and pay off your only bank loan. They'll be impressed and ready to do *ANYTHING* for you.

Now, let's see where that would leave you. You'll still have:

The original $20,000 cash in your pocket (less any expenses).

$50,000 more cash in your pocket, left over from the $100,000 after you paid off your only bank loan.

A second mortgage on your second property for $152,000 at a high interest rate, and because of the higher rate, this mortgage will sell at a higher price, so only discount 15% to sell it.

PLUS: The other $500,000 property, now worth $575,000 and owing $340,000 on it. You paid 400 grand for it and paid $40,000 down and paid the mortgage down $20,000, with an EQUITY in this property of $235,000. Summary:

Property equity	$235,000
Cash	75,000
Second mortgage	152,000
total	$462,000 net worth

ON ONLY ONE DEAL

Against your properties you have a total debt of a mortgage on one property for $340,000 and you don't owe the bank a nickle, but have proven credit with them.

O.K. let's sell the third property and see what happens.

You end up with another hundred grand down on the third property but no bank loan to repay out of it. So, we put that hundred thousand with the $75,000 you already had in cash, and now have $175,000 in cash, plus the second mortgage from the second property for $152,000 and a second on the third property for $135,000. You discount these two second mortgages 15%. Those seconds were written at 15% interest since your buyers only paid you about 15% down. But discounting them 15% your secondary mortgage buyers will make the 15% interest plus the 15% discount, or a 30% return on their money. So, you have $287,000 in notes and sell them for $244,000. Put that $244,000 with your $175,000 cash and you've got $419,000 CASH.

You'll have some tax planning to do but you'll still end up with the money.

So, how large a property can you get with the 400 grand, and how much under value will you get it for, and how much will it appreciate, and where will you be one year later?

Remember that this $419,000 came from only one deal in two years and you (I) didn't invest a penny in that first building. Actually, I bought that building in the middle of my five year program so I was buying properties left and right besides that one, and getting loans and repaying loans in several places. But, you can see how it happens.

Is it really that easy? Yes and no. Yes, all you have to do is *do it.* There are thousands of properties everywhere. There are plenty of people either nervous, tired or in financial trouble who need to sell their properties. There are also lots of people who want to buy property and have the money to do it. You do have to do some leg work to find the properties and be familiar with their values, locations and etc. You have to be on top of your deals so that they don't get away from you. You need to get good tenants, make wise improvements, and manage your properties, but YOU CAN DO IT.

No, it's not easy, in the respect that you have to do the work and be committed to your program. You can see how the loans would fly at the bank but you have to know what you are doing and come across like you do. Then they'll give you the money. If they don't, someone else will, because you won't stop until you get it.

Is there any risk? Following the format we just discussed you can see that near the end of our example you have a substantial net worth. You are also obligated to loans for $700,000 in mortgages. You can buy a lot of groceries for $700,000 and you will owe that much to someone. But you have cash and assets.

The debt will never bother you since you can't acquire wealth without the careful management of debt. You have to borrow. You have to owe money.

Yesterday I called a friend who is a builder and developer, a real mover, and visited about our current activities. He felt VERY solid now since he'd reduced his debt to the banks down to only $14,500,000.00. He felt great. As you do more and more deals the larger figures will become more and more common to you and you'll start to think in hundreds of thousands, and, in that frame of mind, the $700,000 in debt won't bother you.

Risk? Yes, Progress? WOW!! I'LL SAY!! And the deals keep falling together over your five year plan. You'll have a few turn out better and a few turn out worse than this example. You'll have a few windfalls come to you and they all melt into the few slimmer deals. As you apply this to a financial statement you can see how it will, *very quickly,* look better and better and how fast your net worth actually can grow.

As you do more and more deals you'll not only get more real estate to list under assets, but you'll get a lot of mortgages and other receivables, and you'll probably start to collect possessions that will be listed also. Some of these items will be personal or recreational stuff, jewels, equipment, inventory of one kind or another, or just a varied listing of real estate holdings.

In other words, you may be worth a million bucks but if your only listing under assets on your financial statement is this one property, it looks a little narrow and tenuous. On the other hand if you have a number of properties in different areas, a few commercial pieces, some houses, some apartments, some pieces of raw land and so on, it seems like you have a broader foundation. You may specialize in apartments but have several of those properties. You may specialize in lower cost buildings, but have some prestige locations also or you'll appear to be a slumlord. Even if you have one small higher-class property it will spruce up your statement. I guarantee you that you will feel solid and you'll come across as a stable and successful fellow if you have a financial statement with a long list of assets and few liabilities.

One basic rule is to stretch and itemize the assets and squeeze the liabilities. You may have several adjacent properties that could be listed as: Smith Street properties. The best way to list them would be:

6811 Smith Street (house and outbuildings)

6821 Smith Street (house, workshop and garage)

6831 Smith Street (improved house and garage)

Notice the descriptive or more expansive words used to identify the properties. Notice that you also used up several lines on your statement of assets.

You may have three first mortgages on these properties, and three second mortgages, but under liabilities you'll just list:

$108,000   Smith St. mortgages

That visually minimizes the debt and maximizes the assets.

As you apply this idea to your personal possessions and properties you can develop quite an impressive list of assets. All of this may not seem important but it is certainly impressive when you use the financial statement as a tool to cement a deal or swing a loan. Your prospective seller of your lender will look it over, and may ask some questions, but probably won't go over it item by item. This may have something to do with your personal attitude, but I've never had anyone go over any of my financial statements item-by-item. If you have this extensive financial statement, someone will be impressed.

It will be so solid and there will be a great spread between the total of assets and liabilities. The basic way to accomplish this is to be honest, creative, imaginative and be careful to have a valid explanation for every item. Even if your explanation is tainted by your optimism (i.e. "to me that seems to be a very conservative estimate").

And, again, I stress that the greatest way to get the great bulk of assets, both on and off your statement, is to value your properties at 100 times maximum monthly rents.

Here's another example. I found a six unit apartment building which was for sale. This building was owned by a couple who lived out of state and didn't want it. They had a manger but she was moving and they just wanted to get rid

159

of it. There are many situations like this if you look for them.

They asked for about $80,000 which was cheap, I offered them $63,000, $60,000 for them and $3,000 commission for the real estate agent. The sixty may seem low, but they took it. I should have offered them $40,000. Part of the deal was that the realtor wait a year for the $3,000 commission, and I later extended that another year for 10% interest. I paid them $2,000 down, which, with the $3,000 commission, totalled $5,000 down, but I only had to come up with the $2,000.

I hired a tenant as the manager and told him to get every rent on time or evict the tenant. A previous problem had been partial payments and etc. All the tenants straightened up but one and he was replaced. We fixed the furnace for a couple of hundred dollars and raised the rents a little. In the first place the building was way underpriced.

I offered much less and still got it and the first thing after closing the loan I raised the rents. The six rents averaged only $140 each when I bought it and I raised them to $175 each. It was so cheap that they were always full.

This was not a prestige property but money is money. Anyway, six times $140 a month is $840 a month times 100 equals a value of $84,000. Six times $175 a month equals $1,050 a month times 100 or a value of $105,000. On the surface it appears that I raised the rent by only $35 a month. I actually raised the value of the property by $21,000. Besides that I bought it for $63,000 instead of $84,000 (the correct multiple) so I saved $21,000 and made another $21,000 for a cash investment of $2,000 plus $200 in repairs and an instant equity of $42,000. I didn't even consider the $3,000 commission as a debt since I had no intention of paying it out of my own money. I knew that the property would sell within a year or two when the commission would be due. So, in this case, we have a property worth $105,000. Since it's not a prime location property and it's an old building, let's say that it appreciates only 10% a year. At the end of the first year it's worth $105,000 plus $10,500, or $115,500 and at the end of the second year $115,500 plus $11,550, or $127,050. The mortgage will pay down $6,000 in two years to $52,000 and you have an equity of $75,000 all from an investment of $2,000. I don't remember now, but if I didn't borrow this two grand, I should have.

This property had no negative cash flow, no down (borrowed?), no expenses, low rents to insure full occupancy, and I only saw this piece two or three times while I owned it. This was probably the worst property I ever bought but you can see the profit potential even in this bad piece.

Anyway, how do you think the $52,000 debt looked on a financial statement with a corresponding value of $127,050? It looked great, especially sandwiched in with dozens of other equally attractive assets.

You will be solid gold. Did it take money to get it? No. Did they offer it cheap? Yes. Did we buy it cheaper? Yes. Could we have bought it even cheaper? We should have. Did we do well on it? Sure.

What can you do with the money you make on this deal? Since it was an old property it wasn't possible to cash out on it. I had to carry a second or third mortgage. I discounted it and sold the paper. But, whatever the profit in a deal like this, you can use it to close a bigger deal. The possibilities boggle the mind, but if you are working in real flesh and blood deals, it all seems so logical and simple, and is a natural progression.

If you're buying right, how much exposure will you have? How much trouble can you get into paying $63,000 for six apartments? What if the sellers are offended at such a low offer and turn you down? Big deal. You don't need the property anyway. There are lots of others and you have plenty of them already. The last thing in the world you need is another headache (pitch) and you don't want to have to look forward to running down the rent every month from the tenants (pitch). However, you'd still do the deal if they'd go $63,000 or else they can go ahead and hold onto it and try and sell it higher. In fact, you say, why don't they keep it since they'll probably be able to find someone who will pay a lot more for it sometime. Maybe they'd hold it a year but might even get $68,000 (??!!) if exactly the right person came along. So why don't they just keep it? (!)

Then the sellers say, "Well, your offer is pretty close to what we asked and we'd really like to sell it now so why don't we all go ahead with our deal?" 'Nuff said on that idea.

As far as a financial statement is concerned, your listed values are sometimes higher than you may ultimately sell the properties for but they are completely justifiable. As your statement gets larger, later in this book we'll discuss simple and inexpensive ways to improve your properties and raise rents and etc., but, even though the rents provide you with some cash flow the most important benefit is increasing the 100 times multiple for value.

You can raise the rent on a building $50 a month and add $5,000 to your value. Sometimes buildings sell for more or less than the 100 times, but that's a generally accepted figure and, on the other hand, your buildings should rent for 1% of value, per month. This type of structuring makes a fast and substantial difference in your financial statement and will enable you to swing larger and larger deals.

This may all sound too elementary and very simple, but believe me, IT WORKS.

CHAPTER TWENTY-ONE

How Do You Find Properties?

Once you are all fired up and ready to start, today for instance, you'll have all the energy and confidence in the world and you just need to find the good deals. You may not even have one dollar to spend but you'll either put together a deal with no down payment or become familiar with the market.

You'll look at many markets and, before you know it, you'll understand financial structuring and how to recognize good and bad buys. It doesn't cost anything to look, and you can start doing that today.

Basically, in order to find your properties, you'll: Read the want-ads in your local paper and in the papers from the surrounding areas every day. Talk with real estate agents in areas in which you wish to buy. Be confident and positive with them.

They'll be glad to search for properties for you. It's their job. Don't let them rush you and don't believe everything they tell you. They'll show you enough properties and propose enough deals to acquaint you with some values. Remember that they are also working for, in fact are employed by, the seller and want to get the highest price and terms most favorable to the seller. They sometimes are more structured and inflexible than you'd be if you were sitting down in a head-to-head negotiation with the seller himself.

Also, you run small display or classified ads yourself to advise sellers of your needs and solicit calls. Be specific to eliminate tons of unnecessary calls.

Keep your eyes open as you drive around. Not just for "for sale" signs, but for likely properties. Neglected buildings in a good area, for example. Buildings that are vacant are obviously not being put to good use. You'll notice a property that has a great potential but doesn't look like much now. By asking around you'll find the owner and can inquire about the possibility of his selling. I've bought lots of unadvertised properties this way. In fact, I've bought several properties that the owner definitely didn't want to sell but, by gentle expression of interest, getting to know them personally through repeated visits and light discussions (see the chapter division on how to close a deal), they gradually see that they could sell and I'm making a good offer. I've missed out on a few properties I didn't really want, but I've never been unable to buy a property I really wanted. Even if it wasn't for sale.

Many people go to the county recorders office and look through lot book reports and find properties with out-of-state owners. The general thinking here is that these absentee owners may not be too interested in keeping a distant property and they may be unaware of local property values. Often these owners have had the property a long time. People usually buy property near where they live, and

164

you'll see from the county records that most of these properties have only small mortgages against them. So, the owners have lot of equity and a lot of room to negotiate. You can write letters to these owners to ascertain their interest in selling. The replies will provide you with enough information to seriously go over the property and put an offer together.

You'll send offers, or options, with small earnest money checks and agreements for them to sign and return. A certain percentage of these distant owners *will* be interested in selling. Make a low offer. It's negotiable. Point out the good and bad points of the property and the reasons why you feel the price is reasonable.

You'll subtly emphasize some defects that make the property less desirable and suggest that they have a local contractor give them his opinion on the cost of repairs, if they feel like they need another opinion, besides yours. If you ask them to get a second estimate or opinion, they probably won't, JUST BECAUSE YOU ASKED THEM TO.

Don't ever call and talk with someone and read them a long list of defects. It's their property and they probably have some pride in it. Compliment their property in some way and get them on your side. Express an interest in them. It's an art but an easy one to acquire, to learn to talk about the other person. They'll love you and be glad to deal with you, and they'll listen to you forever if you talk about them, and listen to their ideas.

Dale Carnegie relates in *"How To Win Friends And Influence People"* about a party he was at where a woman approached him and complimented him on his great principles of making friends. She was practicing what she had read in his book. She was talking about him. After the first compliment from her, Dale Carnegie said, "Well, thank you. I'm happy that you feel like you learned something. Say, I heard that you've just come back from a long cruise, is that right? That must have been wonderful. Where was your favorite place?" The rest of the conversation was about her. And Mr. Carnegie says she loved it. When you negotiate with a buyer or seller, get them on your side by having an interest in them and getting to know them. Don't avoid talking about the transaction because the avoidance would be too obvious. Let the conversation flow.

I once negotiated with a widow about buying her business and residential properties. She was anxious to sell but couldn't be snowballed or rushed. Don't ever think you are a big wheel, giving some time here and there to the little people. There are many people who simply can't be rushed and are offended by a know-it-all type who overwhelms them. Be real and be genuine.

Many of your sellers will be older people. These are the people who have had properties for a long time and have high equity positions from which to deal. They are older and don't want to take care of the properties any longer and they can't maintain them. That's why they're run down. They are more interested in a regular monthly check than trying to find renters.

They are boggled by the complex tax structures relating to real estate. They remember the low price they paid years ago and often will accept a price somewhere between what they paid and a high current value, just to get the regular payment. These people need security, they don't need to be impressed with your wizardry.

So, when talking with one of these typical sellers, slow down, be considerate and let them talk for a while. With the widow I mentioned previously, spent several visits getting to know her and simplifying my position, offer and proposal. I suggested that she arrange an appointment with her attorney where we could all sit down and discuss the deal.

She was impressed because I was advising her against doing any deal without some advice. I was on her side. I asked about the house and the conversation led to her family and late husband. We discussed him, what he did and I was genuinely interested. Not just for the real estate deal but because here was another person, opening up herself to me, to share her life with me. She was gentle and I learned a little from her. You can learn from nearly everyone if you stop to listen and are concerned. You can't steamroll most people.

Anyway, I listened to this woman tell about raising her family in the house and commented that it must mean a lot to her. Throughout the conversations I would make natural comments about our proposal and how it seemed like it would help her and one or two ways it wouldn't be in her best interest to cash out on the property, because of taxes and etc. Naturally, the way to avoid this big tax bite on a cash-out is to have a small down payment and regular checks upon which she could depend. Even this way of proposing a low down payment seemed to be in looking out for her best interests. And then on about what she would be doing personally after she moved. You can see the unquestioned assumption, on my part and gradually on hers that the deal would go through.

This pattern of interest carried through several visits and reached the desired conclusion: she said she'd accept my offer. If anyone else had called her after the conversations we'd had she wouldn't have considered another offer since I had her confidence and friendship.

It's important, too, to keep this friendship and relationship at a certain distance after the buy or sale is completed. Continue to be cordial and friendly but don't become an intimate confidant of every person you talk to. They may read more into the frinedship than you do. Sometimes, if you sell someone a car, buy an apartment building from them or have any kind of business deal with them, there will be problems arising for one reason or another. It's much easier to take care of these problems in a friendly business setting than to let it become a personal thing between friends. So, be interested, but don't expose yourself or them to potential upsetting, hurt feelings. Life is too short for that.

Another method of finding properties is to keep track of the mortgage foreclosures in the legal notice section of your local newspapers. These notices are usually in county-seat papers, and they usually appear on county lists and records before they appear in the papers, so you can jump the gun by doing some legwork early. Often, while looking over county records you'll see liens and judgements begin to pile up on some properties. This may mean that the owner is in trouble and can't pay either his bills or his mortgage payments.

Many of these people have a good equity in their homes or buildings, but have run into financial trouble and can't keep their payments up. With their credit in such a shambles, regardless of their equity, they can't get a second mortgage sometimes. If they get too far behind, three to six payments, the mortgage holder will begin foreclosure proceedings.

The owner will then have a certain period of time (varies from state to state) to bring the payments current or lose the property, usually at an auction at a title company. At the auction, whoever bids the highest above the mortgages usually gets the property. I say usually because, in some states, the property has to sell for a certain percentage of appraised value. But not so in most states and you can sometimes make good boys at auctions.

The drawback is that you, usually, have to pay cash. You may pre-arrange a permanent line of short-term credit at your bank for this type of purchase.

If you see in the county records or legal notices in the paper that a property may be entering or will enter foreclosure you can go to the owner and make an offer to buy out his position. He's in the situation where he can't make the payments, he'll lose the property, his equity will be gone and he'll have a foreclosure on his credit rating. It looks pretty dismal for him. You offer him a small amount for his equity. You'll catch up the payments and assume his loan or pay it off with your line of credit. He won't have a foreclosure on his credit report, either. He isn't getting much for his equity but his alternative is to get nothing at all.

At the same time you are helping him you are picking up the equity for yourself. I knew a fellow who, in one year, picked up 250 properties this way. I know he did because I saw the county records showing him as the property owner.

The important thing to realize when considering the prospects of finding properties is this:

The whole earth is covered with water or land. You can't do much with the water but the land has always been here and it will always be here. But, the people come and go and everyone leaves the property behind. Real estate constantly changes hands for many reasons. All of the real estate around you right now will change hands. The property is everywhere and you just have to do a little work to find out which piece you'll buy next.

You don't need to go to a big city to get property, either. In the book *Acres Of Diamonds* a fellow left his farm and spent most of his life looking for a diamond field to work, only to find, on returning to his farm as an old man, that there had always been a diamond field right in his back yard. Acres of diamonds.

That doesn't only apply to wealth, but there are plenty of opportunities wherever you are. If you are in a genuinely depressed area you owe it to yourself to move closer to a more energetic and productive area.

In finding your properties the key elements are: first, being in an area with some promise. Second, buying something that will sell when the time comes. Third, selecting a property with an owner who will deal. Fourth, passing over properties that, after further consideration, aren't really great deals.

Within the next month, I am sure you can find at least ten properties that would suit your plans and purposes. You may make offers on all of them, but you only need to close one or two of the deals. GO DO IT!!

CHAPTER TWENTY-TWO

No Offer Is Too Low

Real estate, stereo speakers or jewelry, there are no offers too low. Considering that, usually the first person who mentions a figure will come out behind in the deal.

A few years ago when we had stereo sales, and retail stereo stores, we used to sell some name-brand stereo speakers for $300 each, $600 a pair. These were large hardwood speakers, really beautiful and sounded great.

We bought these speakers for $95 each and thus our gross profit was $205 each or $410 a pair. That leaves some room to discount a little and still make a significant profit. Perhaps we'd sell them for $500 a pair if they bought an entire system and then we'd only make $305 gross profit. Our overhead was about 5%, advertising 5% and sales commissions 10%. That totalled about 20% off the top of each sale, which, on these speakers, left a $200 net to me on each pair.

Anyway, we usually bought a dozen or so pairs at a time, for $95 each. On a buying trip we visited this manufacturer

171

and during our afternoon there I asked the price on this particular speaker if we took 1,000 of them. I was sure he would come down from $95, perhaps to $75 and I'd counter with an offer of $60 each and we'd end up at $65 each. If he went along with the $60 deal, I'd make an extra $30 on each speaker, or $30,000 on 1,000 speakers.

In response to my question of price if we took 1,000, he said: "If you want 1,000 we'll go $16.50 each." I knew he'd made a mistake and I exclaimed in disbelief, "$16.50?" He hurriedly said, "Well, yes, but we'll pay the freight." He thought my exclamation was because his price was too high. So he offered to pay $2.50 freight on each speaker, and he actually got $14.00 each for them, and I was in them $16.50 each. Can you believe it?

That made our wholesale cost for a pair of these hardwood, name-brand speakers only $33.00 but, it didn't change the value, since WHAT YOU PAY FOR SOMETHING HAS NOTHING TO DO WITH ITS VALUE.

These speakers, for example, were still worth $600 a pair. How would this show up on a financial statement? 1,000 speakers times $300 each equals $300,000 in inventory, with a wholesale cost of only $16,500, or to be conservative, you'd list them lower, perhaps at $200,000. If ever questioned, you could show someone the actual manufacturer's list prices, which would give you a value of $300,000, but to be conservative you listed them under value.

After getting such a low price, I still went further and asked for the best terms possible, the longest time to pay. My idea was that if given a couple of months, more than enough of the speakers would be sold to pay for all of them. If we discounted them, and sold them for $500 a pair, we'd only have to sell 66 speakers and the rest of them would be all profit. Sell 66 and pay for them, then sell the other 934 and keep the money. FANTASTIC!! And we didn't have to pay for them for *three* months.

So then we ask ourselves, how can they sell these things so cheap? *Why* is no offer too low? We went back into their factory to watch the assembly line for speakers, and they had a giant machine into which they fed sheets of thin particle board and sheets of veneer. The machine laminated the veneer, split and grooved the particle board and rolled it back onto itself to appear thicker, sprayed the raw edges on the back and assembled the whole box, and spit them out the other end at the speed of light. Almost. Carefully looking at this machine it was obvious that they were only into these boxes a dollar or so each. Then they went around an assembly line where speaker elements were dropped in and screwed into place, covers were slapped on and the whole thing was dropped into a cardboard box. There may have been two or three minutes of hand labor on each speaker.

Later, while listening to two different high grade speakers we asked the plant manager, what is the difference between these two speaker models?

Without thinking he said, "This one has a 70¢ woofer and this one has a 36¢ woofer." And then he corrected himself: "What I meant to say was that this one has a more expensive woofer in it than that one has." Well, the cat was out of the bag. As it turned out we later learned that the speaker elements for the whole speaker only cost about a dollar and a buck for the cabinet and a buck labor. Add another dollar for packaging and etc. and they were in those hummers about $4 each, so they still made a killing selling them to me for $14 each. These speakers retailed at $600 a pair.

We still sold them on sale for $400 to $500 a pair. At first we advertised and sold them for $85 each but no one would buy them. We raised the price to $200 or $250 each and sold them all.

There are several lessons to be learned from this example. Don't mention your offer first, unless you absolutely have to and then make it *very low*. You can always come up. You would be surprised at how little some people have paid for things you want to buy. Property, speakers, apartments or anything else.

For all you know, someone selling a commercial building to you has had it for thirty years, the mortgage is paid off and he only paid $15,000 for it. So, you'll give him $40,000 and he'll have a good profit. No offers are too low.

That building may rent for $900 a month ($900 x 100 = $90,000) but *perhaps* the owner doesn't know what property values are, he may not live in the area and be familiar with the values, he may be old and anxious to get rid of his property or he may be in financial trouble and need to sell it fast. If he knew what he was doing he'd get some high appraisals, give himself a little time and sell it high, BUT PEOPLE, OFTEN, DON'T DO ANY OF THOSE THINGS. They just want out. That is why no offer is too low. EVEN IF THEY WOULDN'T GET ONE CENT many times owners will let you take their position and slide in on a first mortgage just to get out. People get divorces and need to sell fast, they want to move, they need to sell for many reasons but they need to do it soon and often will take a very low offer.

A couple of years ago I was ill and had three operations. That experience taught me a great lesson about physical suffering and for the first time in my life, I learned what unbearable pain was like. I gained a great sensitivity for people who may spend a whole lifetime with pain like that.

Before I became ill I discussed an apartment building deal with a real estate agent and had come very close to closing a deal for substantially less than its value. These were particularly nice apartments and they had high rents but that happened to be their downfull. These units were located in a prime location and really were comfortable but they were in an area with too many vacant apartments. The owner had a high rent figure fixed in his mind but only had a third of the units rented. He wasn't clever enough to see that 100% occupancy at a lower rent was better than 33% at a higher rate. If he'd planned, he'd have been flexible in his rents and filled up the units and either waited out the temporary slump, converted to condominiums and sold (there were very few condos in the area) or he could have painted and papered the walls and raised the rents back up a little in a few months.

But he could only see himself owning a building that he couldn't rent. And he *had* to sell. He felt trapped.

Well, he wanted $800,000 for the building and I had hoped we'd end up at $650,000. This fellow should have purchased the building cheap enough to suffer through a slump and still cover his mortgage and I was determined that, if I bought it, it would allow me some breathing room. As we had some preliminary discussions we were getting close to a deal when I got sick and had the operations. I was ill for several months, taking lots of medication and, as a result, I had my head foggy and certainly wasn't going to buy anything with my mind in that condition.

During this illness the agent who was putting the deal together called me occasionally to discuss the deal and I kept putting him off. He interpreted my foggy mind as being hard to get and my being uninterested in the deal. That wasn't the case at all. I was very interested but in no condition to do the deal. But every time he called the price was lower. The final price, after two or three months, was $440,000 for a property originally offered at $800,000. The property sold for that, of course, and I missed the deal because of my illness.

This seller was scared, he frightened potential buyers by negotiating from a very weak position (33% full and no reason why), and he acted like the wrold was coming to an end. He just didn't know what to do, and he must have frightened buyers at a higher price by acting so negative and uncertain. He should have been confident and AT LEAST figured out some logical reason why he didn't have tenants. i.e. "While it's true that our vacancy rate is higher now than it normally is, it's part of a local cycle that occurs every few years (if that was true) and it's a passing problem. My wife and I wanted to enjoy some of our equity in this property and so decided to sell. In consideration of the higher vacancies, which can be rectified, of course, we reduced the selling price from 1.2 million dollars down to $900 thousand.

Acting strong, being strong. From this position, after negotiating, he may have ended up at his $800,000 figure or even $700,000 but certainly not $440,000. That guy made a big mistake. I don't know what the occupancy is now in that building, but how can you lose paying half-price for a beautiful property?

"Ah," you say, "that's a great story but deals like that don't happen often." Perhaps not quite that lucrative but there are thousands of deals like that WAITING FOR YOU TODAY, AND THEY WANT *YOU*, BUT THEY DON'T KNOW WHERE YOU ARE. They are even advertising for you. The people are anxious to sell to you on *your* terms. Some of the people cry themselves to sleep at night because you won't call them. They want you to own their house, their duplex, their triplex, sixplex, stores, shopping plaza, block of buildings, shopping center, skyscrapers. Fit yourself into that progression wherever you are now.

They want to sell to you *cheap*, but they just don't know where to find you. Some folks want to sell high, like you do, but you can skip them since they want to make some big bucks off you. You don't need their deals. In fact, after a while you don't need any one deal in particular and you can pass over the bad ones without it bothering you. If they don't accept your low offer, that's fine. You're grateful for

176

their time. There are lots of people who will accept your low offer but YOU HAVE TO MAKE THE LOW OFFER.

I once saw an ad for an old car, a foreign limosine, in the paper. They wanted $8,000. I was sure that was a misprint but called to see if it really was that cheap. I drove over to see it and happened to be in a car woth $2,000 and just happened to have the title with me. While discussing the old car, I limited my interest, since the price stays high if you're too interested, and I talked with the owner about how much the restoration would cost and so on.

The fellow gradually wore down and asked why I didn't just trade him cars. A newer car for an old car? That would make him happy.

So, you'd jump at the deal, right? Me, too, but you don't want to appear too anxious so I said, "Well, let me look it over again." So I looked it over, and then traded cars. I advertised and sold the car for a very (!) high price. When the little work needed was done to it, the car would be worth $100,000, more or less. I got less that that, but enough, and the previous owner got a $2,000 car. He was happy, I'm happy and my buyer is very happy since he got a rare car and will make a good profit when he sells it. Unless he gets scared and takes a weak position. I had some low offers on the car and didn't even consider them. I passed over the bad deals and waited for the good deals. No offers are too low. If he wants eight grand offer him one or two.

Do you think that, as the deals get larger, somewhere it magically becomes impossible to buy things for less than their value? Do you think you can buy a car cheap and sell it high but not an apartment building? I bought a Rolls-Royce for more than a nice income property costs and bought it for less than full blast. Cars, apartments, furniture, duplexes; it's all the same and *NO OFFERS ARE TOO LOW.*

I once bought an old motel in a prime location for $135,000. We started out at $100,000 and the guy went up a couple of times. We were so low on the price, anyway, and I went along with him because I wanted the property. He didn't know that he should have started at $400,000 and I would gladly have paid him $300,000.

But this guy had no imagination and he thought he put the screws to me by raising from $100,000 to $135,000. . I laughed for months. Later I'll describe what I did to make this a beautiful property but I got it *cheap*. And then the property next door, too. And then the one up the street and on and on.

Remember that many people either have little imagination or knowledge, are in some kind of trouble, or for other various reasons have to sell fast and cheap and they are just waiting for your call.

CHAPTER TWENTY-THREE

Structuring An Offer

As previously mentioned, in years of making deals, there was never a property *that I really wanted* that I didn't get. This includes properties that weren't for sale, deals in which a large down payment was required and I had none and various other complicating factors.

Not that I'm more clever than anyone else. I'm not, but with patience, persistence and a positive outlook on the deals, they came through every time. It was just a matter of getting the people to think along the same lines as I did and finding the conditions we could agree on.

There are so many flexible ways to structure an offer. You can use price, interest, length of payback, improvements, partnerships, tax structuring, mortgages on other properties, premiums, and so on. Let's look at a few deals and see how some of these elements can be used.

In the previous chapters we've discussed the potential profit spread in many available deals. If you are putting a transaction together that is very slim and tight as far as

179

profit is concerned, it may be difficult to be as creative with your financing. You can't do a lot with the price and terms if they are part of a limited potential transaction. Some people enjoy doing deals and making a few thousand at a time. I, personally, could never get excited about a few grand after I got my financial program going.

As you grow you'll think in larger and larger numbers. Overall, after you get going, you'll pass over the slim-profit deals and go with offers that enable a VERY LARGE PROFIT. That gives you miles of headroom to be flexible and creative on your terms.

For example, let's say that you've found an apartment property that's for sale. It has eight units and is priced at $230,000. From talking with the owner you learn that he owes $110,000 on a first mortgage and $60,000 on a second. He figures his equity at $60,000.

Each of the eight units rents for $260 a month or $2,080 total income per month. He has priced the building at $230,000, or over the 100 times multiple. So, it's overpriced. However, looking at the units, you see that, at $260 a month, the rent is much lower than other available apartments in the area. You know this fact because you've been doing your legwork and you know what the comparable values are. From your own knowledge you think that $300 would be a reasonable rent on each unit. The present owner has had the building for several years and is reluctant to raise the rents. The $40 per month increase per unit is only about 15% and it should raise that much each year just to keep up with inflation.

The present owner is asking for $230,000 and $60,000 down. That's about 23% down. That down payment will cash him out and leave you with the first and second mortgages. So, he feels like it's all a fair deal, considering price and down payment, he'll be completely out and you'll assume his position.

So, how can you deal with this person? Even if you didn't make any improvements the rents should be higher and you'd make some money by increasing the rents and consequently increasing the multiple value of the property.

Your first object in this transaction is to get the selling price down. Do this before you get into terms and conditions. After you have a lower price and you discuss it and negotiate around it for a while, it will seem that that was always the purchase price and the seller won't feel like he has already compromised his position. The price seems high to you because of the rents, the unstable local economy and the question of having full occupancy in the future. You're concerned about the money you'll have to put into the building.

He'll assure you that the building is in mint condition but you'll explain that you've bought several "mint" buildings and you've always had to spend some money on them. New plumbing, new electrical, a new roof. There's always something and besides the unforseen things, you'd like to improve the apartments a little inside and outside. Emphasize that you'd be happy to pay the $230,000 for the building if he would agree to do and pay for all of the improvements you've outlined. If he'll sell lower, you'll pay for the improvements yourself.

He'll ask you how much you think they'll cost and you'll tell him about $35,000. He's trying to get rid of the place and you know that he's not going to spend $35,000 cash. You go back and forth in your conversation and emphasize that, considering the repairs, you'll go on the property for $195,000. That leaves him with $25,000 equity, although he took out a second mortgage and probably used part of the money for himself. He may have taken the second to get some equity out to buy another property. Even if he didn't get his $25,000 in cash he's probably in good shape.

So, in any case, you tell him that $195,000 would be your top offer. He says that you might be able to get it for something like that figure, but it sounds a little low. You mention that amount several times in your conversations and before long both sides will understand that that is the assumed figure. It has become the final price, simply by assumption and repetition.

Now comes the terms. He wants $25,000 now to cash him out. You explain that you'll go on $195,000 *but* you're going to have to spend $35,000 on the improvements and are concerned about having, at the same time, to pay out $25,000 down. To reassure him you tell him that $25,000 down is fair, more than fair and you want to pay it, but would prefer to pay part of it now and part of it in one year. If he'd accept $10,000 now and $15,000 later, you'll pay him 10% interest on the $15,000. Since you'll pay out the $35,000, more or less, on improvements, if he'd take $5,000 now and the other $20,000 in one year you'll pay him 15% interest on the $20,000. He is in a great position because the money you'll spend on the property will increase the value of the property that is securing the debt.

If he doesn't go for this, offer to pay him $200,000 for the building if he'll accept $5,000 down and $25,000 in one year at 15% interest.

Or, you'll go $195,000 with $25,000 down, $10,000 now and $15,000 in nine months at no interest. Or, $210,000 for the property if he'll go $10,000 down and the other $30,000 of his equity if he'll accept it in payments of $10,000 every 12 months for three years at no interest.

There is some way to put the deal together. Your top offer is $210,000, in this scenario, which is $20,000 less than his original offer, and that $210,000 offer only includes $10,000 down.

Now it looks like you're giving *him* everything. He's already agreed to $195,000 and now you're offering him more than that. All he has to do is wait a while for part of his down payment. The reason he has to wait is because of the money you'll have to put into the property. Tell him how you've done this before and how it's always worked out just fine.

You know that you'll be able to do some repairs (minor) or improvements, painting and so on, and raise the rents immediately when you buy the property. You may not be able to get all of the $35,000 in improvements completed before you sell the property.

The property will be resold within a year and you'll never, personally, have to pay the delayed down payment. All the delayed terms, if you're sure you can resell within a year, are all show business. You aren't going to pay anyway, and never intend to. You must, however, be sure that all of this show biz stuff will fit into a reasonable package when you want to resell. All you want to do *IS NOT PAY IT NOW*. You want to get in for as little as possible *NOW*. That's the whole point here. Get in for as little as possible. The building itself doesn't know if you paid $5,000 or $50,000 down and it will keep the tenants just as warm and resell just as fast if you've paid $5,000. When you resell, the sales price won't be any higher because you paid more down now.

So, pay less and offer incentives, that will fit into your profit picture, and premiums to get the low price and low down deal NOW.

Now let's look at the incentives to offer.

CHAPTER TWENTY-FOUR

Structuring The Deal

Since people often don't do what they tell me they will, if someone owes me $100 in six months, but offers to pay me $50 today, I'd probably take it. If, however, this person offered me $300 if I'd wait a year, and if his story was convincing, I'd probably wait a year. If he asked me to wait ten years for a return of $2,000, I'd probably wait the ten years.

If he offered me $40 a year and $1,000 in ten years I'd go along with that proposal. All of this is considering, of course, how believable his story was, and how reasonable his pitch was. If it sounded like his head was in the clouds or he was being deceptive wih me or that his sure deal really had no substance to it, I'd rather take the $50 now. It all depends on how the deal sounded. From his side of the transaction, he is *structuring a deal*. He wants to keep my money and he wants to multiply it and make it work for him, all the while finding the least demanding terms that I'll accept and still let him keep my money. It's the same in any potential transaction, but even more important in real estate.

Let's look at a few examples of financial maneuvering and financial structuring.

In the first example we find a person who is selling a fourplex. This fellow is older and is more interested in security and regular payments than he is in getting a big chunk of cash. He needs to be approached with patience ad deference (defering your own energetic nature to his slower style of doing business). This guy has his whole retirement and future tied up in two or three properties. He's tired of taking care of them and wants to sell. He's not a wheeler-dealer. He knows interest is high but in the back of his mind he still thinks about historical 5% and 6% interests. For this fellow our first objective, as always, is to get the selling price down to rock bottom. Then we can deal on terms. But, first the low price.

He wants $90,000 for the building. We are thinking more along the lines of $70,000. We tell him that we know that he's taken good care of the property, but there are some improvements we'd make and if we paid anywhere near the $90,000, plus the improvement costs we'd be into the property so much that it would never return enough rents to make it work out. We also tell him that we've compared several other buildings nearby and we feel like $70,000 plus our improvements will bring us up to the average selling price in that area. We are interested in the property but it, somehow, has to work out in the figures. In all of our other properties, we have reasonable mortgages and good occupancy and *all* of our sellers get checks on the first of every month, as regular as a clock. This doesn't come out as if bragging, it's just part of a conversation, but it builds his confidence and tells him the most comforting thing in his mind: that he'll get a regular check. After several conversations in which we've gained his confidence by visiting, talking about things that interest him and so on, this fellow wants to make a deal with us, but we are too far apart on price.

Our "final offer" to him is $70,000 at 10½% interest. He counters with $80,000 at 10½% interest. We can then do one of two things. We can either accept his $80,000 offer at 10½% interest, or we can tell him that we can only go $75,000 but, in return for being slightly under his offer we will pay a *premium interest.* We'll go $75,000 at 11½% interest. If we really want the property we'll go at 12¼% or 12½% interest, but insist on the lower price of $70,000. The reason for this is that when we get ready to sell we want as small an assumable first mortgage as is possible.

When we eventually sell, the first question may be what the price is, and we want to have a small first mortgage and a large personal equity. The interest being one or two points higher may not seem as significant as the lower mortgage. The fact is that interest rates are critical and make a big difference, but if the numbers fit into your financial package then the higher interest offer is worth considering.

Remember that this fellow is out of the 1940's, 1950's and 1960's and his ingrained ideas aobut interest are 5, 6, or 7%. We offer him 11½% and it sounds very impressive to him. Put yourself in this guy's place. He's tired, he's old, he doesn't want any more taxes to pay and tenants to chase for the rent. All he wants is a regular check, a good return, like 11½%, on his property sale and time to relax. He knows what he paid for the proeprty and will make a good profit, dollar-wise, no matter what he sells it to us for.

Since we've visited a few times, he knows us and has confidence in his buyer and he wants the deal to go through. The high interest looks good and the repeated off-handed comments about regular checks "make his heart flutter" and he may accept the deal. If he does, it's good for him. And even better for us because we have a $90,000 property for $75,000. We paid a little extra interest but not much and we've got the deal. As far as the down payment is concerned we explain about the improvements we'll make and the estimated costs, and in light of the heavy cash outlay for the improvments, our down payment will be limited to $5,000. Of course, we offer to pay him $15,000 down if he'll pay for all the improvemnts before the deal closes. He certainly isn't going to spend that much money on a building he's trying so hard to sell. We can commit ourselves to complete the improvements within a year, and if they aren't completed within a year he'll notify us by certified mail and we then have an additional 180 days to comply. The fact is that he may not keep track of the year, or he may ask us in a year or so, but not notify us.

If he eventually notifies us, we still have six months to do the work, and as a practical matter, we can see that we usually would have two or three years before push came to shove. If it ever did. And, by that time we'd certainly have the property sold. The reason that he'd probably never force the issue is because he's been getting his regular checks and he's happy with that. He, intrinsically, has no abiding reason to care about the improvements anyway. He can't eat them and they won't return him any more money, or higher payments on his mortgage. As we've been making the payments, his principal balance due is getting smaller and the property is appreciating so he's covered as far as value is concerned. All he *really* wants is his checks and he's been getting them for a year or two, so he's happy. All of this is good for us because it reduces our down payment to $5,000 and, effectively, we won't ever have to spend the additional money. The contract doesn't specify any penalty and we'll sell the property in a year or two and be finished with it. As far as the seller is concerned, however, we have a $15,000 down payment and the only reason he's only gettting $5,000 is because we have to spend the other $10,000 in improvements.

So, when all is said and done, we got the property for $75,000 with $5,000 down and we originally were asked to pay $90,000 and probably $20,000 down. We gave him a 1% interest premium but overall we came out very nicely.

You can see how this deal would fall together. I've done several just like this.

There are many incentives to offer a seller. Once, I was buying a $500,000 property from a fellow and, for some reason, he just couldn't bring himself to close the deal. He had a soft spot for cars and I suggested that, if he'd sign today, we'd go downtown and buy him a new Cadillac, just between friends. That is called an *incentive*. An incentive can be an spiff that isn't part of the deal that is used to swing the transaction. This may be used after a deal is all ironed out, and if there's plenty of profit in it, you want it so badly that your teeth ache, but the seller won't sign. Some times it is so frustrating because it is no longer a matter of price and terms. If that's the case, you may want to offer an incentive. It may not be very business-like and it might be classed as a pay-off, but it sometimes works. I have friends who have pulled out a stack of hundreds and pushed it across the table. Maybe five or ten or twenty-five grand, depending on the deal.

Some people will succumb to the sight of actual cash and sign. This money may or may not be in the contract. I, personally, like to have EVERYTHING in the contract so that there can't be any misunderstandings. This incentive technique also isn't a standard practice. If it came out that way in all of your deals it would seem that you are a little underhanded, offering pay-offs.

This is just a possible offer when everything is done to close a deal but the buyer or seller just won't go through with it.

The third tool, sometimes used, is what I call "kickers." I've tried to stay away from these since they can complicate a simple deal, but I know several people who used this technique often. Let's say, for example, that you have a small duplex for which you paid $40,000 and have an equity of $25,000. You made a good buy on it and made a few small improvements which resulted in your equity. You are now trying to close a deal on a ten unit apartment bulding for $290,000.

You have the price and terms worked out and the deal is good all around, but the seller is still reluctant to close the deal. As a final offer you agree, as part of your contract, to sell him your duplex for $40,000, just what you owe on it. Your equity of $25,000 will go to the seller of the 10 unit building, but your contract won't note any equity transfer.

As far as the contract is concerned you just sold him the building for what it cost you since you could no longer maintain it from the return it provided and you couldn't get any better offers. As a practical matter the seller got your $25,000 equity for free, just for closing the deal. Since you didn't make any profit on the duplex you won't have any capital gains tax and while you've owned the duplex you've deducted the interest from income and had the tax depreciation advantages. So, you still came out alright on the duplex and its transfer allowed you to get the larger property.

You should, however, remember to look at it another way also. You gave your $25,000 equity in a $65,000 property. If you hadn't transferred the property you could have sold it. You probably would have received $10,000 down, maybe more. The remaining $15,000 of equity could have been discounted to $12,000 and sold to an investor. Figure a rock bottom twenty grand cash could have come out of the deal. What could you have done with twenty grand? And, how does that compare with whatever gains you'll realize by getting the ten unit apartment building?

If you could have used the $20,000 as the down on another $200,000 building and ultimately come out ahead, you shouldn't use your equity as a kicker to get the 10 unit deal.

If, however, you have a special reason to want the 10 unit building, and IF IT COMES OUT AHEAD IN THE FIGURES, then it's to your advantage to use your equity as a kicker to swing the 10 unit deal. It's all gravy to your seller because he gets a duplex for only $40,000. It pays for itself, is a nice property and will appreciate and make him money. You really don't have any investment in the duplex, dollar-wise, and it might be sufferable to give your equity away.

You may want the 10 unit building because you can see how the overly-large two bedroom units could easily be rebuilt into 20 one bedroom units. Or how they are available for way under value, or because they are on a property that has space for another 10 unit building and you know of some available mortgage money that could be used to build the second building. For example, perhaps the room for the second building was on a separate, but adjoining property. Part of your transaction in buying the 10 unit building may be that the seller gives you a clear title, free of any lien, note or mortgage on the adjoining piece. You can then approach a lender with a clean title on a piece of property to use as collateral on a loan for the construction of the new building.

In any case, by your imaginative examination, you have a good reason to acquire the property and feel like the transfer of your equity is worth it. Then you give him the "kicker," that is, you transfer the duplex to him.

The fourth financial structuring method we'll look at is the *BALLOON*.

Balloon payments can be good and bad. They are good if you can turn the property before the balloon is due to cover it when it has to be paid. The balloon payment can allow you to get a larger property, using more leverage than you normally might get.

Balloons are bad when you have to pay them, and can't comfortably do it. An example of a good deal with a balloon might be something like this:

You are going to buy a commercial building for $410,000 and the owner wants $160,000 down. He started out at $480,000 and you got the price down to $410,000 so the price is where you want it but, of course, you can't pay that much down. You can see that this building could be divided into small shops with a wide aisle down the middle. This building could become a center for all kinds of crafts and hobbies. In Southern California this collection of shops could be called "Santiago Craft Village" or "Sunshine Hobby Village." In Illinois "Lincoln Craft Village." In Wyoming, "Eagle Rock Craft Village" (That's the one I used.) Think of some catchy name.

In any case, you can visualize that this building, with around $100,000 in improvements or a total cost of $510,000 could be rented for a total of $9,500 a month. $9,500 monthly rent X 100 = a value of $950,000. So there is a tremendous profit to be made. The seller sees a big old building and you see 20 craft shops in a gallery-type building. The only things standing in the way are the down payment and the 100 grand to do the improvements.

Don't worry as much about the development costs as the down payment. Your banker, from your track record, will advance you the hundred grand. If he does it, you can get an option to buy the building, good for six months, then do the blue prints and plans, advertise and get signed prospective leases, contingent on the deal closing, and put all of the above in your proposal to the bank, before you ever buy the building. More on options later.

On the basis of your option and signed leases you'll be solid at the bank. That leaves the down payment. If you absolutely have to, and the chance of a development delay was nonexistent, or if you had a buyer lined up for the finished project, you might borrow the down payment from the bank also. They would also have to be lined up for the development. You may not have the project fully leased and sold in a year and the note would come due. You might pay the interest and flip the loan but you would have some exposure.

So, you decide to propose to pay the $160,000 down payment in the following manner. $30,000 cash down and $130,000 in a balloon payment due in three years with 11% interest. The reason he might go for the balloon payment is because of the tremendous improvement costs needed for the property. The balloon payment will count as a down payment, reducing the balance due and therefore the monthly payments. That makes the monthly obligation easier to live with and you also get to wait on most of the down payment.

If he won't go on that proposal and IF IT WORKS OUT IN THE NUMBERS, you can offer $190,000 down, $30,000 now and $160,000 later. That sweetens the deal. Or, if it works out on paper, you can offer to pay $20,000 more for the property if he'll go on a balloon. There *IS* a way to structure a deal on this property.

There are ways to make it so much more worthwhile for the seller to wait for most of the down payment. Make sure it's an assumable balloon payment, so you can transfer the obligation when you sell the project. Your attorney should always include in any contract you'll eventually transfer that the original owner who sold to you must first agree to a transfer of your obligation, and *approve of your buyer, which approval cannot unreasonably be withheld.* In other words he has to agree to a transfer unless your buyer is a completely unacceptable person. If you plan on keeping the property you should plan ahead on your method of paying the balloon payment when it comes due. If it's a small amount it could be paid out of your cash flow or financial package on another deal in the future, but it's suprising how many deals are put together with little thought on how to cover future obligations. In any case, by juggling purchase price, down payment, interest and so on there should be a way to get a balloon payment.

There are so many variables when using these delayed payments. I've bought properties and deferred the entire down payment to a later time at which I was fairly certain that the property would be sold. I've always been careful to make sure that the balloon payment wasn't so large that it would make the down payment at the time of sale proportionately too large.

If you have a $160,000 balloon payment and a $100,000 improvment loan plus interest to pay and ended up with a $950,000 property, just to come out even, dollar-wise, you'll need $275,000 or more down payment from your buyer. Add to this the cash you want to realize, since you won't take all of your equity on a contract and you'll be trying to get 400 grand down on a $950,000 property. If you have an assumable balloon payment due a couple of years after you sell the project, the down will be less and the balloon still liveable.

I've also bought properties through realtors and had a balloon payment in a year or two to cover their commissions. Another common method of getting in as cheaply as possible with low payments is to structure a deal with a *20 or 30 year amortization*, and a 100% balloon in three, five or ten years.

For example, if you buy a building for $100,000 and pay $10,000 down, the balance of $90,000 would be put on a 30 year payback which would give you low monthly payments. At the same time your seller doesn't trust the economy and doesn't want to get payments for 30 years so the contract specifies that the entire unpaid balance will be paid in full in five years, or whenever mutually agreed upon. You are betting that you'll either find a buyer to cash out the whole balance or find some mortgage money to refinance it by the due date. At times the money supply is loose or tight and buyers seldom cash out on a property so there's a little risk. On the other hand there's a potential profit and you may transfer your position to your eventual buyer, make your profit, and let him worry about the balloon payment.

The next idea to consider is *THE COST OF LIVING INCREASE.* Some of the possibilities for creative financing are more apt to make you sick to your stomach than others, but this one will work better than most. This is a killer unless you have a super-duper, can't fail deal. This method raises the balance due on a note each year by the rise in the national cost of living index increases. This can only work for you in a very high profit deal.

If you have seller who is terrified that the inflation rate will eat up any value he has in his contract with you, you agree to keep the balance up with inflation. If you bought a $110,000 property, paid $10,000 down and the $100,000 balance on a 20 year mortgage, at the end of the first year, on the principal amount you'd owe him $100,000. less the pay-down from the mortgage payments, plus the rise in the cost of living index times the unpaid principal balance.

TOTAL price of property $110,000

Down payment in cash   <u>10,000</u>

Balance payable   100,000

Monthly payments approximately   1,000

First year principal reduced by about $200 per month.

$800 interest plus $200 principal off monthly payment.

Principal reduced approximately   2,000

Principal due at end of first year   98,000

Now here's the killer.

The U.S. Government cost of living index rose this year by 12%, for example. That is used to multiple the

unpaid principle balance.   + 11,760.

New principal balance due is   109,760.00

Now, one year later, your payoff is nearly $12,000 more than the year before. Your payments will increase and can never even keep the balance even. It will grow and grow.

If that's the case, why would you ever use this technique? It would be nearly impossible to sell a property with this financial arrangement attached to it.

The only times it would be good would be if you were buying the property very low and you are *CERTAIN* that you can cash out of the deal, that is sell it for 100% cash within a reasonable period of time. Or, at least, sell with enough cash to cover the original loan and take your equity on a contract. You may also buy it, knowing that you can refinance later on.

There is a lot of exposure in this method, but it *is* a way to get a property from someone who is afraid of their value eroding. I bought a large commercial building with a cost of living increase in it and that cost increase didn't harm the deal at all. It wasn't a great deal for other reasons but the cost increase was alright.

Another technique is to *RAISE THE PRICE AND LOWER THE INTEREST*. People are funny. Many of them would rather sell a property for $150,000 at 9% interest than at $125,000 at 12% interest. They'll have more capital gains taxes to pay at the higher price if they cash out, but on a repayment schedule the payments at either price come out about the same. Mentally, they know they got the higher price and they don't place as much importance on the interest. Many older people place more value on a high interest. Judge the situation yourself and see what is most important to them. If you're following my advice, the building is worth $175 or $200 grand, anyway, so either $125,000 or $150,000 are alright for a purchase price. The advantage to you of going on the lower amount and higher interest is that, while the payments would work out the same dollar-wise, there will be more interest in each payment at $125,000 at 12%, than $150,000 at 9%. The interest is tax deductable right off the top of your income, so that's a plus. On the other hand, if you have a higher sales price, you can allow more money to the building or property and depreciate a larger amount. In that case you have that tax advantage. This is where a good accountant is important.

He can protect you from excess taxes by helping you structure your deals. The interest deduction is important and so is the depreciation. Get an accountant who is careful and covers his rear-end, but who is also creative and aggressive. Occasionally he'll make a wrong choice, but he'll always have a good reason.

If you have an audit he'll have all of the paperwork ready to go. You may have to pay a little interest or penalty here and there but a creative and courageous accountant can save you so much more than a conventional, by-the-book type.

Many C.P.A.'s go right down the book and pass over so many possible exclusions and deductions. A good accountant will tell you about allocating values and depreciation, and a hundred other allowances and make all of them work for you.

I have a friend who got a call from his accountant who told him to push down an old building on one of this properties. He had a week to do it in, and it would save him $60,000 in his yearly tax bill. The accountant had worked and reworked the figures and come up with the need for a small, 100% depreciation. That called for the removal of a building, somewhere, with a cost allocated to the building in a contract, large enough to cover the potential tax he had calculated. He had lots of buildings from which to choose. He needed one that wasn't covered by a mortgage, since you can't destroy loan security. So, they pushed down a little building and eliminated the last $60,000 of potential tax. The deduction could never be questioned since it was clearly valued at $60,000 in the contract, and the building couldn't then be appriased, since it had been torn down.

This accountant was superb in his structuring. It would have taken him five minutes to prepare for an I.R.S. audit since he was always ready with paperwork and explanations for everything.

A year or two before my friend had ended up with no taxes due at all, as usual, except for $11 due to the state. Creative and tenacious enough, and unwilling to let the $11 get away from him, the accountant searched and searched and found a way in which my multi-millionaire friend qualified for a poverty exclusion which eliminated the $11 tax. It was all honest and open and solid. (An update: This year he got back 13¢ more than he paid in.)

Well, the kinds of interest and depreciation advantages which a good accountant and good attorney can generate will be of tremendous help in structuring your deals in the first place.

In our example of the $125,000 to $150,000 contract, either way could be an advantage to you, depending on your situation.

My point here is that sometimes you can raise the price, lower the interest, or lower the price and raise the interest, get the property and have the monthly payments the same at either price. The important thing is to get the property and if the sellers want to go through these gymnastics you can do it.

Another method available to structure a deal with a reluctant seller is to have a *VARIABLE INTEREST RATE* on the contract. In this type of contract, the principal amount stays the same and the interest will rise or fall each year, keyed to the prime lending rate.

In most cases this is a can of worms, since no one has any idea what the interest will be next year. Once again, the acceptability of this method hinges on how badly you want the property, how much you'll make on it and how fast you'll make it. The difference between a few points in interest is astounding. But, it may be a way to get a really great property. If you're contract was written at 12% and you agreed to rise, point for point, with the prime rate, your interest could go up 6 or 8% in one year. Be careful with this just as you are with the cost of living index increases. There are plenty of deals around with low prices, fixed principal amounts and low, fixed interest and you normally won't use these methods unless the deal is so good that it makes your "heart flutter."

You might also use a *graduated mortgage payment.* These payments are smaller in the early years and larger in the later years. The thinking here, is that the rents will go up each year and cover the increasing payments. This can return the full mortgage amount, circumvent balloon payments, and still allow you to acquire the property and have low initial payments.

Insist on an early payoff without penalities so you can take advantage of the low early payments and still refinance or sell the property and avoid the higher payments later.

In summary, there is almost always a way to structure a deal to get a property you want. Maybe you don't have a down payment. You can promise them something later on that is better than a down payment now. There are incentives and premiums to offer and advantages to acquaint them with that will swing almost any deal. But, make sure you are covered and can fulfill the obligations you've encumbered.

All of these methods are tools which, coupled with your positive personality and self-confidence and natural assumption of getting the deal through, will allow you to be creative and flexible. It's all part of your entire approach to the whole wealth concept. *It can be done.*

You just need to find the way and put it together.

CHAPTER TWENTY-FIVE

Making A Silk Purse Out Of A Sow's Ear

As I went to an appointment today I drove by a furniture store that was having a grand opening. It had actually been open for several months but had obviously never really got off the ground. The building was acceptable, I'm sure the products are also fine, but it has one great problem: Location. If that store stays there for a hundred years it will never really succeed because it isn't in the right place. Not that it's on a side-street or anything like that. In fact, it's on the busiest commercial street around.

I've had off-street and side street locations that, properly promoted, were very successful and exciting.Some things are so obvious but no one seems to stop and think about it. People will rent a good building in a poor location and assume it will be successful for their business, and they'll overlook a poor, or old building in a good location.

The location being good has a lot to do with traffic pattern, accessability, proximity to other businesses which are successful and/or draw traffic. But some people just don't think.

I don't know who designed the small Susan B. Anthony dollar, but if they had asked me, or one of my children, first, we could have told them that it looked like a quarter and wasn't designed right. Perhaps they could have left it the same size but made it a definite hexagon. Anything but what they did.

For years American Motors designed odd-looking cars that never kept the same radical designs for long, my recollections are that their corporate performance, except for the Jeep Division, was never great after their hey-days with George Romney. I'm sure that they have a very extensive and skilled design department, but if they had only stopped a ten year old kid on the street he could have told them it was an ugly car. It was so obvious, but they kept on building them. That's a very large corporation and their design and planning always escaped my understanding.

So, as I drove by this furniture store this morning, I thought that it is so obviously in the wrong place. Why would they put a business in there? As I mentioned, I've had off-street locations for my businesses but they had some elements of success. It's not neessarily that they have to be major street locations. In any case, my point here is that while you are looking for properties that appeal to you, in the first place, look more carefully. And in the second place, sometimes you don't have to look carefully at all. Just open your eyes.

It is so elementary but it is overlooked so often. Let me give you two examples from my personal experience. While looking for new rental units to buy I looked at a duplex and fourplex which were priced low enough to consider. As I approached the neighborhood where they were located, I said to myself, before I even found the buildings...."You might as well quit looking, since they could be gold plated and still not be worth anything out here. Anyway, I soon found them and, to my surpirse, they were very nice buildings and the price was quite low for the money invested in them. However, they didn't fit into the neighborhood which was quite run down. For an *extremely* low price they would have been worth considering but they were simply locked into a losing situation.

If a person had purchased many surrounding properties and improved them also and made a large enough island of improved properties, they would have had an appeal, of sorts, but certainly not as they were. They never did sell, even at lower and lower prices. So you may be thinking that that all seems so simple. You could just tell by looking that it was a bad area or a bad property.

On the other hand, a few years back, I saw an old motel property located on a major street. It was very deep, a large property, but very run-down and unappealing. I described in another chapter how I acquired the property. Although it was a real dump and would be viewed by most people as a rat's nest, when I looked at it I could visualize a small shopping center. I saw the adjoining properties and noticed, over a period of time how much business the other stores nearby were doing. I could see some adjoining owners selling to me and the general prices involved. I could "see" what could be done with the property to make a beautiful property out of it. How corners could be cut here and there, some structural changes and lots of cosmetic improvements.

That's really what I could see in front of me when I saw the place. Other people I described it to could never visualize what I told them. To give you a couple of ideas of how to actually make a silk purse out of a sows ear, or a beautiful improved property out of a rat's nest for very little money, I'll describe what I did with this motel property and a couple of others.

The first example is a three bedroom house located in a medium sized city. I bought it very cheaply since it was run down and neglected. If it had only been painted and so on, it would have reflected an increase in value but I wanted to get the maximum spread, of course, so I looked through our magic improvers glasses and "saw" what could create the maximum change for the least money. The sellers could see how run down the property was and they had to move away quickly so the purchase price was right.

Many of the standard changes were taken care of, of course. Paint, vinyl, carpet, a new door or two and trim paint on the exterior. BUT, since I knew we wouldn't own this house forever, we watched our improvements carefully. We could have replaced all of the windows and put in double pane insulated glass, but it wouldn't have returned any greater amount of money. We could have replaced all of the heating system, but instead we just got it cleaned and repaired. I put in a new bathroom sink and toilet. I had a plumber put them in but, of course, didn't buy them from him. As you work on your properties more and more you'll get sources for everything. At first you'll dislike paying retail and, after a while, you'll even avoid paying wholesale. You'll buy things on close outs, out of season, etc. and when you need a toilet for a repair you'll have one stuck away somewhere. So I put in a new toilet or perhaps a used one out of another property.

The garage wasn't well-situated so I insulated, panelled and carpeted the garage to make a family room out of it. That was all very inexpensive, and it added another very large room. A new screen door and yard clean-up and it was complete.

After perhaps only $2,500 in improvements, I raised the rent $80 a month which resulted in our $80 X 100 = $8,000 increased in value in just a couple of weeks. Besides that I bought it cheap and could take some time to sell it at a high price. It was in a fairly nice neighborhood and, when cleaned up, fit right in with the other homes. This is a simple matter of buying a property, a fixer-upper in a good area, and doing what thousands of people have done. Everyone knows about fixer-uppers, but many people fail to see a beautiful home in an old dump.

Many people purchase a home or income unit to fix up, but don't think about the location. I've seen plenty of deals where a person puts a few thousand down on a fixer-upper in a poor location, does the work, only to find that they can't even get *their* money back out, let alone any profit or equity.

Properties in poor locations don't normally appreciate as fast as those in better areas. All of this doesn't mean that the sole criteria for selecting a building is the condition of the surrounding buildings, but how can improving one building change the character of an entire area? Normally it can't. I've had buildings, homes and apartments, in older areas, too, but they either had access to traffic, close to a school, behind a business area, or were in some way isolated from the other properties, so that that property, on its own had some logical selling feature.

You can learn to see what can be done with a property and not judge it for how it seems to be at first glance. I have seen literally hundreds of homes on which a buyer could make several thousand dollars simply by painting it. Or putting in a room of new carpet and nailing up half a dozen sheets of $10 panelling.

There are so many things to do to a property. Often we look at a dilapidated or run-down building and think that the entire structure needs to be rebuilt. Or it seems like it. There are a few ideas, off the top of my head, that I've used many times that are both cheap and dramatically improving.

For example, let's take a simple house. You can spend $300 and put a rough-cut pine wainscot along the front and nail up some shutters to match. The shutters, in this example would be made out of two 1 X 2's nailed horizontally with two 1 X 6's nailed vertically on top of them. In other words the 1 X 1's would be the cross-frame behind the 1 X 6's. This would be very cheap, but the shutters would match the wainscot and the whole front of the house would look 100% better.

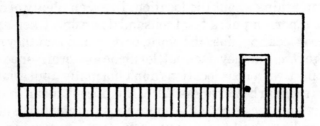

Remember that often your buyers will form quick opinions and this cheap improvement will present a good front. As they enter they see a newly carpeted room, also, to one side, a new $100 cast iron fireplace with some precast brick panels behind will give you that as an additional selling point. And the list could go on and on. But, all cheap, cosmetic and they provide a dramatic difference.

These units are all over the place and the only reason you won't do a lot of them is that you'll progress to larger deals.

But, even on the houses, you can make plenty. You may only buy it for $8,000 under value and improve it for $1,000 but the $1,000 can raise its value $5,000. And if you find the right buyer, one that just *has* to have this house, they'll pay you $2,000 to $5,000 OVER VALUE so you'll end up with about $16,000, plus or minus. If you've put this deal together the way you should have you'd only have paid $2,000 to $5,000 down, hopefull borrowed, or else agreed to pay them the $5,000 down payment plus a $1,000 premium if they'll wait 10 months for the down. Ten months doesn't sound like a whole year. Anyway, in this example you've purchased a fixer-upper in a good enough area, not necessarily the best, but not the worst, and you've made ten or fifteen grand on it. The front appearance was dramatically changed, even though it only involved some rough pine and a can of stain. I've done wainscots like I've described and they can usually be completely finished in one day, with just one or two people working. Saw, nail and stain. Don't let anyone make it sound any more difficult than that. This wainscot idea is also very worthwhile if you've made another room out of a garage, extended a room, closed in a porch or changes like that, since they usually change the surface appearance substantially, are noticeable changes, and need a continuous, end-to-end surface to tie them together and make them appear uniform.

On the motel property I bought, my plans were fulfilled as I had first visualized them in my mind. I paid $135,000 for the property with $40,000 down (borrowed, naturally). I should have paid less down, but the seller insisted on this amount and I really wanted the property. The price was less than half of what I would have paid anyway. When others looked at this property they saw a bunch of run down old rooms. I saw solid walls and roof and sound foundations and the shell of a dozen small shops and stores. My first step was to tear down the motel signs and put up an 8' X 20' sign with an artistic representation of what the final project would look like.

Then I gutted the entire interior of one building, and in the end of that building nearest the street, I put in my own donut shop. I already had another donut shop and wanted one for my project, and it was easy to convince myself on how attractive the building would be when we were finished.

So, the tenant and location were perfect for that business. There was a super-high traffic flow. Since the roof was a gable-type and we wanted a boxy appearance for the shop I had them put a full facade around the entire store. This sounds more difficult than it was. They simply nailed 18 foot long 2 X 4's horizontally around the entire perimeter, put 1 X 12 rough-cut cedar boards, 18' long, on end all the way around the building and put 1 X 2 batts, 18' long over the seams between the boards. They let the ends of the gable roof protrude through this facade, and nailed gingerbread (decoratively cut 1 X 12 and 1 X 6 and 1 X 2 boards, scalloped) on the gable ends and around the top of the facade.

We ended up with the exterior 100% covered, with no trace of an old building.

We then put a wooden sidewalk and railings around the building, added beautiful back lit signs and the entire exterior looked brand new.

Inside, we removed most of the walls, added beams and posts for support, utilized existing electric and plumbing sources and covered every inch of old surface. We used panelling, plastering, vinyl and formica and made sure that all surfaces were covered with new material. Thus, the entire outside and inside were completely new, and no one would have known that inside it all was an old building.

The next unit in that building was an ice cream parlor. Visualize, if you can, two buildings thirty feet wide and one hundred thirty feet in length with a big parking lot between them. The two ends front the street. The end of one building has been rebuilt into a beautiful, old fashioned donut shop. The next section of the building then becomes an ice cream parlor. All exterior surfaces have been covered, but on this one, to contrast with the vertical facade on the donut shop, I left the sloped roof exposed and shingled it with cedar shakes. The inside was completely rebuilt. All interior surfaces were recovered, as in the donut shop, so that it was a completely new building.

If you were to do a property like this one, you have to let your imagination flow with the existing walls, floor levels and what has to be done to make the floors structurally sound, etc. As you let your mind melt into your project you can "see" how it will all happen. You can also "see" how to make it happen cheaply. A pessimist sees a wall that's kicked in and must be removed and replaced. You will see a wall that only needs five sheets of $10 panelling. A pessimist sees a floor that is irregular and must be torn out. You see a floor that needs thirty sheets of $10 particle board over it and $600 worth of commercial carpet, which you got from your cheap carpet source.

A pessimist gets an electrical contractor that only thinks in thousands. You and I find an electrician who counts in hundreds and will give you very low prices for the prospect of continuing work. He's a new fellow in his profession and NEEDS the work. From my own experience $20 an hour carpenters don't pound any more nails than $6 an hour carpenters, if you find the right ones and the $6 an hour guys will usually work harder too. You may not think all of this makes that much difference but you'll save HALF of your rebuilding costs on your proeprties by always *"seeing"* the economical way to improve them. And, if you save half, you can do twice as many projects with the same amount of money.

The last section of this building became a sandwich shop. Inside we removed the ceiling and used the vaulted roof to add a more open appearance. I bought mirrors and reprints in fancy frames for the walls and the finished appearance was very striking. While all of this was going on I bought the adjoining property for $100,000 to continue the same type of reconstruction.

I still had one more motel building, but wanted to get the adjoining piece before the entire project was completed and the adjacent property values raised. On the piece next door, I paid $15,000 down (borrowed) leaving a balance of $85,000, and payments of $900 a month. There was a tenant for the property and the rent paid the mortgage payment and I knew that the tenant would stay until we wanted to double the size of the mall. Where did I get the money for the remodelling and rebuilding? Earnings from my businesses, which I was continuing to operate and expand to provide cash flow, bank loans which were always falling together, buying and selling other properties, and from money saved. When deals are all said and done there are usually a few bucks left over.

After building these first three units in the first motel building, I then built a beauty shop in the second motel building. Since my sign was up showing what the completed project would look like and since the public could see the plan being fulfilled, there were lots of calls from people interested in renting space.

In order to spend as little of my own money as possible on the project, since I was buying income properties every week, I worked out a unique arrangement with the beauty shop tenant. In order to complete the rebuilding quickly I had the tenant prepay the rent seven years ahead. The reasons they would do this are as follows:

1- They could custom design their space.

2- Their lease payments were calculated at a lower rate.

3- Their option to renew the lease was at a lower figure.

4- I had others willing to pre-pay and these people wanted the space.

I used the money from their rent pre-payment to rebuild their space, and had a completed building which I owned and had no investment in. When I bought the property all I paid for was the land, since the buildings were obviously so worthless. So I had no personal money in the beauty shop structure or the rebuilding. If you were doing this but wanted some cash flow too, you could collect a partial pre-payment and get a smaller lease payment to you each month, but, for example, with no lower option to renew the lease. The ways to organize the deals are endless and we'll get more into them later. But you can and I did present a package that will be accepted.

We did the beauty shop unit in a box design, modified from the donut shop and a magic shop next to it with a higher box design to provide the appearance of completely separate stores and buildings. My theme on this project was an old West design and we put covered wooden sidewalks all around the store fronts to give it an authentic appearance.

All of the exteriors were wood with designs copied from books on the old West and the finished appearance looked like a main street from an old West village.

The next unit was an electronic repair shop and the adjoining one was an installation shop for car stereos. In that unit we had to raise the ceiling to 14' and since they had to rebuild the whole roof, instead of using the existing pitched roof, I had them add a second story of apartment-offices.

Most of the existing roofs were hidden behind vertical facades and couldn't be seen. We reshingled the hidden roofs with asphalt shingles and the exposed roofs with rustic cedar shakes.

The next unit was a large store which I designed with four separate exteriors on it and with the interior walls, restrooms and so on, designed so that, for perhaps $2,000 we could add three interior walls and divide the space into four separate stores when the need arose. I used this large space for my stereo store and the need to divide would have arisen when we built our new store across the back of the property.

That left a small shop in the end of the second building which we refinished, giving me twelve rental units in buildings which appeared to be brand new, with relatively little of my own money invested, and full title in my name. I got bids on repaving the parking lot and ended up getting a good job done for half the average bid price. As this project proceeded we got beautiful signs, back-lit with plastic faces, all in varied shapes and old West designs and the completed project really looked fantastic.

I had a sign company look around the country to find a used sign with which to build a large sign for my plaza and they found one. They gave me a price for the sign which was lowered a couple of times, like all the prices, since the sign company wanted to continue doing my work. I think they did about half a million dollars in work for me on various projects, and they always tried to get my business. Anyway, they ended up manufacturing a sign about 90 feet high which was completely rebuilt and refaced and added to the finished appearance of the first property in a grand style.

I've gone into some detail here concerning improving this particular property and how some of the work was done to show you that you can end up with a very beautiful and rentable property when starting out with a very unattractive piece. You don't have to spend a fortune, and just because you may get a good deal on an imaginative exterior doesn't make it any less attractive.

If you do a project like this one, you may or may not want to keep it. ONE PROPERTY like this will provide you with an excellent living for the rest of your life. Or, you can sell it and leverage the money into larger deals. In my next deal after this one I spent over two million dollars on a building. The sky is the limit.

Just for your own information: as I've travelled around the country I've noticed a great opportunity in almost every city; old motels, just like the one I bought and developed.

They are usually near the perimeter of the original city which has by now been engulfed by expansion and they are now in the middle of business districts. They are virtually all on high traffic streets. They have parking lots or property to add parking, and the basic structures are perfect for converting into small offices or retail spaces. You probably will pay for the land and very little for the buildings since they are so old. Motels like these usually generate low incomes so the value of the property isn't predicated on income multiples. These properties are usually deep so when you buy by the front footage on the street you'll come out ahead. These buildings are usually 25' to 35' deep which is an ideal depth for shops or offices.

Plumbing and electric may be usable the way it is. For example, the bedroom in one unit could be an office and the bathroom, rebuilt, could stay where it was. If a large office is desired, take out an adjoining wall and use two units with the second bathroom becoming a storage room. That keeps most of the interior walls intact. Use some posts and beams to vault the ceilings and it will appear to be much more roomy and open. You might add a second floor over part of the structure, not only for additional footage, but for a variable design. On the outside you could leave the exterior surface there but cover it with stone, brickwainscot, wood or anything to give it a new surface appearance.

Pour a new sidewalk and repave the parking lot. Get a cheap sign identifying your project, making sure that the sign looks expensive and professional, and your old cheap motel property has become a new, luxurious commerical space. These motel properties are everywhere and most of them could be converted this way. After I did my conversion a friend of mine converted a motel he owned and ended up with a really beautiful plaza. His theme was an old south, New Orleans style, while mine was old West. There are so many themes to use. A theme serves a couple of purposes. It ties all of the "separate-buildings" together, and it gives some character to the entire project.

There are thousands of other types of sows ears ready to be made into silk purses. Just use your imagination.

When you look at a twenty unit apartment bulding with a basement used for storage, learn to see the basement as four more units, just waiting for completion. All it takes is a few dividing walls, some sheetrock and carpet. Some cheap electrical and plumbing and you have four new units for perhaps one third of the cost of new construction. Even less than one third.

Remember how this reflects on your financial statement. You may spend $10,000 or $15,000 on the four units (learn to think in low figures like this when it's your money or money you've borrowed), and you'll rent them for $250 a month each which raises your monthly income on the property by $1,000 and the value of your building ($1,000 X 100) by $100,000, JUST BY SEEING THE BASEMENT AS FINISHED UNITS.

On another deal I located a property that had ten one bedroom apartments, very small, with a small kitchen and small bath as part of each individual building.

I don't know why these cottages were ever built as individual units, perhaps for more privacy but each of the units was 12 feet wide and 15 feet deep. The buildings were built 12 feet apart on the property and the entire back of the property was unused. There wasn't even a lawn in the back. Each little unit had a gas wall heater and the plumbing was sound and intact. Each unit also had its own power service and meter. The roofs were sound and overall, the property was in good condition. It was old and poorly designed, but sound. Almost anyone looking at this property would see 10 old units renting for $100 a month or $1,000 total monthly income X 100 = a value of $100,000.

Since little had been done to improve the property and it was in a stable area with no great demand or large tract purchases being made, I was certain that it could be picked up, when all was said and done, for about $70,000. When I looked at that property I saw three major possibilities within just a couple of minutes.

First, these units were built at ground level, with the cement pad right on the ground, and a cement floor could easily be poured between each building by just putting 2 X 6's across the front and back and pouring in 2 or 3 yards of cement. You wouldn't have to dig any footings because there wouldn't be any load bearing walls on the new floor. After the floor was in a front and back wall could be placed between each two units. These walls nail together on the ground in fifteen minutes each, literally. You can nail them on the ground, tilt 'em into place and nail into the adjoining secure walls on the existing units. Make the front wall 6" higher than the back wall, nail your flat-roof 1 X 6's into place from front to back and cover with plywood, then tar and gravel.

Thus, you have created 9 new spaces which can:

Second, be used as large (12 X 15) bedrooms or living rooms for each of the existing units. They each already have a wall heater and those units would heat the additional rooms. There would be no new plumbing and the only necessary electrical work was to add one light and wall plug in each room. The wall plugs come through the walls from the existing plugs. One switch and one light in each new area, and the rooms would be complete.

Third, with the addition, across the back of the 12 X 15 space of a small bathroom and small kitchen area, nine completely new units could be created. This would also require new electrical service to each unit so the extra expense would be for electrical, plumbing and the kitchen times nine units.

Let's see how these figures would go together on this project:

Original value	$100,000
Purchase price	70,000

Conversion to 9 bedroom

Units   16,000

For the rear of the property a new sidewalk for $400, lawn for $800 and bushes for $200 make the entire property more desirable, rentable and livable.

Improvement to rear yard $1,400

Three foot rough-cut pine

wainscot across the entire

fronts of old and new buildings

to tie together visually   1,100

Total investment in property $88,500

As you've seen, with 9 spaces between 20 buildings, one unit was left with the small size. So we have 9 units with new rooms. The rooms previously rented for only $100 per month. After improving they would rent for an extra $25 because of general improvements (wainscot, lawn, trees, walk and paint), and $100 more the extra 12 X 15 room. So nine of the units now bring $225 per month and one brings $125 or a total of $2,150 per month. If we had converted the nine separate rooms to nine new apartments the total conversion cost would have been about $20,000 more and the units would have rented for the $125 a month with twenty grand more invested. That's why $25 a month more than the use as additional bedrooms, at $100 extra per month. That $25 X 100 = $25,000 increase in value of the property over the other alternative but we'd have to have spent $20,000 to get the $25,000 increase in value.

So, obviously the best use was for extra bedrooms. So we'd end up being in the property a total of $88,500 with a monthly income of $2,150 or a multiple value of $215,000. In this example we'd make a profit of $126,500 on the property, even though the improvements are new they constitute a general repair or improvement to an OLD property. As for taxes you can depreciate your value very fast, since it's really an older structure, maybe even as short as five to eight years.

When selling, if you need to sell under value, considering this isn't in a prime growth area, you could knock 10% or $21,500 off the price and sell for $193,500 less $5,500 sales commission or closing costs and end up with an equity of $118,000 on your cash investment of $25,000 for six months. They would agree to wait for the down payment for 12 months, considering the substantial improvements planned. When sold the buyer pays 20% down (which is less than the oft-quoted 29%) or $45,000 in cash. He assumes the first of $70,000, owes us $73,000 on a second mortgage. The $45,000 down payment repays us our $25,000 investment and twenty grand besides. Then we have $73,000 coming on a second which we can collect at $800 a month or sell the second mortgage at a discount.

This deal is not only good for us but we sold it to the buyer for 10% under the value multiple. He got a good deal, he has a beautiful property. The tenants are happy because they have new rooms and an improved property. The first mortgage holder is happy because his security, the property, is improved and we are happy because of the excellent return. Besides that, this would be a fun project. Ultimately, I didn't end up doing this particular deal because it ended up in a complicated estate. But you can see how I did the mental planning that would have culminated in buying and improving this property. If you do this type of thinking as you look at properties, their potential and available improvments will qualify or disqualify the deal.

I've done many other improvements like this and the results have always been excellent.

You must always be careful on a project like this one. Some building codes require a complete rebuilding and bringing the *entire* property up to new codes if more than a certain percentage of value is proposed as the improvement. One method to sometimes circumvent this problem is to minimize the improvements and make it appear as a minor remodel rather than doubling the size of the whole project.

Sometimes you'll get a property that may eventually require a complete replumb or rewire, or all new roofs etc. Be sure, before you buy, that you know what HAS to be done to fulfill your plans on your property.

Make sure you don't try this on a dumpy property in a dumpy area. Make it a dumpy property in a nice or average, or at least clean area. If you can "steal" a property in a very neglected area and improve it by getting the work done for nearly nothing, you may make some money but be sure that you don't end up pouring a lot of money into an area with no appeal. Just use your head.

To give you a further idea on the preliminary consideration of a property, I'll outline another deal and how it was viewed by other buyers and myself. I'm recounting a few deals that I didn't ultimately put together simply to let you know how I learned to see potential and figure possible returns, upon which information to form a decision of whether or not to buy. You'll have some very good deals pass by you for one reason or another also. It's all part of the game. But you can get many of the good ones consummated.

On this property there was an even simpler means to drastically change the appearance of the property. You can find properties like this one too. This 8 unit apartment building had been owned by the same family for a long time and from that fact I supposed that they owed little or nothing on the property. They seemed very conservative. They had done a lot of improvements right out of the book, paint, carpet, yardwork, and so on.

The building was very neat, and in a clean neighborhood. In fact if had everything EXCEPT they had overlooked *the* most obvious characteristic. The building shape was very ugly and unattractive. It was a simple box building with nothing to break up the flat surfaces on each side and the flat roof. It was the most obvious thing, but because of its appearance they had been unable to make *ANY* deal on the property. There was one single improvement that the bulding needed to make it extremely attractive and it was an improvement that would cost less than $2,000 and literally take one day to do.

I'll outline this one improvement in detail so you can see exactly how simple and fast a dramatic improvement can be.

Three fellows to pound nails and two trips to the lumber yard could accomplish:

A mansard roof around the entire roof and small mansard overhangs above each window. It's as simple as this: One man carries 2 X 4's to the roof and the other two nail a single 2 X 4 one foot below the upper edge of the bulding and one on the top outer edge of the wall around the entire roof perimeter. Then 2 x 4 angle pices two feet on the pitched side and one foot on the straight side are nailed every two feet all around the perimeter of the roof, anchored into the two previously nailed 2 X 4's. Thus:

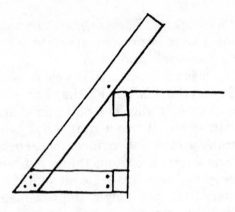

Then 4' X 8' sheets of 3/4" plywood are ripped into 2' X 8' lengths and 1' X 8' lengths. These are nailed under the edge and on the upper angled surface of the 2 X 4 angled assemblies thus:

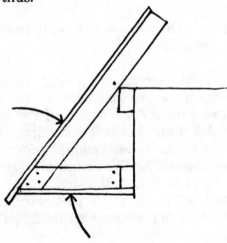

This same idea is also carried out above the windows and 1 X 12 rough pine shutters are nailed on each side of the windows onto two 1 X 2" horizontal boards underneath. The split singles are nailed on the roof surfaces and the underside of the mansard roof is painted very dark brown.

This isn't as much work as it sounds like. I've done this on buildings several times.

This quick and simple improvement would make a DRASTIC difference in the appearance of this property, and consequently in rentability and salability.

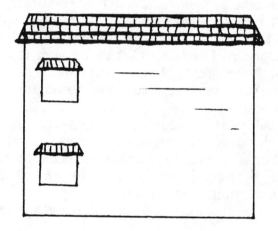

These small decorative roofs would break up the flat surfaces on the building and instead of a box it would look like a beautiful cottage. Whereas the owner couldn't even get offers, even very low ones. They were trying to sell very cheaply, with the bulding rebuilt they could have even sold at a premium. I didn't buy the building because the owner was too uppity. He had many years invested in the property and lots of work and effort in it and it seemed like the whole world to him. He felt badly that no offers were coming in but simultaneously he had an attitude that prevented any real dealing. It was as if we wanted to buy the World Trade Center and I didn't need the heartache so we skipped it. It's still sitting there.

I went into great detail in the previous paragraphs to describe exactly how I'd have done the construction just to illustrate how incredibly simple some of these improvements can be. It really is just as simple as I described. I used this building as an example since this quick fix was the ONLY improvement it needed. On other buildings that I've done this type of roof treatments and so on also required other work and were more involved.

In the case of this mansard roof treatment, since it wouldn't be a load-bearing roof the framing only had to hold the roof up, but not shed or hold water. Since it was not an expansive roof surface, only two feet high, it would only take 2 or 3 rows of split shingles and the shingles shouldn't have to be fire retardant since it wasn't an actual roof, just a decorative surface.

For $500 more they could have made it a cozy English tudor style by nailing stained 2 X 6's over the surface in the box and criss-cross pattern that creates the tudor design. I've never done a tudor design, but I have a friend who did this on a building in one afternoon.

In the previous example the family with the property didn't:

1- Ask a high price, confident that they'd get it.

2- See the most obvious necessary improvement.

3- Make much of an effort to sell and affronted prospective buyers.

4- Weren't flexible in their terms of sale.

But they were distraught that it wasn't selling.

I sold a building to a fellow a few years ago who could have made a good profit on it if he'd done only two or three simple things. He bought the building with only 2 tenants in it and room for two more. He never advertised once for tenants. He never did any repairs but he did make up the cash flow loss each month out of his moderate salary. And he felt really awful that the building wasn't making him money. So he decided to sell.

He asked around but never advertised and as the months passed he became very depressed with the property because it wasn't selling. How could it? All he had to do was clean it, rent it, advertise it and sell it. It was so obvious, just as many minor improvements are obvious, but many people just don't see them. There is equity just for the asking.

The point of all this is to simply see more in a property than it has now. And someitmes, it is cheap, fast and simple.

Remember in these property improvements you do to *KEEP THE COSTS DOWN.* As mentioned earlier you should get a young but able contractor or less expensive workers. Develop your sources for cheaper fixtures and materials and remember that, for the most part, improvements should be cosmetic. You can spend $5,000 removing all of the floor joists and replace them, instead of just repairing the bad ones, but you'll almost never get the non-cosmetic money out at the time of sale.

When you look at a house that has a carport but no garage learn to visualize the carport as two additional bedrooms. All that is needed is one interior wall, two exterior walls, a little cement to level the floor, carpet and paint. Then you've increased your floor space, number of bedrooms and value (rent) but with little money invested.

"See" an old house with small dingy rooms as just needing a few walls removed and some beams installed. I walked into a commercial bulding I was considering buying and, just inside the door, instantly, I could see that if they spent a few thousand dollars *and* put in a lowered, suspended ceiling, the entire building would look 100% better inside and they could raise their rents with their multiples equity raised fantastically. They could have done the ceiling for $5,000 more or less, and raised rents $40 a month on each unit. No one would have complained much since they could see the tremendous improvement in the appearance their monthly net would have been $400 more times 100 equals an instant increase in equity of $40,000 for $5,000 invested.

They'd have their $5,000 back in one year, the heating and air conditioning bills would have been less since the higher air space didn't have to be heated or cooled. And all of this was so obvious but no one had thought of it. I once built a very beautiful business in an awful looking building which had been flooded. The entire ceiling area was a mess and most people would have rebuilt it. Instead, we cleaned it and put in a suspended ceiling which covered all of the visible sins. No one ever saw the terrible mess above the ceiling. In this building, lowering the ceiling was great cosmetically and very simple. Everyone else saw the awful mess. I saw the new ceiling. Look for it.

You can learn to see properties this way. You don't have to make your money ten grand at a time. If you can buy and improve your properties as I've described, you'll get your wealth in larger and larger chunks.

I just read a book about real estate dealing in which the author outlines deals in which he'd made $10,000 or so in profit.

That's fine and ten grand will buy a lot of food but you should learn to watch every dollar carefully but think in larger and larger amounts. I don't gamble now and haven't for a long time, but when I did gamble my friends and I progressed from flipping a coin for a few dollars a flip, to a hundred a flip, then to a thousand a flip. A couple of times I flipped for ten grand and it all seemed normal because of the progression from smaller to larger amounts. I'd suggest that you don't gamble at all. Flipping like that was one of the most careless things I've ever done, but my point was that you can learn to think in larger numbers and be at ease with them. Before long you'll be counting in hundreds of thousands and then millions. You can make your money in bigger chunks and one way to do it is by seeing the potential in properties. You can make your largest stacks of money by making something out of nothing, as opposed to making a small stack out of natural appreciation on a property that is already something. Look around you and you'll see the opportunies.

CHAPTER TWENTY-SIX

Options, Etc.

I met a wealthy fellow a while back who, as far as I know, made all of his money in real estate without ever buying or selling one piece of property. He carved out a niche and a bit of expertise in buying and selling only options.

Options to buy are agreements from a property owner to sell you a certain property at a designated price within a certain period of time. You pay him a deposit which secures the deal. If you don't exercise your option the money is forfeited but you aren't obligated further. You don't have to consummate the sale and have paid a certain price to have the option to buy the property. I've used options a few times and they have always worked out just fine and accomplished my goals. I've only let one option pass and not exercised it. In my own cases I used th options to secure a property to buy it, and not to go out and find a buyer before the option expired. I used the option time to line up financing or fit the new property into my program.

You may find an excellent piece of property but lack all of the down payment or else lack the ability to carry a negative cash flow. The few months or weeks or years you have to exercise the option may give you the time you need to structure your deal. If it doesn't come together you forfeit your deposit but aren't bound to buy the property. This has exposed you to the opportunity the property affords without the responsibility.

The option is good for the property owner since he can't lose. If the sale falls though, he has your deposit. If it goes through on the other hand, he's sold the property for prearranged terms. After signing you will ALWAYS GET AN OPTION RECORDED ON THE TITLE.

In fact, every rental agreement, lien, lease option or other legal document pertaining to a property you own or are acquiring should be taken to the county recorder at the court house and attached to the title on the property. It will cost you a few dollars but will legally bind the property owner or his successors, including potential purchasers, to the terms of your option agreement or lease or whatever. If you are the property owner don't remind anyone about this. Give yourself all the flexibility you can.

I once leased a building from a fellow and made some lease-hold improvements in the amount of about $100,000. This entire amount was credited toward future rents. In addition, when the pre-paid rents ran out I got a couple of options to renew the lease at very small payments. This deal was good for the owner since I put a hundred grand in his building and good for me since it was all credited toward rent. It may sound like a poor investment, a hundred grand in someone else's buiding, but I put in a solid-gold business that generated a tremendous profit, so it was all worthwhile. I got the hundred grand back lickety-split and still owned the business with no lease payments. Anyway, as soon as I got the lease signed I had it recorded on the title so the lease would go with the property in case of a sale.

Sure enough, sometime later the owner was trying to sell and I was contacted about why we had the attachment recorded on the title. I explained it and refused to release it. Another buyer may or may not have been bound by the lease but when it was on the title he could only get the title subject to the lease.

All together we had the building tied up for eighteen years, and the lease payment in eighteen years would only be $1200 per month. It was a good thing I had it recorded. Always get your options recorded. Then if the owner makes any other effort to sell the property the interested party, alerted by the title search, will have to wait until your option expires or buy it from you.

Typically, to buy an option, you would approach a property owner trying to sell or willing to sell his property. Often, a piece of property that has no for sale sign, isn't advertised or listed with an agent, will still be for sale at the right price. Options, psychologically, have an advantage sometimes over a direct offer to buy. It makes the transfer seem more distant and inconclusive. The sale won't necessarily go through and in the mean time the owner has some of your money. If you buy options on property while never intending to ever purchase it yourself, you are just betting your deposit that you'll find a buyer before the option expires.

Let's assume that the aforementioned is your program. You are only interested in buying options, not properties.

You find a twenty unit apartment builidng that is for sale for $600,000. Using the methods we've discussed you got the price down to $500,000 and you've got the terms acceptable to both sides: $75,000 down and the balance on a 30 year payout at 12% interest. Your proposal has given you a good deal but you don't have the down payment. Because the property is in a prime location and because you got a hundred grand off the price you feel certain you could turn the property within three months.

229

So, you inform the seller that you are considering the deal but would like a 180 day option to close the sale. You'll pay him $2,000 up front for the option. If you go through with the sale, he's sold his property. If not, he keeps the $2,000. He has a live body (you) interested in his property, with some cash in hand, and he goes along with the option deal.

In your option, you include in the wording for "buyer" the following: "John Doe, or his assigns." Assigns would be anyone you assigned or transferred your interest to. This language is rather innocuous and shouldn't alarm anyone but allows you to legally sell your option or position. The logic for settling for a seemingly small amount for an option is that you wouldn't pay for the option if you weren't interested in the property. The option isn't a down payment. And it's his to keep in any case. Normally even a $100,000 bulidng would only require $500 or $1,000 for an option. Maybe even less.

A small duplex option may only cost $200 or $300. They want a buyer and you are a buyer willing to pay a little cash. It's a good deal. You may also agree to a little higher price if they'll take an option.

For example: You've found a duplex for sale for $60,000. Naturally you first get the price down to $50,000 or less. Let's say you ended up at $50,000 with $5,000 down. You've offered $500 for an option good for 120 days but the seller is reluctant. You've gone over the deal with him several times and he's nearly forgotten the original $60,000 figure. You've forgotten the higher price too, and act as if $50,000 always was the price.

He wants to sell to you and the price is alright but he wants more for the option, let's say $1,000. You're 90% sure that within four months you'll have the $5,000 down, the property at $50,000 is a good buy and you definitely want it, but you only have $500 for the option. If he'll accept the 120 day option you'll raise the price, if necessary, to $52,000. The price is still low. All of these possibilities hinge on how badly you want the property and how many *"spiffs"* it can support. The variables are innumerable. You may pay him only $100 for the option but raise the price $1,000 and offer a $5,000 balloon payment off the unpaid principal in five years. That is a slight complication when you sell the property. You'll have to pass on the balloon. The important thing here is that you've locked up the property. Now you can go out and find your buyer or leasee, someone who will rent or lease the property once you have the title in your name. Or you will have found a buyer if you're only interested in flipping the deal.

Within four months all you have to do is find another party to take your position. It's not as hard as it seems, but in any case your only exposure is the option payment.

Let's say that you settled on $50,000 with $5,000 down and the balance at 12% on a 20 year contract. The seller has a first mortgage for $30,000 and he'll carry a second for his $20,000 equity. You arrange an escrow account at his bank and when the payment comes in each month, the bank will send the first mortgage payment to the first holder, send the second to the seller, and keep track of all the payments and interest. Most banks charge $2 to $5 a month for this service, and that fee is usually split between the buyer and seller. The advantage of using a bank is that they keep accurate records and are less likely to foul things up. When you sell your position your buyer will feel more obligated to timely payments if they go through a bank. Anyway, as soon as you have your option signed, you advertise and search for a buyer.

You offer the property at $2,000 under value ($60,000) or $58,000, with $8,000 down and the $50,000 balance on a 20 year contract at 14%. This *is* under the $60,000 value and the down and interest are reasonable so you'll stick to your guns on this deal. You may have to flex a little but not much.

231

You have four months to *AGGRESSIVELY* pursue a buyer. By burning up the road you'll find your buyer and make money three ways on the deal.

In the first place they'll pay you $8,000 down and you only have to pay $5,000 down, as specified in your option, so you have three grand cash in your pocket.

Secondly, you'll still have a $5,000 equity in the property. This $5,000 will be paid to you out of the monthly bank escrow payment for 20 years.

Thirdly, you've added 2% to the interest rate. This will raise the entire principal amount payments each month and in addition to the payments on your $5,000 equity you'll get about $100 a month on the higher interest you charged. You have all of this potential for an investment of only $500 for the option.

Of course, instead of 20 year payments you can easily discount that amount and sell the contract.

Another common method utilizing the use of options is to arrange the purchase and get an option for as long a time as possible and use the time to find a partner on the property.

Your half of the partnership is to find the property, get the price down, get the terms arranged and secure the option.

Your partner's half of the deal is to provide the down payment on the property. The logic that would lead a person to be your partner in such a deal is that you have used your expertise for finding good, high profit deals, you bought the property well under value at excellent terms, and you are offering half of an excellent investment opportunity to your prospective partner. The down payment he'll make is relatively small, anyway, less than half the normal down and you're willing to accept half the responsibility. It's a super deal for him.

You may be able to structure a deal with a partner that will give him a very good return, in interest, on his investment, but he'll have no actual share of ownership in the property.

Many potential investors don't end up putting deals together because they lack the talent, inclination, or time. Many are professional people, doctors or lawyers. If they realized the money they could make they'd give up their practices and pursue careers that would pay them better. Many of these people simply can't put these deals together. After one or more good experiences with you, many of these investors will continue to fund your investments. If you go this partnership route, you'll collect half of properties right and left with no cash investment on your part.

Personally, I feel like partnerships of any kind are one rung below a five-to-life prison sentence but, in the abstract, there could be some good partnerships. There is so much exposure for misunderstandings, arguments, dissolutions and bad feelings.

I've never met anyone who was involved in a partnership that worked out, but I've read about some.

If you could somehow keep it copasetic and cooperative though, through using this method you can acquire tremendous equities in real estate with no investment except time. If you use the options to secure these deals while you're looking for a partner, they'll be easier to sell on the idea since the property is already on the hook and your exposure and liability for the option is limited.

CHAPTER
TWENTY-SEVEN

More Options And
Interest Spreads

There are many specialties in real estate. A person can isolate one type of deal he enjoys and develop his skill in one area and do very well specializing in that one thing.

A friend of mine buys and sells property all the time, and almost always buys and sells a piece for the same price or very near the same price. He always buys it at a good price, he always gets 90 to 120 days to close the deal, and he usually gets only one or two thousand dollars more than he paid or else the same price he paid.

So, how does he make money? Through an interest spread. He may buy on an assumable contract for 11% interest and sell at 12 or 13% interest. He'll pay $100 to $500 in earnest money. As little as posssible. After he signs the loan agreement he has three or four months to find another buyer at nearly the same price he paid. He may get a little for closing costs etc. and if he doesn't find a buyer he can either close the deal and keep the property for himself or until he finds a buyer, or he can sacrifice his earnest money.

If you do this make sure your only liability is the amount of your earnest money. You should insist that that is in the purchase or earnest money agreement. Also have the agreement drawn up for *you* "or your assigns." That wording lets you negotiate a sale to someone else. A way to back even your earnest money is to either have it noted as refundable if the sale is not consummated for any reason, or to put something like this in: "Sale subject to buyer's inspection and approval of electrical and plumbing." That's a way out. If you don't find your buyer in three or four months, declare the plumbing below your standards and cancel the sale. If you do get your buyer, he'll get a good buy and, even on a small property you can make $100 a month in the interest spread. Make sure your interests are fully assignable and that you won't retain a liability for payments.

Normally, in this type of deal you would establish an escrow account at a bank to make the divided payments each month.

Seller's price	$90,000
First mortgage	60,000
Second mortgage	30,000

Monthly payment on the first and second mortgages is $916 a month.

Monthly payment to you is $121.

When the person who buys from you sends in his payment, the bank, for a $2 or $3 a month fee, will send the mortgage payments and your interest difference to you. You really aren't being paid for your equity since you bought and sold the property for the same price. Your payment is the difference in the amounts collected for the interest rate you charged your buyer and what your seller charged you.

Your seller has agreed to release you from all liability but you are still in the escrow payments for receiving a check every month. You have no investment, no risk and a monthly check for twenty years. Do this dozens of times and you have a steady flow of small checks. Or bigger checks on bigger deals. After a year or so of doing this on a contract, you can either sell your position to someone for cash, since it's proven itself as a regular pay, or you can approach the person who bought from you to cash you out. Or, you can package your debt portfolio and sell it to an investor.

You may run across deals that have an extremely low interest, (don't be surprised, no offers are too low) and you may be able to get a 4 to 6% difference in interest rates. That could be hundreds of dollars a month. It happens every day. The interest spreads I've done have been only one or two percent, but still very worthwhile.

CHAPTER TWENTY-EIGHT

Refinancing Or 2 + 2 = 5

Through juggling mortgages, positions and equities you can, on some deals, come out with money in your pocket as well as owning a property. There are several aspects of refinancing which range from worthwhile realizations of equity into cash, to ending up owing 150% of the value on a property.

I know a fellow who had dozens and dozens of properties, and a substantial portfolio of income sources, but has virtually no equity anywhere. Some people are contented to have a property with a 50% equity in it, and they feel secure with their equity. Others feel comfortable owing 100% of the value of a property against it. Some others, including the fellow I mentioned, don't feel good until they have 1½ times the value out of a property.

There are good and bad aspects to this method. It almost always results from *refinancing*.

First, let's look at an example. You've found a four-plex for sale for $125,000 and you've got the price down to

$110,000 with $10,000 down. The down payment is only a structural aspect of the contract since it will never be made. That is, you personally won't pay the money, although when the deal is completed the seller will have ten grand in his pocket. This seller will get $110,000 for his building and he has a first mortgage for $40,000 and a second for $5,000. He got the five grand a year ago to improve the property a little.

So, the seller's equity is $110,000, less the $45,000 against it or $65,000. He'll get $100,000 after your ten grand down and carry a third mortgage for the $55,000 balance. The seller's primary interest is to sell, to get his down payment and to be secure in his position. You have secured a source of financing on the property, perhaps a Savings and Loan. They'll go on a *second* mortgage, after the $40,000 first, but not after the existing second and certainly not after the third position the current seller wants to take. The S. & L. will loan 75% of the value of the property. The value may be $125,000 but let's say, to be conservative, we use the $110,000 reduced price you are paying for it. So, the S. & L. will loan to 75% of $110,000 or $82,500. There is already a first mortgage of $40,000 against the property, so in effect the S. & L. will loan $42,500 in a second position and still be within the 75% value.

With this loan arrangement you can then propose to the seller the following:

That instead of being in the third position after a first of $40,000 and a second of $5,000 you'll offer him a premium if he'll take a third position for his $55,000 equity balance after a $40,000 first and a $42,500 second. The premium is that you increase his third mortgage by $5,000 (or $10,000) to $60,000. He'll get slightly higher payments on his third mortgage, you'll pay off the existing $5,000 second mortgage and he'll still have a secure third position. If the deal falls together it will look like this:

FIRST, SECOND AND THIRD	$142,500

$32,500

ACTUAL VALUE	125,000

PURCHASE PRICE	110,000

LOAN VALUE	82,500

```
First.................... $40,000
Second................. $42,500
Third ................. $60,000
```

As you can see, the seller's *UNSECURED* part of his third mortgage amounts to $32,500. That is how much you'd owe him above the actual purchase price of the property, and $17,500 above what you believe the property is really worth.

The reasons that the seller would hang himself out in this position are these:

1- He is selling the property which he wants to do.

2- He has a large equity and is not risking cash already in his pocket.

3- His monthly payment from you will higher than it would be if he didn't go along with this deal.

241

4- His effective selling price will be $5,000 (or $10,000) higher than he had agreed upon.

5- He knows that you'll make some improvements which will increase the value substantially.

6- In two years inflation will have raised the property value to surpass his total exposure and in less than the two years he'll be full covered by value.

7- You're paying off the current $5,000 second.

The deal will be good for you because you'll end up with some cash, as well as having the title to the property in your name.

New second mortgage	$42,500
Less paying off old second	-5,000
Balance of available cash	37,500
Less down payment on property	10,000
Cash to you	$27,500

Here are some good and bad points on organizing a deal in this manner.

Good aspects:

1- You have *no* money invested.
2- You end up with $27,500 in cash.

3- If you've limited your total liability TO THIS PROPERTY *ONLY* you have *NO* exposure. In other words if you have absolutely no personal liability other than the value in the property itself.

4- you end up owning a property that will eventually surpass the total of mortgages and will make you money through appreciation.

For example:

Using lower value $110,000

Appreciation at 15% (10% to 20%) *compounding*.

First year   +$16,500 = $126,500

Second year   +$18,957 = $135,475

Third year   +$20,321 = $155,796

Fourth year   +$23,369 = $179,165

Fifth year   +$26,874 = $206,039

In five years you'll have an estimated value of $206,039. The mortgages will have declined the principal to $122,000, and your equity in five years will be $84,039. This equity position could even be greater.

If the real value to begin with was actually $125,000 and you made $10,000 worth of creative improvements resulting in an increase of $25,000 in value you actually have something like this:

Improved full value $150,000

Appreciation at 15% (10% to 20%) *compounded.*

First year	+$22,500 =	$172,500
Second year	+$25,875 =	$198,375
Third year	+$29,756 =	$228,131
Fourth year	+$34,219 =	$262,350
Fifth year	+$39,352 =	301,702

Full appreciated value in five years	$301,702
Mortgage, declined, in five years	$122,00
Your equity in five years	$179,702

So, even though you've borrowed heavily against the property you still have a tremendous potential for profit. As far as the $10,000 in improvements are concerned you can take care of those out of your $27,500 and still have $17,500 cash in your pocket with an improved property in your portfolio.

As far as disadvantages are concerned, if you've limited your total liability to the property involved you have no potential for personal financial loss. However, if you were to default, since you have no equity to lose, being over-mortgaged, the only negative in that regard would be your loss of pride having defaulted on loans and being foreclosed. That doesn't bother some people but others feel that iron-clad performance is important to their credibility and track record. The idea being that a foreclosure and bad publicity may preclude other opportunities. Were you to have a deal like this fall through and foreclose it might be more difficult to make other deals if it became known that this type of structuring hasn't worked well for you.

That reason isn't a real concern as long as you keep the property and make all of your payments. Making the payments is the second negative aspect of these over-mortgaged deals. Since you are mortgaged over value and since rents and incomes usually are keyed to around 1% of appraised value per month, your income probably won't cover your mortgage payments. In that case you have to be willing and able to pay into a negative cash flow.

If your payments are:

First mortgage	$410 month
Second mortgage	$469 month
Third mortgage	$630 month
Total monthly payments	$1,509 month
Taxes and insurance	
Total obligation	$179 month
Income at typical 1%	$1,684 month
of appraised value	$1,100 to $1,250 month

So if these figures hold, you'll have a monthly loss of about $484 to pay out. Of course after you make the $10,000 in improvements, resulting in an equity increase of $25,000 and assuming that you bought the property $25,000 under value, after the improvements your actual value would be $150,000 and your justifiable and expected rental income will be $1,500 a month. In this case your monthly loss will be about $200.

Of course offsetting this will be your tax advantages to you might well come out even if all of these elements fall into place.

Usually, though you'll end up with an actual out-of-pocket loss on over mortgaging. You can either plan on paying this loss until you can eventually raise your rents to cover it or you can arrange to have accelerating payments on your third mortgage.

The first mortgage is already in position and an S. & L. on the second mortgage probably won't go on gradually increasing payments, but the property owner, if motivated and rewarded, might well go on increasing payments on the third. In this way you'll lower the early payments in the contract and have higher and higher payments as the years pass. Theoretically the rise in rents each year will surpass the increase in the third mortgage payments.

Remember also that you came out of this deal, even allocating $10,000 of the $27,500 second mortgage net proceeds to you, with $17,500 in cash which would carry the loss while you are making the improvements and raising the rents. It's all a juggling act but everyone can end up happy if it falls into place.

Your only challenge when over-mortgaged is not to allow the monthly loss to cause deliquency of payments. As you build and expand your wealth program you'll have lots of properties that provide excess monthly funds. I've used this surplus money each month to make up the deficit in my negative flow properties, or to close more deals. I haven't had too many "loss" properties since it's against my inclination to lose money on anything. Even if it's made up on tax savings I don't like it. What I enjoy the most are large tax savings *PLUS* some spendable money each month. But, some properties will have a loss and I've always had the other positive flow properties to cover the loss. You will, too. It all fits together like a puzzle.

My last comment on refinanced and over-mortgaged properties is to be careful with any money you realize. In our example you could spend the $27,500 on one vacation to Peoria if you spent it like water. Be careful. If you spend it foolishly you'll only have a $110,000 property with $142,500 owing against it.

As I mentioned, I knew a fellow who bought more and more properties like this all the time. He spent some of the money on improvements and the rest to live, but he was floating large losses each month. As his previous deals matured they would pay the losses on newer deals. He had to keep getting more deals to give him chunks of cash to pay losses not covered by other properties.

That is too much anxiety for me. I'd recommend that if you do over-mortgage deals, you make them a part of your balanced program.

Other aspects of re-financing are very common and useful. If you are looking at a property with first and second mortgages on twenty year contracts at 14% interest and you can find some thirty year mortgage money or money at a lower interest rate, by getting a new mortgage you'll end up with lower payments, obviously, but also a better selling position.

When the time comes for you to sell, the longer contract and lower interest will give you more flexibility. It can also substantially "clean-up" a deal to re-finance. After all we've discussed about options, balloon payments, cost of living increases and so on, all of these exercises and methods can complicate a title. If you are offering a property to a buyer it's important to make the deal sound as clean and simple as possible. You can have a balloon or cost of living increase and etc. But you should project and convey simplicity. Even a complication can be made to seem less important if it is approached in an assuming way.

For example: "There is a cost of living increase in this mortgage, however the property values and equities are so high that the increase doesn't affect your position." That's an assuming and straight-forward comment and is disarming enough to get by a potential obstacle. If, however there are so many liens, taxes, balloons, increases and mortgages permanently attached to a property, refinancing can clean up all the loose ends and lower the monthly obligation and leave one or two mortgages.

The entire game of refinancing is to find or develop sources of long term money at reasonable interest rates. Often, somewhere in the figures, there is at least a few thousand dollars more for you.

The whole idea of building your wealth quickly is to use every possible tool to get money, leverage it, and get more and more property in your name. All the while, of course, leaving yourself a way out and covering your rear end. If you can't cover it, at least moderately, in a deal......don't do it.

CHAPTER TWENTY-NINE

Legal Problems And Exits

If you buy a new car, before you've gone too far you'll likely have repairs or service performed on it. It's also likely that at some point in your ownership of that car you'll have some misunderstanding with the dealer. What he promised when and so on. We have problems ordering food in restaurants, dissatisfaction with a washing machine, and troubles with many small and large things that affect us every day. Misunderstandings are an inherent part of our daily activities.

It makes sense then to assume that while acquiring millions of dollars in real estate you'll run into a few problems.

There are, however, ways to simplify and avoid many of the potential difficulties. Being optimistic, in a hurry and off like a rocket you may always assume that everything will always work out alright in the end. Ultimately it will, but when you depend on people, public tastes, business trends and fulfillment of all promises you will often be disappointed.

Generally you can't depend wholly on anyone. Situations arise that change the character of a deal and inject complications into it that could prove terminal.

To circumvent the potential loss or damage you should always have the most detailed contingencies outlined in all of your contracts and agreements for every transaction you enter into.

A perfect example is in organizing a partnership. When you are considering entering into an investment or business with a friend it seems like you understand each other so clearly. You can't imagine how any serious problems could arise and if they somehow did, you understand each other and communicate so well that the problems can be talked out! That doesn't work. When the time comes that serious problems arise no one involved will be objective in the least. Everyone will only see that they have kept their end of the bargain and how they've been wronged by someone they trusted.

I've been through it enough times to know exactly what I'm talking about. I'd recount some personal instances but I don't want to place blame on anyone but myself.

But let's suppose that you and your friend are going to start a carpet cleaning business to get your nest egg together for your wealth program. You've been friends for so long, just like brothers, and it's a natural partnership. Where have I heard that before? You both agree to the terms of your new business agreement and feel like such small details need not be included in a contract because they are so obvious and reasonable. When the end comes there will be hurt feelings in this deal because both parties will rely on their recollections.

To avoid this make *EVERY* contract as completely detailed as is posible. I had one partnership agreement that specified my responsibilities in the business which was to build buldings and provide funds for future growth, and my partner's obligations which included how many hours each day he was to devote to the business, how much he'd be paid, amounts of any potential raises, other benefits, performance figures, daily duties, timely payment of all obligations, limitations of amounts of encumberable debts, payment of legal costs in case of litigation, personal tax responsibilities, and on and on. Everything that could ever have a bearing on the busines partnership, including buyout procedures in case the partnership didn't work out, insurance coverage on each other and lots of similar details.

If you do this and things fall apart you don't have to rely on your recollections, just go to your contract and it will all be spelled out there in great detail. Hours, dollars and etc.

The same idea applies in any real estate transaction. While many people use blank forms from a printer or office supply for their contracts, I prefer to have a new legal document drafted for each deal. As well as including as many details of the transaction from both points of view. I usually have the documents prepared by my attorney, whether buying or selling, and I have him include as many protections and escapes as possible.

Some contract details of mutual interest:

Exact legal description.

Exact price and down payment.

Exact allocation of values to building and property.

Prepayment options.

Current tax liabilities and who will pay them.

Do you share escrow and legal fees?

Who carries the insurance?

Some inclusions for your benefit:

Have grace periods of 60 days so that if payments are late a few days you won't be seriously in default.

Specify that if payments are later than this 60 day period, the property seller must notify you by certified mail of the default and give you 60 days to correct it. If not corrected within 60 days the seller must then notify you by certified mail that you have failed to correct the default and have defaulted the contract. You specify that during the default and foreclosure you, the buyer, are still entitled to any rents or income the property generates. You then have whatever time is legally allowed in your state, usually two to six months, while the property is in notification of foreclosure or actual foreclosure to bring all payments current or, in some cases, the entire unpaid balance is due.

The first notification stages of this exercise gives you four months of flexibility and all you have to do is bring the payments current. If you can incorporate, write the contract with the corporation as the buyer to limit your personal liability.

If you can get a reduction in price for prepayment, specify that. If you can ever refinance this will be extra cash to you, assuming that your refinance will either be at lower interest or you can get a gross price reduction. The logic for this is that, *in the future*, the other party may prefer cash to a long-term contract and a price reduction may motivate you to prepay the balance sometimes.

Always load the contract in your favor. You may have to eliminate some items but you'll end up in a better position if you give yourself every advantage. The above example was for buying a property, and in selling you'd be careful that your buyer didn't include many of the personal benefits you used in the buying example. Many buyers and sellers are anxious to close the deals and some details have little importance to them.

If you have employment contracts, treat them the same way. An exact definition of duties, pay, benefits and responsibilities.

In your written offers leave such escape clauses as:

Offer subject to approval of partner. Anyone could be your partner and they could disapprove for any reason.

Offer subject to re-survey.

Offer subject to inspection and approval of floors.

Offer subject to inspection and approval of plumbing and electrical. You may declare them unsuitable.

All of the above can be disapproved and the deal cancelled if you change your mind.

You might also specify a long closing time: "Sale to close on...."(four months away).That will give you time to round up financing, down payment, a partner or to decide not to close the deal. Specify that if, for any reason the transaction is not consummated, all earnest money and deposits will be refunded. Sometimes you can do this and sometimes the earnest money is forfeited, but you can always try. If the earnest money in your state must be forfeited, pay only a small earnest money deposit, perhaps $100 or $200. If they demand a larger amount leave the $100 or $200 in place as the earnest money and pay the additional money "*not* as earnest money, but as a separate deposit against the purchase price." With that wording it would have to be refunded if the sale wasn't completed. Also by using a smaller amount for your earnest money deposits you'll be able to make more offers with limited funds. By leaving the exit you'll have a graceful way out of a deal that was accepted at the wrong time, perhaps when several other deals came through, or for any reason has become undesirable to you.

The last topic we'll discuss in legal transactions is what to do when a lawsuit is threatened.

Personally, I make every effort to avoid conflict and bad feelings. Curiously, though, I am very litigious, meaning that I am given to lawsuits or litigation.

Years ago when I was starting, I thought that the ulitmate threat I could throw at a person was that if they didn't do so and so, I would sue them, and it may have had that effect on some less-experienced people. But the guys who had been around to block a few times didn't care at all.

One of the first people I ever threatened with a lawsuit told me "go ahead, but you'll have to stand in line."

For any reason, never feel intimidated or threatened when someone tells you they are going to sue you. Half of suing and being sued is pure show business. Half of the time you're bluffing and half of the time they're bluffing. When threatened with a lawsuit I always smile and tell them that I am home most mornings, if they want to catch me to serve papers. I then tell them that I have never lost a lawsuit in all the times I've been in court and, in fact, I sort of enjoy going to court.

They are always disarmed because I refused to be threatened by them. If they continue I tell them that if there was any question at all we could settle it between us, but since I'm certain I'm right in my position, we should have a judge decide. Then I assure them that a lawsuit is definitely the right way to pursue it. This alone will take the wind out of their sails.

If they've talked to an attorney they may still go for it. That's fine with you, too. Once you get the hang of legal procedures and have gone to court a few times, it will all seem less frightening to you. I've always enjoyed the drama and legal jousting in a trial. It's fun to see the sides try to prove their points and see the logic develop. Of course my appraisal of trials is a little biased since I've never lost a court case. I've never lost one that even came close to going to court. I did let a couple go to default once, but they weren't viable cases and they had no recourse in those cases anyway.

But I've never lost and it's entertaining. You can feel the same way and, when you do, you won't feel apprehensive about the threats. Remember that, regardless of the proposed action, much of the legal talk is a bluff. Call their bluff.

A few years ago I owned a retail store and, shortly after we changed insurance carriers, we had a small burglary. We lost about $5,000 worth of merchandise. I called the insurance agent after the burglary was discovered and he rushed right over. He gave me his condolences and told me that, unfortunately, there was no burglary coverage on that store. He showed me the policy and my signature and, sure enough, there wasn't any coverage on the stolen items. But, I recalled specifically that he'd mentioned burglary coverage on that store, and that it would be included. This, inspite of the fact that it wasn't in my written agreement, was enough for me to insist on the payment for loss. Naturally, the company declined. I wouldn't let it pass by because I knew that my position was right. I had my attorney trade a few letters back and forth with their home office and he then notified them that we would take it to court.

We all met for sworn depositions in which, under oath, both the insurance agent and myself told our own versions of the story. This procedure brings out both sides but it is also part of the bluff. I'm showing them that I won't give up the lawsuit just because my written contract didn't include the coverage.

255

They are showing me that they aren't going to be forced to pay a claim, no matter what I do. We're bluffing to the extent that we're both exerting pressure to see our respective positions vindicated. After the depositions we proceeded to trial and the day before the court appearance they offered me a check to cover the loss. So, I got the check.

They expected me to give up all along but I wouldn't give in if I was right in my position. You can do the same thing in your legal encounters. If you're wrong, pay up and forget it. If you may be wrong, admit it and work out a settlement. But if you are right stay with it until you win. The only exception to this, unless you want to prove a point and uphold some principal, is if, even in winning, you won't come out money ahead.

As another example, I had an illness that cost me $13,000, and an incidental expense from one doctor was for $160. I paid everyone but this fellow and he didn't deserve it since I felt that his advice and service was incompetent.

Rather than pay the $160 and forget it, which would have been the easiest thing to do, I refused and he sued me. Our counter suit against him for such shoddy medical practice was for $300,000. Because we were right and would not accept the unfair thing. We might ultimately pile up a significant legal expense on this case, since it has yet to be decided, but the important thing is that we are sticking with the right position. Clear to the end. Sometimes it is better for a person to swallow their pride, pay the bill, have a nice dinner and forget the problem. Then the next day you can get on with your wealth program. Some problems aren't worth five minutes of your time.

The above remarks shouldn't be meant to demean medical doctors in general, although I think it's very humorous how they have become elevated, in this country anyway, to a position of reverence. Overall, because of the common arrogance in many doctors, I don't regard them too highly. There are many good ones, and they all go through a lot to become doctors, and give lots of time for their practices after they become doctors, but they are so darned arrogant. I sometimes think that there isn't a group of people more widely respected and less deserving than M.D.'s. And they make so little money for the time they spend in their work. I hope they are happy. If they will listen to you, you can help them make some real money. The reason I mention doctors in this chapter is to encourage you to purse what is right, even against someone as highly regarded as a doctor, having no consideration of position, reputation, profession or anything else, except your own ends. IS IT WORTH YOUR TIME TO PURSUE IT? That's the question.

I was once threatened with a lawsuit for $25,000. I was busy and offered $5,000 just to avoid the hassle. They wouldn't take the $5,000 and said they'd go to court. That was fine with me. I told them thanks for saving me the $5,000 since in court, there wasn't any way in the world they'd win.

We then had depositions and traded letters back and forth. They decided that they'd settle for $10,000 and I told them I wouldn't pay them one cent. Because I was right. You have to really believe in yourself and believe you are right. Get your thinking tight. It will all come out in your testimony and manner and you will seem so obviously correct in your thinking.

Well, we went to trial, all day long,and I won. It couldn't have ended any other way.

My point in this is not to show you that I've done well in court. It's to show you that you can be threatened with a lawsuit, right up to going to court, and if you'll be strong, you'll often win. On the other hand if you're suing another party, run with the ball all the way to trial. Most of your opponent players will drop out of the game before you get there. If you have a difference of opinion on a contract or transaction, tell them you'll have to handle it legally. Thank them for their time and excuse yourself. Be pleasant. They won't know what to do.

This procedure has always worked well for me and I recommend it to you. It's saved many many thousands of dollars, and many arguments. There is no reason to argue since it will all be settled by a disinterested third party.

Remember, too, that many problems can be avoided by having the smallest details included in your contracts. Then you can simply turn to the file instead of going to court. Realistically, you have better things to do with your time. Don't forget that it's mostly someone bluffing or calling your hand and your sticking with it until you win. If it's worthwhile.

Lastly, remember, when drawing up agreements and contracts, to give yourself every possible flexibility in terms, notifications, defaults, pay-offs, discounts, recourse and every element that could be in your favor. Verbally minimize your advantages. Mention and pass over them. Assume and accept them and the other party will be inclined to go along, if it seems right, and your manner and confidence can convince them that it is.

CHAPTER THIRTY

Bookkeeping And Records

It's difficult for a free spirit like you, particularly when you're running on all eight cyclinders and at 5,000 R.P.M.'s to keep good records. It is often the least exciting aspect of getting rich.

There are several good reasons for keeping accurate records. You want to accurately chart and assess your growth and financial position. If you keep separate files on each property and chart declining principal balances, increasing equities and value increases from improvements you'll always have a visual reference to inform you, at a glance, where you're at financially.

In each property file you'll have original documents (or copies) of purchase, all correspondence, all contracts or agreements that relate in any way to the project, bids for work to be done, summaries and thoughts on improvements and utilizing the property for its best use and development and all other notes, letters and papers that relate, in any way, to the property.

You'll keep every receipt for work done, all income (rental and lease) records and receipts. Also all receipts for repairs and improvements. You'll also want to chart income and keep line graphs to plot pending balloons and etc. Even though I have great difficulty keeping my schedule regimented, I still like a lot of *clean* paperwork to keep me in touch with what I'm doing.

Then when questions come in on a piece of property I can pull the file and have everything relating to it in front of me. If I want a general overview of all properties I can turn to a general ledger in which the figures relating to each project are entered.

You should also have summaries of financial condition to instantly show you variations in trends, vacancy factors and cash flow.

Graph your financial growth, all asset figures and net worth figures. The importance of this is not to burden you with paperwork that bores you but to keep you organized while you get bigger and bigger. It's too easy for things to get away from you. At the end of this chapter there are some sample forms you can use or modify to suit you.

You also need to keep sufficient and accurate records for tax planning. There are, for example, capital gains taxes that are short term and long term, and plotting will organize your scheduled selling. In my recommended reading list are a couple of excellent tax books and your accountant will help you plan your buying and selling. You also need to plot your depreciations. If you get a property on which you can accelerate the depreciation (if it has a particularly short life for some reason) and you can write off 100% of the value in just a few years, you'll want to do it and dispose of the property when the tax advantage is used up. When you sell it you'll buy something else and that's the way the government keeps the economy rolling. By giving you incentives to buy and sell. You are the one that keeps the country running and the government rewards you with little or no tax bill.

But to take advantage of these rewards you need a good acountant and some good books. If you have an extremely competent accountant who has *PROVEN* himself over a period of time you may want to depend on him a little and let him do your tax planning.

MOST of the C.P.A.'s and accountants don't dig as deeply as they might. It isn't their money, and who cares about a few bucks anyway. For this reason it will be worth your while to get a basic understanding of the basic tax laws and their applicability to you. If you keep your own summaries and portfolios you'll feel close to and be in touch with your program.

Thirdly, you'll need good records in case you have an I.R.S. audit. You're going to be making a sizable amount of money and you won't fit into the normal profile. You may draw a little attention to yourself, and your fast growth could trigger an audit. I've never had a tax audit, although I was always expecting one. If you keep *everything* in organized files an audit will be a breeze.

DON'T EVER KEEP DOUBLE BOOKS. Lying to the Feds is against the rules and can result in heavy fines and free vacations. I've made mistakes on taxes and so on, but when asked, I've always told them exactly where I was at. If I didn't know the correct procedure I told them so. I was always open with them. A good attorney would tell you never to tell them anything unless they ask you specifically. A lot of people tell them things they'd never find out if the taxpayer would keep his mouth shut.

That's good advice, but don't lie to an I.R.S. agent or auditors. Take *ALL* of your tax advantages and don't pay a dime you don't have to but be able to show, from your orderly records, how you arrived at your return figures.

261

Many people have cash deals on the side. Cash spiffs from sales, cars bought and sold and cash coming in here and there with no record of it. Most of these people don't declare these cash deals on the side, and use these funds as pocket money. It's difficult for anything to ever come of these cash deals since there aren't any records and no way to pursue or follow up on the transactions.

However, the problem with being deceptive and lying is that it's hard to remember what your lies are and to keep the story straight. An honest person who tells the truth and occasionally makes a mistake is on solid ground. A dishonest person who lies all the time has to always remember what his story is. If he lies part of the time he has to remember which time he told the truth and when he lied. I'm not smart enough to keep track of more than one story.

Whatever you do with your cash deals is your own business but I'd suggest you don't juggle your books and have openly vacuous items or entries which can't be supported. Keep it clean. You're going to make plenty of money anyway and you needn't resort to blatant dishonesty. On the other hand don't pay anything you don't absolutely have to.

Your books, records and charts can keep the whole program clean and organized while you are building your fortune.

CHAPTER THIRTY-ONE

Be Nice To Them On The Way Up Because You'll Meet Them On The Way Down

There is always one thing you can always be sure of and that is that you can never be sure of anything.

Years ago, after some financial success and failures I had a bankruptcy filed against me. I never would have filed a bankruptcy myself but a couple of people I had dealt with on a deal got hot pants and filed a motion with the court. At that time a fellow owed me $1,300,000.00 and didn't pay me. I really trusted the guy. See the Chapter on "Whom can you trust?" I owed about half of that to these guys and they wouldn't wait for me to put the money together another way. I had my cash tied up in other deals and they wouldn't even wait for a month. They filed in two weeks. If I hadn't trusted the guy to pay me the 1.3 million dollars I wouldn't have had that exposure but if you play the game you have to go along with the rules and risks.

I should have known better and learned a lot from that lesson.

If that same situation arose again, I would have petitioned the court for a reorganizaiton, but at the time I wasn't fully aware of the options. We all learn. Anyway I got over that bad experience quick enough, and it all turned out just fine.

We are all big boys and have to pull up our boots and kick ourselves in the rear-end and start over. So I did. A great lesson I learned was to be nice to 'em on the way up because you'll meet 'em on the way down. It might interest you to know, also, that a bankruptcy can result from cash flow problems, not just insolvency. You can have millions in assets but if you have a liquidity problem (no ready cash equal to your potential maximum needs) and three people file a claim against you, it can result in a bankruptcy.

Overall, bankruptcy doesn't have to be a bad thing either.

Some people structure their bankruptcy and use it to further their fortunes. That isn't honest and is unnecessary since there are plenty of legitimate ways to make money. Bankruptcy also has some social connotations but that aspect is fading rapidly. It isn't what it used to be at all. Since my own experience with it wasn't caused by a total lack of assets, but simply from cash flow problems, it didn't interrupt my activities much.

To acquire wealth you must take risks but they should be calculated risks. And somewhere along the line you'll make some mistakes. *MOST* people who eventually acquire great wealth go through significant financial problems at one time or another. It's simply a part of what happens. It may be bankruptcy, some forclosures, lots of lawsuits and on and on and on, but it happens.

Be Nice To Them On The Way Up Because You'll Meet Them On The Way Down

As you continue to build your empire keep a reserve of self-confidence and energy to get you though the hard times. Also, keep some friends. Many people cast their friends and families aside as they ascend the ladder of wealth. They feel progressively more distant and detached from the "little people" and they often lose sensitivity with the problems the people around them have.

This can manifest itself in a divided marriage, social segregation and a lack of ease with neighbors and friends. It's understandable how this happens, since you are doing big deals, building big buildings, going places and doing exciting things and you have a little trouble getting excited about the gas consumption of a new lawnmower. All of this mental stuff has about as much real substance as fog but is equally as hard to see through when you're in the middle of it.

When you're making ten to twenty grand a year it is easy to be at ease with others earning that much. As you earn millions and millions and characteristically surround yourself with the trappings of wealth, it is too obvious that you are doing something different from the twenty grand a year folks. This is usually interpreted by both sides of the friendship or relationship as the richer person gaining in intelligence or status and progressing while the other remains behind. That's how friends are often cast aside.

When you are poor it is easy for you to be interested in a friend's inability to pay his phone bill. When you have millions it is beyond you why anyone doesn't pay his bills for living expenses, and you can't find the time to listen to why he can't.

Small problems to you may be big problems to someone else. As my years and wealth progressed I became distant from my wife's concerns. I've always been very affectionate and complimentary with her and never let a day go by without telling her how beautiful she was and how much I loved her. I also took her out once a week or more and bought her lots of clothes, presents and personal things so she'd feel special.

However, that wasn't what she needed. I wasn't in close enough touch with her to stop and just listen to her more. I've seen the same thing happen in other families. The same thing can also happen in friendships.

Don't ever be above people, only above problems. You are greater than any problem but no better than any person. Treat them that way and, if your great financial crisis ever arises, you'll find yourself with a great circle of people you are, and always have been, "in touch" with.

CHAPTER THIRTY-TWO

Structuring A Bankruptcy

From seeing a number of bankruptcies first hand I can give you the following information and advice.

As you grow financially you will use optimism as a great tool and that personal quality will be your best friend. However, *ALWAYS COVER YOURSELF.*

Typically the complete optimist thinks that everything is going to come out alright, even when it is headed in the wrong direction. The optimist knows that bankruptcy is impossible because he looks at his financial statement and he sees "wealth" but overlooks some immediate cash problem that should have been covered in more ways than one and wasn't. If someone owes me over a million dollars and I depend on that payment to me, and obligate myself to pay something else out of the million, I am totally dependent on the person to pay me so that I can pay the third party. I should cover the third party debt in a second way, just in case the first person defaults. But it always seems that the first party is such a nice guy and has repeatedly reassured me that the money will come in on time. But it doesn't and I haven't covered myself. That's when a problem develops.

Leave yourself a way out. During the years of building your wealth as you start to get more and more money, learn to do favors for a few close people around you. Don't ever count on the favors being repaid, but if worse comes to worse, you'll always have what you need.

Pinpoint a few rising stars who are just getting off the ground and *give* them some help. Don't co-sign loans or make direct loans to them. *Give* them some help, finanical and otherwise and if they ever pay you back, fine. If you do this for a number of people, you'll always feel comfortable going to them later on when they have a roll going and, this time you need a favor. All you are doing is covering yourself.

Give a friend or relative some cash once in a while, as a gift. They can put this money in bank deposits, bonds or some other liquid asset. This will be their money since it was a gift. If the need ever arises they'd draw it out and give it to you, but it could never be considered an asset of yours. This will represent small dollars when you are "rolling" but substantial funds if you ever really need it. There isn't anything wrong with this line of thinking. It's just doing favors while you can. After all, it's your money and you can do with it what you please. You are sharing when things are going your way and someone else will share with you if things turn against you.

Can you trust these people to cooperate if you need them? Maybe not, but give it a try. The only other alternative is to stick money away in hidden accounts (out of town banks, using false names, etc.) safe deposit boxes, sacks of diamonds and various other fiscal gymnastics to hide your own funds. This places you in a position of either having to surrender those assets if you become bankrupt or of perjuring yourself while under oath which could result in some hard time if the truth ever came out. Do the favors for others instead.

Perhaps I shouldn't expand on the prospects of a bankruptcy in a book about MAKING MILLIONS but it is worth taking a little time to protect yourself. Some dishonest souls structure bankruptcies by buying all they can and borrowing everything they can, never intending to repay it. They float along like this, getting more and more, knowing all the while it will end in a declaration of bankruptcy.

These sorts usually have the money all tucked away and have it all planned from the beginning. That is much different from really trying to make it successful and having problems develop.

Even if you have the "Big B" hit you, you'll get over it. Things were never better than after my bankruptcy, even though it never would have occurred if I hadn't been so trusting. Learn from my experiences. Remember to cover yourself on the side with a few friends. How can you decide who to depend on? Flip a coin. They are never as they appear to be. Perhaps a member of your family is a good bet.

But remember that YOU ARE GREATER THAN ANY PROBLEM and there isn't *anything* that can happen to you to abort your progress. *YOU WILL NOT ACCEPT FAILURE*. You don't even know what the word means.

There are a couple of things to keep in mind as you prepare for the very slight chance that someone will pull the plug on you or you'll have to pull your own plug.

One is that you should never have transactions which could appear to be in defrauding your creditors. If you go bankrupt in March you should not have gifts and deals of questionable value in January. From what I understand, they can go back one year from your filing date and re-examine *all* transactions during that twelve month period.

269

All gifts may have to be returned, and value must be established on real estate and other transactions to see if there was preferential treatment or circular deals involved.

Preferential treatment would be if you show preference to one creditor over another within a short period of time before filing, in paying an obligation. If you owe company A $10,000 and company B $10,000 and deed a property to company A to settle the debt but leave company B hanging this transaction could be reversed or upset in a bankruptcy. Likewise if you have a property with an equity of $50,000 and sell it to someone, realizing $10,000 out of your equity, this also could be upset, if you can't show a good reason why you had the reduced value. This would only happen if the transaction was within the twelve months preceeding the bankruptcy.

As you go along you can give gifts and sell properties to friends and relatives here and there for very low prices and the only deals or gifts in question would be in the year previous to filing. If you have an income property that you paid $100,000 for, which had a real value of $130,000 and you did some repairs or renovations and arrived at a rental multiple of $180,000 you could easily sell this property to your father or mother or some other family member for $100,000. It will be great for them, since they can depreciate the property and use the tax deduction. We are assuming that your parents are of more modest means than you are. If the property "cost" them $100,000 and was an older building they could value the land at $10,000 and the building at $90,000 in their contract with you and give the building a life of, say, twenty years. The idea being that in twenty years the building will have no value at all. So the building will be used up in twenty years so is worth ($90,000 — 20) $4,500 less every year. If your parents are in a 33% tax bracket, they can take $1,500 a year right off the top of their taxes.

Since you are well-protected, by this time, as far as taxes are concerned, you don't need the deductions, but your parents, or other persons, do need the deductions.

Were it ever questioned, if you went bankrupt within a year of the sale to your parents, you could show that they paid $100,000 for the property, exactly what you paid. Therefore there is no preferential treatment and the deal would hold. If asked why you sold for a hundred grand when the building was worth more, the answer would be that you wanted out of the deal, offered it to several investors for $100,000 and no one would take the deal. Your parents had the time to manage the property and you assured them you'd help them so they bought it in order to start an investment program.

The one important criteria for this or any other deal is whether it was entered into when the principal, you, knew he was insolvent, if he was behind on many contracts or bills, and if he generally knew that he was going down and gave better than normal deals to preferred people, within a year previous to filing.

In the above example your parents would have paid you $5,000 or $10,000 down on the deal. Of course through the years you will have given them plenty of money as a gift from you, and this five grand *could* have come from their own money. After you get the down payment from them you may continue to do favors for them and give them monetary gifts. You may even end up giving them the five grand back. Meanwhile, they have the property, the depreciations and deductions for taxes. Besides the depreciations of $4,500 a year and the corresponding reduction of $1,500 a year in taxes, if their mortgage payments on the property are $1,200 a month, which will be covered by rental income, they'll be paying $1,000 a month or more in interest and that is also tax deductable. So, they'd have $1,000 a month times a 33% tax brcket or another $330 a month deducted

271

from their taxes or a total of $455 off their income taxes on just this one property every month.

Later on, if the going gets rough, you know that your parents will transfer this property back to you. So you are in a position of having a property with substantial value, selling it to your parents for what you paid for it, with no preference. And there won't be any capital gains taxes since you sold it to them for exactly what you paid for it. You've helped your parent's tax situation, you have a property that is really accessable if you need it, and you have some security which can transcend the "Big B".

If you do this a few times you'll have a few favors to collect if you ever need them, you'll be helping people in the interim and it is all legal and moral since you believe in sharing your wealth while you have it. If you never need any favors from anyone that's even better. The idea is that you shouldn't be so greedy while you're getting rich that you ignore others and restrict your generosity. If you do that and ever need a hand yourself, there won't be one available.

It's important to have documents showing that all sales and transfers were legitimate and completed legally. If your sister buys some buildings from you, be prepared to show where she paid you for them in accordance with your contract with her. If a court asks to see the check you'll have the cancelled check she paid you with, from her files. You'll also have an explanation of what happened to the money she paid you. This would only have to be accounted for if a bankruptcy came within a year of the contract date. You must be very careful to AVOID A CIRCULAR DEAL. If she paid you $40,000 for your building and you produced a cancelled check from her to you for that amount, the deal may not hold up if, in examining her bank records and statement it showed a deposit a day or a week later for $40,000 from unaccountable sources.

If her subsequent deposit was from a third party for some viable reason the deal would hold up. But, if it appeared that she paid you $40,000 and a week after she got the money back (circular), from you to cover the deal, it probably wouldn't fly. Often, however, no one goes to the trouble to explore more than the first layer on any deal, but you'll do your groundwork in case they do.

All you are doing is providing for every possible contingency. Even if it's only a few thousand here and there, it will be signficant to you if anything upsets your apple cart.

The main idea is to have a good reason why every deal is legitimate and you'll never have to worry about fraud, preference or anything else. I didn't do that extensively but did depend on a few people I'd helped get started to get me into high gear again. If nothing ever happens that you need it, so much the better, You've helped people who needed it and felt more secure at the same time.

Another thing to do is to put second, third or fourth mortgages on property in favor of some close friends or family.

This can be to secure a debt, money they've "loaned" you, to secure payment for money you owe to them for work they've done on this and other properties, and for securing their interest in a commission due them for organizing the deal. Thus, if you have a property with a $100,000 first mortgage and $60,000 in equity you could easily owe $30,000 in "work and commissions."

So they take a second mortgage for $30,000 and you have a mortgage totalling $130,000 or more. Thus, if the sky falls, you may lose the property but this friend or relative can either:

1- Collect their $30,000 when the property is sold at a sheriff's auction for more than $130,000 or,

2- Assume the first mortgage for $100,000 if the property sells for less than $130,000.

You are covered either way, assuming that in light of the great favors you've done for this person, and considering your bankrupt condition, he gives you the property back for a fresh start. The day after your bankruptcy is filed you can start over on another fortune. They can't take a dime from you after you file, if the bankruptcy is granted. They are seldom turned down, but if they are it's usually because you either aren't bankrupt or because they have evidence of fraud and won't protect you from your creditors.

Have plenty of legal documents to support whatever you do. These would be loan documents, agreements to provide a second or third mortgage to secure the payment for all of their time and work on the project, real estate sales contracts and etc. Then put it in the file and forget it. If it's ever questioned, never volunteer any information, just answer their questions.

Considering that the *only* way to get ahead is through risk taking, and considering the fact that you'll do larger and larger deals, you'll have a greater and greater risk. Since your net worth should be increasing, too, your exposure, percentage-wise, should be the same. Whether you're playing a poker game with $1 chips or $1,000 chips has nothing to do with the outcome of the game. Same cards, same bluff and same winner. Just larger stakes.

Since risk is an inherent part of what you're doing, you should prepare for the possible result of the risks you take.

Incorporation is another route to take in protecting your assets and wealth. If you incorporate properly and follow the rules and requirements for a corporation, your individual businesses and projects can become entities and individuals themselves You can receive dividends from them, and use them to your advantage but they must operate as individual persons.

274

The money you take out of a corporation is regulated but the big plus is that the risks you take as a corporation can only affect the assets of that corporation.

For example, if you own a bicycle shop and personally operate as a sole proprietor, you personally will be liable for all debts incurred. You personally will sign the orders and be liable to pay for the bikes you order and receive. If, on the other hand, you operate your bicycle shop as John Jones Bicycles *Inc.* and sign *FOR* the corporation, another individual, then the corporation is liable, *to the extent of its assets*, for the corporate debt. In the latter case the corporation is liable for the bills and, if they aren't paid, the corporation can be sued to collect the bill. You, personally, can't be held liable and in this way the corporation has protected you. There are a couple of exceptions to this. If the corporation is a shell, a sham, a creditor could "pierce the corporate veil." They could show that, although incorporated, the project or business was, all along, just your own game. That could be because it never operated as a corporation, never had meetings, never kept the necessary records, had no assets, no real operation and was obviously put together to defraud others involved in the enterprise in some way. The way to keep that from happening is to do the things a corporation requires. Meeting, records, taxes, abiding by money handling rules and regulations. When you incorporate an attorney can give you the requirements.

Lack of record-keeping and irregular money withdrawals are the greatest downfalls of most terminal corporations.

A corporation can isolate your exposure and limit your liability but must be taken care of. You may, someday, have to bankrupt one of your corporations but your only exposure will be your investment in it. Often, when a corporation is sued, however, they include as plaintiffs, the officers and sometimes stockholders in it. I did that a few times when suing corporate entities simply because when we sue we like to sue everyone in sight. If we get a dozen people involved in one way or another it may ring a few more bells. At the same time you have to have a good enough reason to sue someone. You can't enter lawsuits just for the fun of it. Some people think that being a corporate officer is a good enough reason to sue, but usually only if you seem to have been running the corporation as your own self, not as a separate entity. So, keep the rules and protect yourself whenever you can sign as a corporation.

There are a couple of drawbacks to that practice. On your financial statement you can list the stock in the corporation as an asset, but not the total assets or net worth of the corporation. In some cases if you own all the stock, you could list the net worth of the corporation as the value of your stock. Your attorney will steer you on this, for your own situation.

The only other drawback you'll find on this corporate protection is that, often, when you want to buy a property or whatever, a corporation, even if it has a great net worth, your seller will want you to sign a *PERSONAL* guarantee. That puts you on the hook personally for the debt, in which case all of your assets are on the line, too. This evaporates the protective advantage of the corporation. If you enter your deals in a REAL POSITION OF STRENGTH you can refuse to sign a personal guarantee. They may say, "If you don't sign the guarantee we won't do the deal." Then you can decide how much risk this would be to you and if you really need it. If it's a marginal deal, one that you would allow corporate but not personal risk, pass it by. As you grow financially you don't need every deal anyway. Also the tax structure for a corporation is much different than your personal tax.

The corporation may pay a corporate tax on its earnings and then you may have to pay tax again on your personal dividends.

276

A way around this tax problem, in many deals, is to make t a sub-chapter *S* corporation in which *all* of the corporate earnings are distributed as dividends and are only taxed once. Ask your attorney. If it seems that he doesn't really know *ALL* about incorporating, find one who does. I've always had the best legal advice and representation, and if they don't know about something, they tell me and find someone who is an expert on the problem in question.

You should get good advice before incorporating. If your corporation qualifies and if you can structure an offering you can issue and sell stock in the corporation, too. This can provide funds for growth into new projects and areas, using someone else's money. This dilutes your percentage of ownership but may increase the stock value significantly.

The Security and Exchange Commission (S.E.C.) regulates stock offerings and securities trading. Be careful when issuing stock to follow the rules.

There are *BILLIONS* of dollars waiting to be invested in promising new corporations. Perhaps yours is one of them. In any case, incorporating may offer some protection to you and you should consider it.

Use all of the available tools and methods to provide for your long-term security, even if a bankruptcy comes along. There are plenty of ways to cultivate the kind of help that can carry you past your bankruptcy and on up the mountain of millions.

CHAPTER THIRTY-THREE

Recovering From the Big B

If you make your millions in a five year period and within that time develop a terminal problem which results in a bankruptcy, you have several consolations.

Since you've made your wealth so quickly there is no great time loss. Since you started with nothing, there isn't a monetary loss either. You've learned *how* to make money quickly and no one can take that knowledge away from you. If you did it before in five years, this time you can do it in three.

If you've followed the suggestions in the previous chapter and have "favors" all around you ready to collect, you already have a platform upon which to start over.

Some of these people may not come through for you, but some will. There are two approaches to recovering from a bankruptcy.

You are either completely on your own or you have these favors to depend on. If you have these people, when the bottom falls out if it does, and your cash flow from your income units and businesses stops, then these friends can resume your cash flow. First for living expenses and then to get your investment program going again.

Personally, I never considered for a minute the remote possibility of bankruptcy and never intentionally made gifts or favorable transfers to anyone with the thought of the "Big B" in mind.

I did, however, do a lot of people a lot of favors, just to help them. And, when I needed it, everything clicked into place and I was able to rebuild my investment program and carry on with my living without any great interruptions.

If you haven't been generous as you put your riches together, and the Big B hits you, you'll be on your own, but with tons of knowledge to get you going again. If you end up penniless or near it, your first objective would be to provide for your family and put together a few thousand dollars to start over at the beginning again. The trick, at this point, isn't how to make the thousands. You know how since you've done it.

The greatest challenge is to get your head straight. The first thing you have to realize is that *a bankruptcy is not a failure. There is no failure.*

No, the bankruptcy is only a step to your eventual wealth. Some folks go though that step and some don't. It's all a part of the risk. If you flip a coin and it comes up heads when you've called tails, it really isn't your fault. Of course you'll say that you wish you hadn't flipped that time or bought that property or made that deal, but you did and it came up on the wrong side.

Sometimes our financial misfortunes come from our own stupidity, trust in others and so on, in which case we learn from our mistakes, which is good. When our problems are caused by our own bad judgements and mistakes we should look at the problem head-on, admit the mistake to ourselves and then make sure we don't make the same error again. We can never grow if we *always* blame our bad fortune on the wrong flip of a coin. Sometimes it's us.

Whatever happens it's no reflection on you personally, and you certainly aren't going to let a common step in the growth process (that being bankruptcy) hold up your progress. It's all part of the game. You'll get over it.

At this point, if you are just beginning your wealth program the best insurance is to be generous with friends and family as we have previously discussed. If you are already into your program of riches, start now by feathering your nest.

There is quite a mental process involved in overcoming something that could be considered significantly disappointing. A problem with our minds is that we look back at all of our successes as being the end results of many positive experiences. We compare that idea with our current toubles and see our present difficulties as sure signs of decline and decay.

We forget that there have always been problems and our troubles now are nothing more than what has always been. Don't dwell on the negative, don't lament the problems endlessly but don't forget that *YOU ARE NOT DECLINING* just because your immediate problems seem so real and your past problems seem so vague.

Also, it will be to your great advantage to look at a world globe or look out through the stars and contemplate something larger than one person or one program in the here and now.

Life is very broad and deep and, although sometimes our personal difficulties distort our perception of life in general, the nature of life is that eons of time have come and gone and some things remain constant. Nature, friendships and families. These have nothing to do with money and a financial upset can never cloud an appreciation of things that transcend everything.

If you are thinking of killing yourself you are taking life too seriously. *Life is just long enough for one good laugh.*

Enjoy yourself, relax, and reassess, then go after it again. Don't languish in self-doubt or self-pity. It will consume and destroy you. In *Brave New World*, Aldous Huxley observed that "rolling in the muck is not the best way of getting clean." Learn from the past but don't be dragged down by it. And realize that our time here is short and our problems temporary.

You can experience a great joy and euphoria, a natural high, by seeing what your life experience could be. Step back and look.

Remember that that is why you're making your millions in only a few years. So that you can get on with more pleasurable and significant things. More worthy pursuits.

Thus, *any* setback has no significance to you. I hope that you never have a bankruptcy but if you do, pull up your pants, take a fresh breath and GO FOR IT.

CHAPTER THIRTY-FOUR

Leaving An Estate

This is a short chapter and could be summed up in one word: "Don't."

In the book *Acres of Diamonds* the author observes that there is no surer and more certain way of guaranteeing someone a miserable life than to leave a lot of money to him. We all want money. We want our relatives to leave it to us. We want gifts. If only someone would give us a million. But, inherited wealth usually debilitates the recipient. His own creativity and drive dwindles and he cuts back to one or two cylinders.

I believe in helping people. While living, you can give your money away to your family or to good causes and see how it is used.

You can *give* a nest egg, even a large one, to each of your children and they'll be grateful but if you're gone and they get millions of unearned dollars, you've cancelled their ticket to happiness. Get them started, but don't carry them through life.

Give them a hundred grand or more if they need it and can take care of it, if they can use it to start and develop *their own program*, but don't carry them past their own growth by letting them live *off of your program*.

The problem in leaving an estate or a fortune behind is that you're not actively able to oversee its use. Being dead and gone they probably won't ask for your advice. In any case dead people are notorious for living in the past and not keeping up with current investment trends, so your advice would be worthless even if they did ask.

While you are living there are plenty of charities and service organizations worthy of your money. I have no connection with the Salvation Army, and I don't understand their religious tenets, but I don't think there is a more worthy organization for all available help. Their members are, uniformly, more sacrificing and their organization provides more essential services in more places and to more people. It's amazing. They are everywhere. They can use any excess millions you won't need, and there are many other charities that can also. As long as you won't be paying some administrators inflated salary. Why should he benefit from your hard work?

If you have small children whom you haven't been able to help get started you might set aside a sum of money for them to use after you're gone. I really believe in being generous but you have to be careful not to spoil them since there is so much satisfaction in making it themselves.

If you've given each of your children a big chunk, either now or after death, for a good start you've done your best.

If you leave them millions they may become lazy and unproductive. Your family and friends could also use a little help to get going and you can easily share with them now.

Be generous, enjoy, give and spend. There is little doubt about your not needing money when you're dead. So use it while you're living.

CHAPTER THIRTY-FIVE

Creating A Personal Image

We all know that the external and superficial stuff has little or no value but on a practical basis, many people will get ahead financially, further and more quickly, if they look the part. We've already discussed this in other chapters but here are a few summarizing points we should cover.

There is a certain demeanor or attitude that you can cultivate that will attract people to you, encourage their confidence in you and help you close deals. This attitude has little if anything to do with your appearance, and that permeating attitude can and will overcome any physical appearance, handicap or difficulty.

As discussed previously, regardless of any outward abnormality, your great confidence and self-assurance will come through. At the same time, although I didn't pursue my wealth this way, there are a few things you might pick up along the way for decorations.

Some people form first opinions and make some immediate character judgements from your appearance. Yes, these ideas can all be changed. I never played this end of the game until I could buy everyting I wanted, and then I didn't have to impress anyone to swing deals. It might have some value for you.

As far as these decorations and wealth indicators are concerned you might get a few of these things AS YOU CAN AFFORD THEM OUTSIDE OF YOUR WEALTH PROGRAM. You'll never take the two grand you can pay down on a duplex and buy a diamond ring, unless you already have lots of duplexes and no diamonds. If you want the bauble get a stone as a spiff on a real estate deal but don't sacrifice the appreciation of a duplex just to have a diamond on your finger. Or get an imitation stone if you really feel like you need a flashy ring. The point is that you shouldn't give up a lot (appreciation) for a little (a diamond).

HOWEVER, if you'll visualize this scenario you'll also appreciate the reasons to pick up a few of the items our society has prescribed as symbols of financial success.

Have a confident, moderate attitude. As you acquire a Cadillac or Lincoln don't let your head inflate. Act excited but sure of yourself and your Cadillac will fit into your appearance of success. Before your Cadillac come some reasonable, nice clothes. Not $500 suits but make sure you don't have pants cuffs six inches off the floor. In other words stay away from Hawaiian shirts. Dress as well as you can afford so that your first appearance will be good.

Start with clothes and then add a little jewelry. Don't load yourself up with rhinestones. One nice bracelet or ring is nicer than tons of cheap stuff. As you have more and more properties work a nice car in somewhere. Then get a nice home for yourself as an investment as well as for comfort and appearance. Add a nice office when you can and a versatile secretary to manage your properties as well as the regular secretarial duties.

As you add more and more buildings, build a luxury office for yourself and invite potential buyers and sellers to your office to discuss your transactions. You can visualize the natural progression of this acquisition of comfort and affluent appearance.

But remember that a poorly dressed but confident and aggressive fellow in an old Chevy will close more deals than someone who thinks he's a high roller and above everyone (sure signs of insecurity) who's driving a new Lincoln.

But the best of all, as far as appearance of material success is concerned, is to be an aggressive and self-confident, but not arrogant, guy in an expensive car. If you put it all together, nice person, nice clothes, nice jewelry and car and a beautiful home, then you seem to have a well-rounded wealth and demeanor.

That person, YOU, can go through each day buying properties and becoming wealthy while enjoying the pleasures of life.

You'll note, once again, that the aforementioned characteristics didn't include physical attractiveness, a whole body, a brilliant mind and so on. Just get your self image tightened up and THEN you may want to add a few comforts and indicators of affluence.

I hope, when you reach your wealth goals, you'll drop the "decorations" you acquired to impress others and further your program, and that will leave you with all of the comforts and things you enjoy without having to create an impression for anyone.

Then that will just leave the real you.

CHAPTER THIRTY-SIX

How To Wade In

Depending on how many dollars you have in your pocket today you are either ready to launch into your wealth program or lay the groundwork to do it.

TODAY you can start building your credit as outlined in the chapter by that name. You can start seeing properties and become acquainted with property values in your area. If you are in a dead-end job that doesn't allow you to save up a nest egg of $5,000 or $10,000 within a reasonably short time, seriously plan on finding a more lucrative opportunity.

You can do plenty of deals with "nothing down" but normally in these deals you'll borrow the money for use as a down payment. In that case you either have to be a confident talker, have a good deal or have some established credit.

We've talked about how to get all three of those but the important thing is to do it *today*. Borrow some money today to establish credit. Make some proposals on property this week. You can get forms for offers at any legal supply or most stationery or office supply stores. Get the forms today.

Read the ads today and make some calls today. Fill out your personal ambition forms. Set your goals today.

If you're married talk with your spouse today and reach an understanding about the time you'll necessarily devote to your wealth program

Don't rush into a bad deal but don't wait around looking for the ideal solid gold investment property. Find a good property and work on the terms and price as outlined in this book. Do it today. Buy a property soon.

Advertise your services today. Try to find partners who will back you financially if you don't have your nest egg put together. Get a second mortgage on your home as you personally can repay it or if you have a property that will generate the income to repay its own loan and your second.

See many properties now so that you can say, with assurance, that this property you're looking at *really* is a good deal. That's how you'll get partners. That's how you arrange your second mortgage. But do it *NOW!*

You may have to start small. Maybe just a single family house. But that's fine. Next month you'll get a duplex and in a few months your first apartment building. Start small if you have to but START.

If you feel a little uneasy because of your lack of knowledge start reading and talking to people now. Get the knowledge. It will amaze you how fast you'll fit into that frame of mind.

Years ago when I started my first retail stereo business I felt bewildered by all the business and technical details. But, at the same time, I knew that within a month I'd feel at ease with the store and products, and be able to take care of everything.

You'll be the same way in the investment game. In no time at all you'll be discussing deals with all the confidence and vernacular of a long-time investor. But that can't happen if you don't put your heart into what you're doing and give yourself some exposure to properties nad proposals. You'll make a few mistakes, but you'll be careful not to repeat them.

Clear a space, today,for your work area. Get some business cards printed today. Become a professional investor NOW. In two or three months you'll have some property that is appreciating and making you money. You'll also have a good understanding of the business. If you plan on starting a business to make you some money for a nest egg, you can start today to explore the opportunitites. There are tons of businesses that will make you a hundred grand a year and that's plenty to launch even a very ambitious investment program. You don't need the hundred grand and you can make great wealth in real estate with little or no money, but you'd have to live and the cash flow is nice to carry and improve properties. You may live in less comfort now than you'd like to and less than your friends or neighbors. I know you want to impress them all with how well you're doing, but live below them now and soon you'll be so far above their standard of living that they'll never reach it.

They'll be higher on the graph than you are now, but you'll rise dramatically and pass them in a year or two and then there will be no stopping you. It will probably be of some help to you to live modestly now and use the freed money to get into investing. If you have extra cars or vehicles that you could somehow get along without, sell them. You can own a $3,000 piano or a duplex. A car or a four-plex.

Decide TODAY if you need to part with something and then follow through with it. It's really up to you.

Don't be discouraged that you aren't buying $100,000 or $600,000 properties at first. You'll be able to see where you're going by looking at your growing assets on your financial statement. Regardless of your standard of living, assuming you'll live modestly while you get rich, you'll see your net worth rising through the thousands, and into the hundreds of thousands and millions. Meanwhile a few years will have passed and you'll be as young, because of your great self-image and confidence, as you are now, and besides that you'll have several millions dollars.

Imagine the freedom at that time.

When you get into your investing full-time it will amaze you how quickly the deals fall together and how your skill has developed.

So, *wade in today.* You may not want to dive in off the high-dive right now, but start at the shallow end and in weeks or months you'll be swimming all over the place with complete confidence in yourself and your abilities.

CHAPTER THIRTY-SEVEN

It's All In Your Head

Most of us are so bound by habit that we can't envision ourselves being anything but what we are now.

Look around you at the number of overweight people. This may be because our society demands less physical labor from us or because we are generally quite idle, but a lot of it has to do with what we eat. It isn't necessarily that we don't care about ourselves but we get into bad eating habits that are hard to break and we end up with sluggish and unresponsive bodies.

When we appease our minds in the same way, giving them non-nutritive material and thoughts, they grow sluggish also.

If you don't exercise and challenge your body it will become more and more dysfunctional. It will be more susceptible to disease. Our minds are the same way and we can become stronger and healthier mentally if we'll learn to work hard and challenge ourselves mentally.

It isn't easy to lose weight and it isn't easy to reorganize our minds either. A very key element in your success in becoming a wealthy person is to learn to *think* of yourself as rich and successful.

To lose weight a person should learn to think of themselves as thin, rather than fat. I know from personal experience what it's like to change that self-perception. Until a couple of years ago I had always been overweight, as previously mentioned. At least for the last ten years, I'd always thought of myself as a heavy person, built stocky and just accepted that idea.

My relatives had a tendency to be a little heavy also and I *KNEW* it was a family trait that had befallen my genes.

We accept our present position even if we don't like it. We are, in fact, afraid of change.

I've read a study that postulated that one of the greatest obstacles that alcoholics have in recovering from their illness is in getting their spouse and friends to *let* them change.

A wife whose husband is an alcoholic *KNOWS* how she hates it, but at least it is a known quantity. As much as she *hates* her present position she has an even greater *fear* of what he would be like if he quit drinking. Because of this fear of change she manipulates him into drinking again. She might say "Honey I know it's difficult for you to get through each day and if you had a drink or two I'd understand." Or she may intimidate and intentionally upset him to cause him to want another drink.

Well, she won't let him change.

A woman who is inhibited and dysfunctional sexually may have a husband who, more than anything, wants her to turn on and let herself go and enjoy herself. But, at the same time, he may be terrified, internally, about how he'd perform and his own ability if she did fire up her furnace. So he may actively do things that would cement her inhibitions and encourage her continuing unresponsiveness.

We often prefer the known evil to the unknown joy. When I was heavy (fat) I didn't like it but accepted it. Interestingly, I knew, and had a consuming confidence in everything else I was doing but never considered this weight problem as a challenge to pursue. After all, if you're fat, your're fat and if you're poor, you're poor. Right?

Well, finally, with a 45" waist and a round face I suddenly decided that I'd be the first person who was genetically fat, big boned and incurably plump to become thin. In three or four months I lost 75 pounds and 14" off my waist. From 45" to 31". From 245 pounds to 170 pounds. AND GUESS WHAT? I wasn't a fat person after all. I was thin. I always was thin but had become so clouded in my own physical self-expectations.

I thought I had fat legs, but they were very muscular, with a layer of fat over them. My stomach hung out and I knew it was because my grandfather's stomach hung out. Well, after the weight was gone there was no more stomach. It was simply gone.

The point of this is that we are not necessarily what we now perceive ourselves to be. Physically and mentally it takes some exertion and exercise to get out of our misconception and realize our real potential.

Physically, I quit eating all the fodder that I'd become used to. I started eating health food, fruits and vegetables.

Mentally, we quit reading and participating in literature and activities that either just consume our time or actively deaden our self-conception of success and excellence. We give up the junk food and the junk activities.

Physically, in one week I lost seventeen pounds which is extreme and I don't know how it could happen physiologically, but it did.

Mentally, in one week, you'll buy three income properties and feel the same elation. I saw and you will see that we are not what we have always thought ourselves to be.

I was thin waiting to get out and you are rich waiting to get out.

After we overcome the feat of changing and realize that we really can be something greater, then ALL WE HAVE TO DO IS DO IT.

This process of mental control is a marvelous talent. *YOU HAVE THIS TALENT AND ABILITY*, but we are so ingrained with and cemented into the self-conception we've developed that it's sometimes a great struggle to break out of it. It's all in your mind. The power of thinking is great. You can think your way into elation or depression. You can sharpen your mental capacities for talents beyond your present conceptions.

I stayed in an Austrian hotel for a couple of weeks during which time a fellow from Cairo, Egypt was also there. We played cards every night and became quite well acquainted. This gentleman was well-educated and well-travelled. Although he was intelligent I didn't think he was especially brilliant. But this man knew how to use his mind and he'd cultivated some unusual abilities.

After a few days of friendship one night as we were playing cards he asked if we'd be interested in some entertainment. He explained that he had some mental abilities that would be fascinating to us. Obviously, it seemed like a set-up for some magic but we went along.

First of all he told us, in turn, what cards we held in our hands. Not that impressive. Then he told us just to think of cards and he'd tell us which cards we'd thought of. Then he had us to take *any* book and read it to ourselves and he would tell us the words we were reading. This became very fascinating.

His last great mental feat was to tell us what we were thinking. He had two fellows carry on a mental

298

conversation and he voiced the words for each of them. He told me to concentrate and he voiced some of my thoughts including my doubts and amazement at his talent. He told us that he reasoned out in his mind, many years ago, that a person's mind could tune into some cosmic thought flow and hear the mental images just as we hear words, and to "see" radiated energy patterns radiating from books and objects.

Purely from his mental reasoning he *CULTIVATED* this talent to read minds. He said it took him some time to do it, but it was purely a learning process. His twenty year old son was with him and his father was teaching him to be in touch with these thought waves and organized energy that even radiated from books and cards. His son could do the same exercises but with less definition and articulation.

Some folks may think he was in touch with a devil. I think he was just in touch with his own mind and its great capacities. If a religious person feels like God represents intelligence then he must also reason that ignorance must be some kind of devil. Well, I don't think this fellow was ignorant. I don't think that he had any greater natural intelligence than any average joker on the street. He had simply learned, *IN HIS MIND*, that his thoughts could overcome all.

I've never seen, but have talked with credible people who have seen people use their mental powers to levitate themselves off the ground. I believe in the reality of disease but some religions teach that disease and illness are mental irregularities and can be overcome by holisitic medicine or mental conditioning.

My object in recounting these mental performances and capacities is simply this:

If these people can heal, levitate and vocalize thoughts totally by mental acuity, doesn't it make sense that we can at least organize our minds enough to get up earlier in the morning?

To read papers, to make calls, to see properties, to think thin, to think successful, to envision ourselves, not as mental puppets of society, but as masters of our destinies?

These ideas of self-concept, self-control, self-confidence, ability and self-respect are all in our minds.

After you master this self-control and confidence, really *BELIEVING* in yourself and after you've applied this attitude to a few real estate deals, then you need only to continue it and let your dynamic self pursue its natural course.

The deals will fall into place in a very natural way. Because you have discovered this great and successful self inside, the same way I discovered a slim and healthy person inside of me.

When Sir Edmund Hillary finally scaled Mr. Everest he accomplished a great victory that had escaped many others. He had preparation and knowledge but, even so, don't you envision that he had many moments when the struggle was simply greater than he could bear? That assumption seems reasonable. But he had that great and indefatigable drive inside which could not fail him. He was a plain sort, like you and me, who had enarmored himself with a determination NOT TO FAIL. And this spirit of success made him great.

Attila the Hun rode, with his men, on an army of elephants across the Swiss Alps. He plundered and destroyed but completed this impossible journey from sheer will of his forceful mind. Of course many of these military and political tyrants met their just ends. Even their belief in the inevitable success could not overcome their evil ways.

But *YOUR SUCCESS* is not predicated on oppression of others, control over other's personal freedoms and so on.

Your success encourages others and provides them with opportunities.

You can originate this great self-image by cleaning the cobwebs out of your mind. Each of us have mental limitations and psychological conditioning imposed on us as adolescents. We have some self-doubts so ingrained in our minds and we must root them out.

Examine your developing years, the good experiences and the bad ones. Reason out how the bad experiences may have tainted your self-image. Think through how those experiences, regardless of their unsavory memory, may have surfaced in some self-defeating behavior. Realize that regardless of whatever has come before, today you are breaking out of that mental state and are becoming the great and prosperous person you have always been meant to be.

I'm no psychologist and there may be a few cracks in my analysis but these ideas are all common sense. If you uncover or recognize personal habits or traits that you dislike for some reason you can do one of two things. In the first place, you can be assured that all people have weaknesses and many traits you consider faults which are really nothing more than normal characteristics that should no longer weigh you down. None of us are perfect and many human frailties are part of a normal profile.

When some of these traits arise in a self-examination we should realize that they are normal and not be troubled by them. The way to differentiate these non-critical weaknesses from actually critical and debilitating problems is whether or not they prevent you from functioning in the ways you would like to.

If they prevent you from functioning and freely pursing your interests or if they are a noticeable weight on your mind, then they should be corrected. After you carefully sift through the mental hardware and set aside frailties that would be part of a "normal" profile, you may be left with a few real problems.

The second approach is to either use the strength of your mind to eradicate the tainted parts of your psychic, or get some professional psychiatric help. The reason that I go into such detail on this general idea is because I've met so many people who want so badly to do well financially and for personal happiness but can't find their way around these mental roadblocks. Each of us must reason out that these problems are behind us. They are in the past.

Some of them are based on unfortunate experiences that have left hurt feelings and mental scars but there can be no good purpose served by continuing to let our yesterdays destroy our todays and tomorrows. By your own will power you can rechannel your thoughts out of these ruts. When the same destructive or limiting thoughts START to develop, think about something else. Divert your thoughts to your positive projects, think about happier ideas and *THINK* your way past the problem. It can be done!

YOU CAN DO IT!!!

If any significant problems remain call the county mental health service for nearly free service or call a psychiatrist in private practice if you can afford it.

To summarize on mental conditioning:

Your financial success is not in your pocket, it's in your head. You have mental abilities so great that they may even tune into the laws of nature and use them for your benefit.

The great importance of this point is that when you get this expanding feeling inside, it will show on the outside and further your interests. Decide how you want to feel and feel that way. Decide what you want to be and be that way. Even the sky isn't the limit. There are no limits.

You will be as great as you make up your mind to be, regardless of what others may think. Their problems are in their heads.

Your success is in *your* head. Let it out.

CHAPTER THIRTY-EIGHT

Forms For Self Analysis And Property Evaluation

So where do you start?

TODAY! TODAY! TODAY! Do it now! Don't wait until next month or even tomorrow. There are lots of things you can acomplish today to get you on the road to your wealth.

1- Before you start be sure you have your inner happiness intact. If you don't the wealth will never make you happy in a lasting sense.

2- Decide where you want to go. How much money do you want to make?

3- Decide how long you'll take to get there. How much time will you allow for your wealth program?

4- Decide how you'll achieve your financial goals. How many properties will you buy this year?

5- Contemplate what you'll do after you have achieved your objectives.

6- Carefully assess your own feelings of self-worth and think about your strong characteristics. Think through the ideas of your inevitable success. Gear your mind to optimism and get on the positive frequency.

7- Toss aside the negative observations and comments of people with less vision and imagination than you. These people enjoy failure and you can't discuss failure with them since you don't understand what the word means. Ultimately, inevitably you will be successful simply because there is no other possibility for you. You are destined for success.

As a little organizing tool, use the forms on the following pages to outline your steps to success. This may seem very elementary to you, but it might help you see where you are now, where you are going and how you'll get there. Check off and comment on the steps as you take care of them, if you want a visual evidence that you are following these steps to wealth.

SELF-ANALYSIS   DATE TODAY:

NAME:

PRESENT ADDRESS:

PRESENT OCCUPATION:

DOES THIS PRESENT OCCUPATION PROVIDE
ENOUGH MONEY TO FUND MY FIRST
INVESTMENTS?

IF NOT, WHAT WILL I DO TODAY TO BE IN A
POSITION TO HAVE THE NECESSARY EXTRA
FUNDS TO INVEST?

1-

2-

3-

4-

5-

CAN I SIMPLY ASK FOR A RAISE?

HOW WILL I APPROACH IT?

WHEN WILL I ASK?

IF MY PRESENT OCCUPATION PROVIDES THESE
EXTRA FUNDS, HOW MUCH CAN I PUT ASIDE
EVERY MONTH FOR INVESTING?

WILL I HAVE TO SACRIFICE TO PUT THIS MONEY ASIDE?

WHAT WILL I HAVE TO GIVE UP?

IF THE ABOVE AMOUNT DOESN'T INVOLVE SACRIFICING, IS IT WORTH GIVING UP SOME IMMEDIATE PLEASURE FOR A LONG-RANGE GOAL? WHAT COULD I SACRIFICE TO BECOME A MULTI-MILLIONAIRE IN FIVE YEARS?

WILL I PAY THAT PRICE?

HOW COMPLETELY DO I REALLY WANT TO BE RICH?

WHAT IS MY GOAL FOR ONE YEAR FROM NOW?

TWO YEARS?

THREE YEARS?

FOUR YEARS?

FIVE YEARS?

DO I WANT TO SPEND MY WHOLE LIFE THINKING IN SMALLER FIGURES AND MAKING CAR PAYMENTS?

WILL I DO WHAT'S NECESSARY TO MAKE MY
FIVE MILLION DOLLARS IN ONLY FIVE YEARS?

CAN I BECOME THAT SINGLE-MINDED?

WILL IT DAMAGE MY PERSONAL
RELATIONSHIPS?

HOW CAN I PREVENT THAT FROM HAPPENING?

IF MARRIED, HOW CAN I INVOLVE MY HUSBAND
OR WIFE IN MY WEALTH PROGRAM TO AVOID
FEELINGS OF SEPARATION?

AM I HAPPY TO BEGIN WITH?

I FEEL LIKE, WHEN I'M WEALTHY THAT I'LL
FEEL:

I WILL STOP WHEN MY NET WORTH IS:

WILL I THEN KEEP SOME PROPERTY OR WILL I
SELL IT AND USE THE MONEY IN ANOTHER WAY?

WHAT WILL I DO WITH ALL THE EXTRA MONEY?

WHAT WILL I DO WITH MY TIME AFTER I AM
RICH?

I REALIZE THAT MY NET WORTH WILL GROW
GEOMETRICALLY. I WILL ACHIEVE MY GOALS BY
START TODAY TO:

1- Start and build credit references.

2- Call realtors and agents and see properties.

3- Read want ads, call and see available properties.

4- Structure my life to have time and attention for my projects.

5- If I don't have a job or business that provides *cash flow*, I will *START TODAY* to organize a new business, get a new job, or do whatever is ncessary to break the chains of a low-paying job.

6- I will improve my appearance.

7- I will read about and immerse myself in ideas and literature that encourages my success.

8- Regardless of how tired I am, I will never stop until I reach my goal.

9- I absolutely will not pay attention to negative thinkers who are geared more to failure than success.

10- I will not listen to all the reasons why it can't be done.

11- When it gets the worst I will try the hardest.

12- I will talk to myself every day and simply convince myself that there is no such thing as failure, and that I am *1000%* destined for financial and personal success and can do nothing about it. It will happen. Let a deal fall apart, let the world fall apart. I will put it back together and own it.

13- I will read current books and periodicals on the latest real estate ideas, investments, and financing methods. I will learn and understand about business, money and wealth.

14- I will not let my plans fade away. I will review them often and make sure I am on track for my goals. I can do it!

REAL ESTATE EVALUATIONS

Have a quick printer reproduce the following forms for you. You may want to modify and re-type them to suit your own uses. Using them will encourage a systematic approach to your evaluations of available real estate. If you use form one for each of the properties you see or are considering, the unifrom layout of each proposal will simplify your comparisons and all of the necessary information will be in front of you. As you make calls from the want-ads you can write down the information given to you and add to it after you see the property.

I, personally, have always liked a lot of printing when used to organize and systematize my projects, businesses, and activities. It adds a certain stability, professionalism, and support to mental organization. You'll come up with many other useful forms, charts and property summaries which will be of help to you. Use your imagination, get them printed, use them and get on with your program. The money is waiting.

PERSONAL FINANCIAL STATEMENT

TO _____

MARITAL STATUS	DEPENDENTS
☐ MARRIED ☐ UNMARR.	NUMBER ___

NAME IN FULL | SOCIAL SECURITY NO. | AGE | DATE MARR. ☐ SEP. | AGES ___

RESIDENCE ADDRESS (NO., STREET, CITY, STATE, ZIP CODE) | YRS. AT ADDRESS | TELEPHONE & EXT. | YRS. OF EDUCATION (CHECK ONE) ☐ UNDER 12 YRS. ☐ 12 YRS. ☐ 13-15 YRS. ☐ 16 YRS. AND OVER

PREVIOUS ADDRESSES IF AT ABOVE ADDRESS LESS THAN 5 YEARS (NO. AND STREET, CITY, STATE, ZIP CODE)

(1) EMPLOYER | (2) ADDRESS (NO. AND STREET) | CITY | TELEPHONE & EXT.

SPOUSE INFORMATION SECTION

SPOUSE'S NAME | SOCIAL SECURITY NO. | AGE

SPOUSE'S EMPLOYER | ADDRESS (NO. & STREET) | CITY | TELEPHONE & EXT.

FINANCIAL CONDITION AS OF _____, 19 ___

ASSETS			AMOUNT		LIABILITIES			AMOUNT
CASH	El Cajon Valley Bank	Office		NOTES PAYABLE TO BANKS	El Cajon Valley Bank	Office		
	Other Banks				Other (Itemize, Schedule 4)			
STOCKS AND BONDS	Listed (Schedule 1)			OTHER NOTES AND ACCOUNTS PAYABLE	Real Estate Loans (Schedule 2)			
	Unlisted (Schedule 1)				Sales Contracts & Sec. Agreements (Sch.4)			
REAL ESTATE	Improved (Schedule 2)				Loans on Life Insurance Policies (Sch.4)			
	Unimproved (Schedule 2)			TAXES PAYABLE	Current Year's Income Taxes Unpaid			
	Trust Deeds and Mortgages (Schedule 3)				Prior Years' Income Taxes Unpaid			
LIFE INSURANCE	Cash Surrender Value				Real Estate Taxes Unpaid			
ACCOUNTS AND NOTES RECEIVABLE	Relatives and Friends (Schedule 4)			OTHER LIABILITIES	Unpaid Interest			
	Collectible (Schedule 4)				Others (Itemize, Schedule 4)			
	Doubtful (Schedule 4)							
OTHER PERSONAL PROPERTY	Automobile							
	Other (Itemize, Schedule 4)				TOTAL LIABILITIES			
		TOTAL			NET WORTH			
					TOTAL			

ANNUAL INCOME	(Refer to Federal Income Tax Returns for Previous Year)	ANNUAL EXPENDITURES	(Refer to Federal Income Tax Returns for Previous Year)
SALARY OR WAGES		PROPERTY TAXES AND ASSESSMENTS	
DIVIDENDS AND INTEREST		FEDERAL AND STATE INCOME TAXES	
RENTALS (GROSS)		REAL ESTATE LOAN PAYMENTS	
BUSINESS OR PROFESSIONAL INCOME (NET)		PAYMENTS ON CONTRACTS AND OTHER NOTES	
OTHER INCOME (DESCRIBE) (Alimony, Child Support,		INSURANCE PREMIUMS	
Maintenance — Reveal At Your Option)		ESTIMATED LIVING EXPENSES	
		OTHER (Alimony, Child Support, Maintenance)	
TOTAL INCOME		TOTAL EXPENDITURES	

LIFE INSURANCE	FACE AMOUNT	BENEFICIARY	COMPANY

Give details of any contingent liability as endorser or guarantor, or on suits or judgments pending. (If necessary, use separate sheet.)

Do you do business with any other bank? _____ If so, give details _____

Have you ever filed any petition under the Bankruptcy Act? _____

Are any of the assets listed on this statement held under a Trust Agreement? ☐ Yes ☐ No _____

Have your Income Tax Returns ever been questioned by the Internal Revenue Service? _____ If so, most recent year _____

SCHEDULE 1: LISTED AND UNLISTED STOCKS AND BONDS OWNED

NO. OF SHARES OR PAR VALUE	Description	Issued in Name of	Joint Tenancy Ten. In Common Comm. Property	Market Value
LISTED:				
			TOTAL LISTED	
UNLISTED:				
			TOTAL UNLISTED	

Are any of the above listed securities pledged to secure a debt?

SCHEDULE 2: REAL ESTATE OWNED   (DESIGNATE: I=IMPROVED, U=UNIMPROVE...)

Location or Description	Title in Name of	Joint Tenancy Ten. In Common Comm. Property	Cost	Present Value	Trust Deeds, Mortgages or other Liens			
					Unpaid Bal.	Rate%	MONTHLY PAYMENT	Held By
		TOTAL			X X X X X X X X		X X X X X X X X X X	

SCHEDULE 3: TRUST DEEDS AND MORTGAGES OWNED

Name of Payer	Legal Desc., Street Address, & Type of Improvements	Unpaid Bal.	Joint Tenancy Ten. In Common Comm. Property	Terms	1st or 2nd Lien	Value of Property
	TOTAL			X X X	X X X X	

SCHEDULE 4: DETAILS RELATIVE TO OTHER IMPORTANT ASSETS AND LIABILITIES

Date Signed _____ , 19____   (Sign Here) _____

(Sign Here) _____

<u>FORM ONE</u>

DATE:

TYPE OF PROPERTY:

LOCATION:

DIRECTIONS:

AGENT:

OWNER:

COMMISSION SELLER?

DESCRIPTION OF PROPERTY:

SIZE OF LOT:

SQUARE FEET IN BUIILDINGS:

IMPROVEMENTS ALREADY MADE:

IMPROVEMENTS NEEDED: COST ESTIMATE:

EXISTING FINANCING:

LIENS, TAXES DUE:

YEARLY PROPERTY TAX:

APPRAISED VALUE:

ESTIMATED VALUE:

HOW FLEXIBLE ARE THEY ON PRICE?

HOW FLEXIBLE ON DOWN PAYMENT AND TERMS?

WHAT IS THE ASKING PRICE?

IS THAT PRICE JUSTIFIED BY EXISTING LEASES
AND RENTS?

WHAT IS THE OCCUPANCY RATE NOW?

HOW COULD IT BE IMPROVED?

WHO ARE THE CURRENT TENANTS?

TERMS OF LEASE OR RENTAL AGREEMENTS
WITH TENANTS:

COULD THE RENT BE RAISED NOW, WITHOUT
IMPROVEMENTS?

HOW MUCH?

COULD THE RENTS BE INCREASED AFTER
IMPROVEMENTS?

HOW MUCH?

SELLER'S PERSONAL FINANCIAL CONDITION:

REASON FOR SELLING:

CONFIRMATION OF REASON TO SELL:

DISCUSSION OF FINANCIAL FLEXIBILITY AND
POSSIBLE OFFER:

DISCUSSION OF FINANCIAL FLEXIBILITY AND POSSIBLE OFFER:

319

YEARLY COST ESTIMATES

LOWEST PROJECTED ACQUISITION $ _____
PRICE

LOWEST PROJECTED DOWN PAYMENT $ _____

LOWEST PROJECTED MONTHLY
PAYMENT $ _____

YEARLY PROPERTY TAX DIVIDED BY
12 MONTHS $ _____

YEARLY INSURANCE DIVIDED BY
12 MONTHS $ _____

YEARLY MAINTENANCE DIVIDED BY
12 MONTHS $ _____

TOTAL PROJECTED MONTHLY COSTS $ _____

TOTAL PROJECTED MONTHLY INCOME $ _____

MONTHLY PROFIT OR LOSS   + or — $ _____

POSITIVE CASH FLOW WILL BE USED FOR:

NEGATIVE CASH FLOW WILL BE PAID BY:

CHAPTER
THIRTY-NINE

Life After Wealth Or How To Stop Making Money

How does a great pianist suddenly quit playing? How does a great artist put away his brushes and quit painting? Once you have mastered the ability to accumulate wealth how do you put that talent aside?

In the 1970's there were three friends who had all achieved some financial success in business who all concluded that their continuing to pursue more wealth was fruitless. They reasoned that they had had enough of the material orientation we're subject to, so they decided to get completely away from it. They also decided to leave their families since they felt that they had outgrown the need for those types of supportive relationships.

So these fellows decided that they would completely remove themselves from all of these conventions they had come to accept. They all went to a small island in the South Pacific, there to live out their days in idyllic glory. This island was populated with natives who passed the time eating coconuts and relaxing.

They had little commercial development and no real commerce. They lived in a temperate climate and enjoyed one the most accomodating situations and locations anywhere in the world. These three men melted into this style of living and realized their dreams: relaxing in a wonderful place with no responsibilities. BUT, true to form, these fellows, at heart, were hard drivers. They were thinkers and doers and it was their cultivated nature to look at anything and see the opportunity and utilization in it. They had been there only a few months when they realized that the very thing that attracted them to the place, the freedom and comfort, had fantastic commercial possibilities. If they enjoyed it so much, just think of how many people would pay to enjoy it for a short time. Others could experience the same feelings they had.

Obviously, the way to pursue this was to acquire vast areas of land and to begin developing the area.

They did that and when they had ownership of key acreages and ocean frontages they arranged, back in the real world, financing to build hotels and resorts. The reason this happened is because of the talent they had acquired to see in a property its potential for development.

They were only doing what they had trained themselves to do. They contineud their development and their island has become an emerging prime tourist destination.

While they all felt that they had outgrown their family situations and they tired of the responsibility, one of their interesting achievements was the acquisition of new wives and children. They were surrounding themselves with what they had always had, what they knew how to do and what they felt comfortable with.

Whereas they went to the other side of the world to get away from society, they couldn't get away from their talents and developmental personalities.

You'll remember that our first premise in this book was that money and wealth really meant so little in life, but because it was necessary to live and exercise our freedom and explore our desires, we wanted to make some. Since we certainly weren't going to spend our whole lives working for something that meant so little we reasoned that it made sense to make more than we could ever need in a short period of time.

Thus, we concluded that if you made five million dollars in five years that would satisfy your needs and desires completely. You would obviously have the cars, homes, bank accounts, trips and on and on, that money buys. You'd have all the free time in the world since you'd sell your properties, or most of them, buy some high yield bonds or in some way protect your five million from erosion by inflation. And you'd settle down to enjoy your family and life in general.

Wonderful thoughts, huh? Then why doesn't it usually turn out that way?

If I walk along a stream bed in Brazil, I see at the bottom of the stream and strewr along the banks, only pebbles and rocks. Another fellow walking along the same stream may see opals in the rubble. What appears to me to be a worthless rock, to him is obviously a precious stone. It only needs to be polished (developed or improved) to reveal its true potential.

Well, once this gentleman has trained himself to recognize these gems, how can he ever again see them and just walk by them? There is so much unrealized beauty and value there and it simply can't be overlooked.

I talked with a fellow in Hawaii who had done exactly what I postulated above. He *was* walking along a Brazilian stream and found an extremely large opal for which he later was offered over $500,000. If I'd seen the same stone I would have overlooked it. But he had the training and vision to pick out these gems as he passed by them.

You will acquire the ability to pick out the real estate and investment gems as you pass by them and it will become a part of your nature. That being the case, in five years when you have your millions, how will you pass by a property that you can see such a great potential and promise in and not look into it? It will be an unnoticed gem.

You'll see as you've been seeing that it only needs to be developed, improved, refinanced, enlarged or just managed and its value will double. The temptation and tendency to do what you have always done are sometimes difficult to overcome.

Remember how we've discussed, at length, that the real challenge in getting yourself to acquire wealth is to overcome thinking along the lines you are used to. To get rich you must break out of the habit of thinking unproductive thoughts and small ideas. You must remove the self-imposed limits to your success and achievement. You can only be financially successful when you change the negative ways you think.

You can only stop the process of making more and more money by changing your thought processes again. Not back to negative ideas that will impede, slow and stop your progress and utilization of your ideas, but by RECHANNELING YOUR ENERGIES in other positive directions.

Your great experience and exposure will give you a broad base upon which to expand your family. If you've started this wealth program when you're twenty-one, now at twenty-six you're ready to get married and divert your attentions into your marriage and family. You can muster the same excitement for non-financial pursuits that you aroused for getting rich.

You may make efforts to raise others up. Not as a compulsive, driving ambition but as an avocation during your years of enjoyment, alternate work and relaxation. You'll still work but that word will mean something different to you. It *won't* be work for money. It *will* be work for enjoyment and fulfillment.

I've been playing with my five children for two years now and have never been so happy. I still see the opportunitites at every turn but let most of them pass by. They mean little to me now. The period of time when they were most important and required or demanded my attention is past. This is a different period in my life and, while I'll invest here and there for fun, have seminars, write books, counsel investors and arrange deals here and there, the period of compulsion to riches is past.

It isn't just real estate opportunities that continue to call out for you. There are so many manufacturing ideas, retail businesses and services that are such great opportunitities. *ALL* just waiting for someone to do them. I see these opportunitites every day and you will too, when you get yourself immersed in your wealth program.

When you get your five million you can sell or dismantle your organization and break the wealth-producing cycle you have so devotedly put together.

There are family activities, service to others, travel, adventure, philanthropic projects, hundreds of worthwhile things to do with your time. But not for money.

Why should you work to produce more money at that point? You already have more than you will ever need. Look around and do something more worthwhile and enjoyable.

CHAPTER FORTY

Now The Challenge Is To Make Something Of Yourself

In the first chapters of this book we talked about raising your sights and accomplishing more than you ever really thought you could. We discussed the vacuous feelings if a person acquires wealth without some internal happiness first.

Then we looked into the mechanics of getting the bucks and in the previous chapter we talked about life after wealth.

In the total consideration of really getting your life organized before, during and after attaining wealth, make this great committment to yourself: To overcome the average, to reach, to stretch and to have an exceptional life experience.

I've heard the story several times about the author Russell Cornwell and his exceptional life. When he was a young man he had a close friend who contracted terminal cancer. His friend knew he was dying, he was only a teenager, and he shared his final thoughts with Mr. Cornwell.

His greatest regret, he related, was that he had determined that he'd spend his whole life in the service of others and his deadly disease would prevent him from realizing the achievement of his life's goals. He was heartbroken, not at his own misfortune in being ill, but that the great plans he had so carefully prepared for wouldn't be fulfilled.

So, his young friend, Mr. Cornwell, made him this promise: That he, Russel Cornwell, would live his friend's lifetime for him and accomplish the objectives and reach the goals he had set for himself. Shortly after making this promise his friend died, and Russell Cornwell was left with his promised obligation.

Each day, to fulfill his promise, the first eight hours of work were devoted to the interests of his departed friend. In these eight hours Mr. Cornwell gave his whole heart and soul, including the necessary mental conditioning, and OVER A LIFETIME did everything his friend would have done, had he lived. He became a minister, a great speaker, a reknowned philanthropist and he served his fellow man in every selfless way he could.

The second eight hours of each day Mr. Cornwell worked for his own interests which were more inclined toward excellence in business. On his own time he became wealthy and influential. He was a great leader in business and finance and, for his own life, accomplished his goals in a grand way. That left him eight hours a day for eating and sleeping and so on.

Here is my great question to you:

IF THIS MAN CAN LIVE TWO GREAT AND SUCCESSFUL LIFETIMES IN ONE, EACH A REMARKABLE ACHIEVEMENT IN ITSELF, CAN'T YOU AND I LIVE JUST ONE LIFETIME IN AN EXCEPTIONAL WAY?

If he can live for two people, can't we live for one?

Think of the fullness of life and the consuming joy in really making something of ourselves. This is not meant in a material way, although money and material possessions can offer us exceptional exposure to some philanthropic, family and recreational and travel opportunities.

The excellence I'm talking about, although also manifesting itself in material success, is more than conquering our material world. It's not in being affluent, but in being good. Not in arrogance, but in consideration for others. Not in seeming to be better than the common man because of our wealth, but in having our own solid self-respect and the realization that we share existence with everyone else. We are individuals. We excell. We grow but we never outgrow life and its simple pleasures.

So often when we think of this idea of excellence, it seems solidly structured in an organizational sense. I don't believe excellence is having filed finger nails, a three-piece suit, an all-knowing countenance and an organizational or corporate acceptance.

I have little admiration for corporate types and company-men. Free spirits fly alone. They don't have limited hours, they don't enjoy long meetings and they don't shine for recognition from a group of associates. These corporate souls, while we need them to add stability and uniformity to our projects and businesses, aren't eagles. They are all kinds of birds, but not eagles.

Typically, the entrepreneur, the aggressive developer who will make millions, flies alone. He does as he pleases with his time and resents controls on his energy, talents or freedom.

The company-man is working his way up in the club. While recognized in the community as a stable soul, his progress is calculated, his growth regular, his schedule predictable and his every word right out of some book. He is well-regarded and probably feels some security in his well-fixed station in life. Once firmly attached to his status level, he has only to wait and let the years pass.

But where is the excitement and magic? This person is excelling in the organization but not in himself. He is expanding the business but not his own soul. When he does grow he moves in inches, not in miles. He passes by the whole idea of freedom.

Some great people find little need to be socially recognized or have any money at all. These people may suffer through mundane jobs to support themselves and find their happiness *in* themselves, not in their work. I have so much greater an admiration for a dishwasher who does his job well and is happy with his mental growth, than for an anxious corporate type who is troubled by his slow movement up the company ladder.

These company types may be doctors, lawyers, vice-presidents or bank managers. All structural and defined positions.

I'm not as critical of these people as it sounds. There are many fine people in these professions and many of them work hard at what they do, but their lives seem to be beyond their control, as if they've surrendered themselves to a pre-arranged assignment.

I think it's humorous to observe how these folks see themselves as the cream of our society while, in reality, the biggest joke of all is on them. They'll spend their lives conforming to some sociological and material values that ultimately mean nothing at all.

The free spirit, the excellent person, while pumping gas, sees into the universe. This person may choose to become wealthy, he may decide to become a mountain climber, he may wash cars during the day and read at night. He does whatever he wants to.

This person demands excellence. He may not meet society's demand for financial excellence washing cars, but he doesn't care.

If he wants wealth, as *you* must since you are reading this book, he'll get it. Nothing can stop him.

His pursuit of excellence is in doing what he wants to do and in becoming his best self.

Yes, you can and will be rich. You'll enjoy all of the pleasures of life, but don't let the money and possessions become ends in themselves.

When your final day comes all of the riches in the world won't bring you peace of mind. But that great consuming peace will permeate your mind and heart if you've lived life to the fullest, had your freedom, lifted others to health and joy and passed the greatest of all tests: being true to your best self.

Although imperfect, your heart will not be weighed down. You won't have devoted your life to wealth that, at this last moment, can't buy you immortality.

But peace will be yours. All the happiness in the world is already in your mind. Just tune in to it. All of the riches in the world are within your reach, just take them.

Be true, be honest, be wealthy, be generous, sensitive, strong and considerate and you'll be happy.

When you get what you want in your struggle for self,
And the world makes you king for a day:
Just go to the mirror and look at yourself
And see what "the man" has to say.
For it isn't your father or mother or wife
Whose judgement upon you must pass.
But the fellow whose verdict really counts in your life
Is the one staring back from the glass.
He's the fellow to please, never mind all the rest,
For he's with you clear to the end.

331

And you've passed your most dangerous, difficult test
If the man in the glass is your friend.
You can fool the world down the pathway of years,
And get pats on the back as you pass.
But your only reward will be heartaches and tears
If you've cheated the man in the glass.

The world is waiting for you. It wants you. It needs you, and it will reward you. You can get yourself going and make yourself great.

Just do it.

RECOMMENDED READING LIST

Acres Of Diamonds by Russell Cornwell: This short book can help you realize that there are opportunities everywhere, even in your back yard. Only takes an hour or two to read.

How To Win Friends and Influence People by Dale Carnegie: This book has been around for a long time and can help you learn to listen and cultivate friendships.

The Greatest Salesman In The World by Og Mandino: This book can give you some insight into self-confidence, self-image and realizing your great potential.

The Power Of Positive Thinking by Norman Vincent Peale: This is an old standard about controlling your mental patterns.

The Power Of Possibility Thinking by Robert Schuller: This fellow's writings are full of energy. This book, and his others, can give you a new perspective on being successful and finding the very best in the very worst situations.

Think And Grow Rich by Napoleon Hill: Another dose of positive thinking and harnessing it to further your interests.

Mental Millions by Ross L. Anderson. My second book explores motivational blocks and isolates and eliminates mental hangups that limit your progress. It provides a step-by-step course on reorganizing and intensifying your motivation to lead you to greater happiness and wealth.

Mountains of Millions, Organizing New Businesses and Real Estate Pyramiding by Ross L. Anderson. Half of my third volume lays out detailed plans for starting new businesses and making them successful. The last half of the book details using the generated profits to pyramid you into great material riches.

How To Buy A House At Auction by Joseph R. Rusignola. This easy-to-understand book outlines foreclosures, auctions and other ways to find and buy real estate for less than value.

Think Like A Tycoon by Bill Greene. This fellow thinks big and has many valid ideas on buying property, avoiding taxes and increasing your wealth.

Real Estate Exchange And Acquisition Techniques by William T. Tappan, Jr. Mr. Tappan has some expertise in exchanging parcels of real estate and he outlines in this book many ways to structure exchanges.

Nothing Down by Robert Allen: This is a great book on the mechanics of organizing offers and deals. Lighter reading than the following book.

How I Turned $1,000 Into Five Million In Real Estate by William Nickerson: This gentlemen has the same five million dollar figure, but outlines ways to take a little longer to get it. In fact he proposes a very conservative ten or twenty year program to get one million dollars. This is a great volume on the actual mechanics of real estate deals. It's a textbook approach, outlines tax structuring, exchanges and other methods outside of my experience and, therefore, not covered in depth in my first book. You really should read this for depth in understanding the various ways to consummate a deal.

Glen W. Turner, Con Man or Saint, a biography: Rags to riches to rags to riches to....... This remarkable fellow will never run out of gas. He could go around the world on an empty tank.

The Funny Money Game by Andrew Tobias: This humorous book will give you some insight on how promotion can make a very big something out of a very small nothing. You'll enjoy it.

Be My Guest by Conrad Hilton: This gentleman is very conservative in a lot of ways, which I don't particularly recommend, but this book outlines and proves the value of hard work and dedication.

Moneypower by Ben Stein: How to use inflation as a vehicle to wealth. A short book with some usable ideas on pyramiding assets.

To the above book list, it might be added that reading magazines like *Fortune* and others geared to national business enterprises may elevate your business perception. They can help you think in larger numbers and understand how larger businesses operate.

To continue your motivation, it may energize you to read additional books on real estate fortunes and business successes. Do whatever is necessary to keep your spirits from lagging as you climb your mountain of millions.